Robert Penn Warren

Genius Loves Company

Robert Penn Warren

Genius Loves Company

Edited by Mark Royden Winchell

Copyright 2007 by Clemson University
ISBN 978-0-9796066-3-2

Published by Clemson University Press in Clemson, South Carolina

Editorial Assistant: Amy Bickett and Kara McManus

To order copies, please visit the Clemson University Press website: www.clemson.edu/press.

Versions of the eleven chapters of this book first appeared in the following issues of *The South Carolina Review*: 38.2, 39.2, and 40.1.

Photographic images of Robert Penn Warren used on the front and back cover, the frontispiece page [ii], and page xiv of this book appear by courtesy of the Robert Penn Warren Collection, Kentucky Library, Western Kentucky University, Bowling Green, Kentucky.

Contents

Preface vi
by Mark Royden Winchell

"Strange Caterwauling": Singing in the Wilderness with Boone and Audubon, Elizabeth Madox Roberts and Robert Penn Warren
by H. R. Stoneback 1

Robert Penn Warren, Thomas Wolfe, and the Problem of Autobiography
by Patricia L. Bradley 13

Cleanth Brooks and Robert Penn Warren: A Beautiful Friendship
by Mark Royden Winchell 23

Robert Penn Warren and Albert Russell Erskine, Jr.: A Sixty-Year Friendship
by James A. Grimshaw, Jr. 37

Warren and Pasinetti: A Study in Friendship
by William Bedford Clark 56

Apocalypse and Redemption: The Life and Works of Robert Penn Warren and Robert Lowell
by Tony Morris 65

Warren, Bellow, and the Changing Tides
by Joseph Scotchie 76

"A Friendship That Has Meant So Much": Robert Penn Warren and Ralph W. Ellison
by Steven D. Ealy 83

A Pair of Moles: Robert Penn Warren and William Styron
by Robert Cheeks 94

Modern Primitives: Merging in the Poetry of Robert Penn Warren and James Dickey
by Daniel Cross Turner 104

Robert Penn Warren, David Milch, and the Literary Contexts of *Deadwood*
by Joseph Millichap 114

Preface

by Mark Royden Winchell

One of the most astute literary critics of our time—J. D. Salinger's Holden Caulfield—asserts, "What really knocks me out is a book that, when you're all done reading it, you wish the author who wrote it was a terrific friend of yours and you could call him up on the phone whenever you felt like it" (18). Although this may not be true of all great authors (I can't imagine wanting to phone John Milton or go out for a beer with Ralph Waldo Emerson), some writers seem to exude ethos. As impressive as his work may have been, Samuel Johnson is probably best remembered as the protagonist of Boswell's *Life of Johnson*. (One of my classmates in graduate school saw him as a cross between Henry James and W. C. Fields.) In fact, some writers live in our collective memory more for who they were than for what they wrote. This would seem to be the fate of Edgar Allan Poe and Truman Capote and the later Hemingway. Although Robert Penn Warren was not such a public figure, people who knew him seemed to seek his company at least as avidly as they did the product of his muse.

Probably since the dawn of the Romantic era, the poet has been pictured living a lonely life, isolated in his garret. But common sense tells us that writers are not invariably hermits and misanthropes. As human beings, they crave the company of other human beings; as artists, they need the stimulation of other artists. (Norman Podhoretz once wrote that, for Edmund Wilson, the Republic of Letters had "an existence at least as palpable and concrete as the Republic of France" [35].) In many ways, Robert Penn Warren was a model of the writer as social animal. As a precocious sixteen-year-old sophomore, he began attending meetings of Nashville's Fugitive group. Decades before creative writing workshops had become a fixture on university campuses, these gifted amateurs would meet on alternate Saturday nights to exchange drafts of poems they were writing. The critical attention no doubt improved their verse, while the shared sense of community solidified their commitment to the literary life. (From 1922 to 25, the group even published a little magazine called the *Fugitive*.) During his time at Vanderbilt, Warren formed life-long friendships with such older mentors as John Crowe Ransom, Allen Tate, Donald Davidson, and Andrew Lytle.

This volume examines the literary relationships between Red Warren and a wide range of writers over the course of the twentieth century. We begin with H.. R. Stoneback's discussion of the affinities between Warren and his fellow Kentuckian Elizabeth Madox Roberts (1881-1941). Although the two novelists were acquainted, they were not close friends. (Roberts was more than a generation older than Warren and suffered from ill health during much of her later life.) Nevertheless, both writers shared the matter of their native state—particularly a fascination with Daniel Boone and John James Audubon. Stoneback conclusively demonstrates Warren's debt to Roberts, as well as his crucial role in bringing her work to the attention of the larger reading public.

At first glance, no writer would seem less amenable than Thomas Wolfe (1900-38) to the strictures of the Nashville New Critics. Wolfe was a bardic novelist who appeared never to have had an unrecorded emotion. When asked to cut or revise a work of fiction, he was apt to expand it by several thousand words. Although Warren took him to task for the excessively autobiographical nature of his work, Patricia Bradley shows us that the later Warren became increasingly sympathetic to writers who drew upon their personal experiences as a source of literary inspiration. Even when he gave every impression of being an orthodox New Critic back in the thirties, Warren himself was the sort of writer who would rather put things into a poem or a novel than take things out. For his part, Wolfe acknowledged some justice in the criticism that Warren had leveled at him in "A Note on the Hamlet of Thomas Wolfe." When the two Southerners were together at a writer's conference in Boulder, Colorado, in the summer of 1935, Wolfe noted that he "had been pleased by favorable reviews but had also learned much from the more critical ones." Turning to Warren, Wolfe said that the one review that had taught him more than any other was written by someone "at this table" (Donald 335).

Perhaps Warren's longest and closest friendship was with Cleanth Brooks (1906-94). They met during Brooks's freshman year at Vanderbilt and renewed their acquaintance five years later when both young men were Rhodes Scholars at Oxford. They first began making their joint mark on literary history in the mid-1930s, when they were teaching at Louisiana State University. It was there, in 1935, that they founded the original series of the *Southern Review* and began to collaborate on a series of influential textbooks.

Baton Rouge, Louisiana, was also the place where Warren's personal and professional relationship with Albert Erskine (1911-89) started to flower. Having met Red at Southwestern College in Memphis in 1930 and followed him to Vanderbilt in 1931, Albert became an instructor in the LSU English department in 1934. A year later, he was present at the founding of the *Southern Review* and soon became the magazine's business manager and an unofficial editor. James A. Grimshaw, Jr.,'s essay focuses on Erskine's long tenure as a senior editor at Random House, where in addition to Warren, he worked closely with Eudora Welty, Ralph Ellison, James Michener, John O'Hara, William Styron, and—during the last fourteen years of his life—William Faulkner. Through an examination of the Warren-Erskine correspondence, Grimshaw reveals the editor's painstaking attention to Warren's novel *World Enough and Time* (1950). I suspect that the next frontier in literary study is the unseen role of editors in shaping the books we read. When that frontier is more fully explored, the reputation of Albert Erskine will undoubtedly soar.

The subject of William Bedford Clark's essay —Pier Maria Pasinetti (1913 —2006) —is probably unknown to all but specialists in Italian-American literature or the history of the Baton Rouge literary community of the early 1940s. Although Pasinetti never became a widely known writer, he is one of many examples of Warren's patronage and generosity. In fact, Brooks and Warren thought enough of his story "Family History" to include it in *An Anthology of Stories from the Southern Review* (1953). The editors of that journal always prided themselves in the sort of Olympian disinterestedness that would reject Nobel Prize winners and accept college sophomores, all on the strength of the work itself.[1]

I

Tony Morris's contribution to this volume suggests some of the similarities and differences in the view of poetry taken by Robert Penn Warren and Robert Lowell. (1917-77) Both poets began their careers writing formal verse under the influence of John Crowe Ransom and Allen Tate. By the mid-fifties, however, both had begun writing more open and personal poetry.² While Lowell was marking time as an undergraduate at Harvard, his psychiatrist—the former Fugitive poet Merrill Moore—suggested that both his literary ambitions and his mental health would be better served if he transferred to Vanderbilt to study under Ransom. Because Ransom was already on his way to Kenyon College at that point, Lowell never matriculated at Vanderbilt, although he did audit some classes in the spring of 1937.

It was during that year that "Cal" Lowell appointed himself protégé to Ford Madox Ford and began following Ford around the country. In April, with the fall term at Kenyon still several months off, Cal appeared at Benfolly, the Allen Tate home in Clarksville, Tennessee, where Ford, his mistress, and his secretary were all houseguests. Knocking over Tate's mailbox when he drove up, and stopping just long enough to urinate on a tree in the front yard, Cal invited himself to join the already crowded household. When Tate facetiously told him that they would have to put him up in a tent, Cal went to the local Sears, Roebuck store and bought a pup tent, which he pitched on the lawn, and stayed for the next three months.

Lowell began his three years at Kenyon sharing a room in Ransom's house with Randall Jarrell. Before too long, however, he ended up rooming with Peter Taylor in a literary enclave called Douglass House. Taylor remembers Lowell as being "not unappealing as a person, but . . . awful looking. He never cut his hair, he never took a bath. His shoes often had the soles divided, and were just flapping. He looked terrible. Though he had what he called his good suit, which hung in our closet at Kenyon always, as a sort of sacred object" (McAlexander 35-36). Lowell played tackle on a spectacularly unsuccessful football team, majored in classics, and continued to write poetry (often on the back of papers diagramming football plays). As Jim Prewitt in Taylor's autobiographical story "1939," Lowell comes across as arrogant and insecure but generally likable. Despite his bohemian ways and indifferent grooming, the real-life Lowell was capable of charming virtually everyone.

Upon receiving his B. A. degree at Kenyon (Phi Beta Kappa, summa cum laude, and class valedictorian), Lowell thought seriously enough about graduate work at Harvard to write a letter of inquiry to the university's president, his cousin Lawrence. Unfortunately, the situation in his immediate family was such that Merrill Moore advised Cal against returning to Boston. The logical alternative was to continue his Southern odyssey and enroll at LSU. In his letter of recommendation to Brooks and Warren, Ransom wrote: "Lowell is more than a student, he's more like a son to me" (Hamilton 72).

The one thing Baton Rouge offered that Cal Lowell had not found at Kenyon was a religious heritage radically different from that of his upbringing. (Like the Lowells themselves, Kenyon College espoused a bland and respectable version of the Episcopal faith.) According to Peter Taylor, "In Louisiana, very French, Catholicism was in the air" (Hamilton 78), Lowell began to inhale this Catholicism through his reading of Hopkins, Newman, Pascal, and Gilson. Then, one day, Red Warren asked the university's Catholic chaplain, the Reverend Maurice Shexnayder, to speak to his sixteenth-century literature class on the subject of the Reformation. Cal Lowell, who was one of the students in the class, followed Father Shexnayder into the hall and asked him for instruction in the Catholic religion.³

As happy as they were to acquire a student of Lowell's promise, Brooks and Warren were even more pleased to secure the secretarial services of Lowell's new wife Jean Stafford (1915-79). When Ransom wrote to his friends at LSU to recommend the young couple in the summer of 1940, the *Southern Review* had just lost its secretary, Mae Swallow. Brooks wired back: "PLEASE ADVISE BY WESTERN UNION IF MRS. LOWELL KNOWS SHORTHAND, LETTER FOLLOWS."⁴ Although her shorthand was only passable, Jean was a first-rate typist and bookkeeper, who almost immediately began to bring order to the chaotic operations of the review.

The South was just as strange a place for Jean Stafford as it was for her husband. A native Westerner, she had grown up in Colorado, the daughter of an odd and shabby family. (Her father was a half-mad aspiring writer, who lost a small fortune in the stock market.) Cal met her at a writer's conference in Boulder, where she was attending the University of Colorado, in the summer of 1937. (As the featured speaker, Cal's idol, Ford Madox Ford, distinguished himself by delivering an inaudible ninety-minute speech on his relationship with Jozef Korzeniowski, whom he failed to identify as Joseph Conrad.) Despite, or perhaps because of, the disapproval of the Lowell family, the romance flourished, even surviving an accident in which Cal crashed his car into a brick wall and broke Jean's nose. The wedding took place on April 2, 1940, at the historic Episcopal church St. Mark's in the Bowery, in Greenwich Village, New York. The honeymoon consisted of a train ride back to Ohio, where Cal finished his final two months at Kenyon. Shortly thereafter, the couple moved to Baton Rouge, where they sublet an apartment from Red and Cinina Warren.

According to one of her biographers:

> [Jean complained] that in those days before people routinely installed air-conditioners, the mildew and damp macerated book bindings and made the *Encyclopedia Britannica* she had sent to Baton Rouge so "edematous" that all the volumes would no longer fit into the wooden case in which they were stored; that the humidity warped phonograph records and gave salt "the consistency of sherbet."; and that "every surface was covered with a mysterious fungoid slime." She also loathed the numerous cockroaches "the size of hummingbirds" that abounded in their apartment and "ravenously devoured the glue in the spines of books, particularly the collected works of Cardinal Newman." (Goodman 116)

In a letter written in June 1940, Jean sounded similar complaints in describing her first few weeks in the South to Peter Taylor, who would soon join the Lowells at LSU. "It is hot and steamy," she writes, "but there are no snakes. There are, however, cockroaches. Cal killed one as big as a calf last night. . . . The job isn't bad and Erskine and Brooks are nice to work for. The office looks like a hogsty with an accumulation of manuscripts (there are some here, really, that were sent in 1938) and magazines and review books and third class matter for Mr. Warren" (Stafford 27).

At the end of the academic year, the Lowells left Baton Rouge for New York, where Cal went to work for the Catholic publisher Sheed and Ward. The marriage had survived some rough times, including an evening in New Orleans when,.enraged, Cal had hit his wife, breaking her nose for a second time. The increasing ardor of his newfound religious practice also widened the breach between husband and wife, a theme that Stafford would treat in her autobiographical short story "An Influx of Poets."

Throughout her frequent illnesses, bouts of alcoholism, and marital strife, Jean Stafford always maintained a witty and sardonic view of life. This is evident not only in her published fiction but also in her letters to friends, including Cleanth Brooks and his wife Tinkum. These go a long way toward revealing the essential Jean Stafford and suggest her continuing affection for her former employers at the *Southern Review*. They also shed considerable light on her husband's eccentricities.

In an undated letter from the early 1940s, Jean describes Cal's continuing obsession with religion:

> The janitor spent an evening with Cal quoting St. Thomas to him in Latin. He is a Catholic refugee from the Rhineland. This, if nothing else, recommends our building to Cal. There was a period when he regarded the place as needlessly luxurious and seriously wanted, after I had described the environs of the Catholic Worker, to go down and live on Mott Street. I argued the general insanity of such a move, the bedbugs, the proximity to the Bowery, the high rate of tuberculosis, scurvy, etc., the stink, the general affectation of it, but nothing would convince him and I truly believe that we would be living there now if it hadn't been that a priest whom he much admires stopped in at Sheed and Ward and laughed at the idea, saying that Cal's métier was obviously intellectual not sociological. Mrs. Sheed has little use for the Catholic Worker, I'm happy to say (she's English and the worker people are all strong isolationists and this doesn't go down very well with her) and I'm pretty well shut of that now. Blessedly I have the flu lately which has kept me in bed for a week and I have been able to postpone any more "good" work but it is blackly written on the books that soon I am to go help in a friendship house in Harlem, run by a Russian Baroness. It sounds much more attractive than Mott Street anyhow.[5]

II

After a new administration at LSU summarily suspended the *Southern Review* in 1942, Red Warren accepted a $200 raise and an appointment as director of creative writing at the University of Minnesota. As Joseph Scotchie tells us, this is where he first met the future Nobel laureate Saul Bellow (1915-2005). As different as the two may have been in background, Warren always argued that there were similar reasons for the flowering of Southern literature between the two world ward and the Jewish American Renaissance after World War II. Like his friend and fellow Fugitive poet Allen Tate, Warren believed that, in the twenties and thirties, traditional Southern culture began to disappear. It is precisely at such a moment that writers become aware of what they are losing and depict it for a variety of purposes from irony to elegy. (Walter Sullivan has called this the *Gotterdammerung* theory of Southern literature.) A similar thing was happening in Jewish-American culture in the period immediately following the Second World War.

It would appear that the relationship of Warren and Ralph Ellison (1914-94) was even closer than Red's friendship with Bellow. It is certainly unfortunate that Warren's position on race was defined for so many years by an ahistorical reading of "The Briar Patch," his contribution to the Agrarian manifesto *I'll Take My Stand* (1930). This essay was—first and foremost—a plea for economic and social justice for the black man. Warren's great sin was that he assumed that, in the South, this would have to be achieved within a system of racial segregation. Although there was nothing in his argument that Booker T. Washington would have disagreed with, enough time had elapsed since Washington's Atlanta Exposition speech at the turn of the century that Northern liberals (black and white) questioned the possibility of justice in a segregated society. This is a position that Warren himself came to accept in the 1950s, much to the consternation of old friends still fighting to maintain the old dispensation. As Stephen D. Ealy makes clear, however, it was not just their shared commitment to civil rights but also a similarly ironic view of history and literature that made Warren and Ellison soul-mates for so many years.

Any list of important American novelists from the fifties through the seventies would include the name of William Styron (1925-2006) somewhere near the top. Although a native Virginian who wrote about the South, Styron was probably more closely identified with Northeastern literary culture than with his home region. Nevertheless, Robert C. Cheeks argues persuasively that Styron's irreducible Southernness was always brought out on his relations with Robert Penn Warren, another member of the literary establishment who could never forget where he came from. Both men had the misfortune of writing historical fiction at a time when the genre was falling into critical disfavor (even as the "nonfiction novel" was on the rise). Although Red admired Styron's controversial novel *The Confessions of Nat Turner*, one of that novel's harshest black critics thought that Warren himself could have made a "more interesting attempt to conceive of the world of a black, Old Testament-type Messiah" (Harding 29).

Unlike both Styron and Warren, James Dickey(1923-97) never left the South. If anything, he tried to project an image of the redneck as poet with his drinking, hunting, and general ribaldry. (As Daniel Cross Turner points out, the more genteel academic term for such a persona is "primitivist.") Like Thomas Wolfe, Dickey turned sheer appetite into a kind of aesthetic virtue. It is therefore no wonder that, of all his forbears at Vanderbilt, he found most to admire and emulate in Robert Penn Warren. In fact, Dickey wrote the best single description I have ever read of Warren's poetry. In *Babel to Byzantium,* he observes: "Opening a book of poems by Robert Penn is like putting out the light of the sun, or like plunging into the labyrinth and feeling the thread break after the first corner is passed. One will never come out the same Self as that in which one entered. When he is good, and even when he is bad, you had as soon read Warren as live. He gives you the sense of poetry as a thing of final importance to life" (75). As his verse was bursting the shackles of formalism and finding its own distinct voice, it is no wonder that Warren the critic would develop a similar admiration for Dickey's poetry.

In Joseph Millichap's essay, we meet the most recent and most unusual of Warren's friends to be highlighted in this volume. David Milch was born in 1945, sixty-four years after Elizabeth Madox Roberts's birth and four years after her death. (Interestingly enough, Warren's own career as a publishing writer lasted exactly sixty-four years—from 1923-87.). As a television writer and producer, Milch might be lucky even to be considered an artist according to the standards of high modernism. If Warren ever subscribed to those standards, however, he had long since ceased to do so by the time that Milch was a graduate student at Yale in the 1970s. Milch's advisor R. W. B. Lewis collaborated with Brooks and Warren on the textbook *American Literature: The Makers and the Making*

(1973). It was during his work on this project that Warren revised his view of such premodernist literature as the poetry of Whittier and Melville and the fiction of Dreiser. As early as the 1940s, Warren had shed any pretense to elite culture by beginning to write a series of bestselling novels in unabashedly popular genres.[6] Milch did much to close the culture gap from the other direction in his literate contributions to *Hillstreet Blues, NYPD Blue*, and (most recently) HBO's *Deadwood*, a series that gives a whole new meaning to the concept of "Adult Western."

In a memorial tribute to Warren in the fall 1990 issue of the *South Carolina Review*, I wrote the following:

> The career of Robert Penn Warren virtually defined the term "man of letters" for twentieth-century America. In terms of sheer longevity, "Red" Warren was the magnificent redwood of our literature. From the time he published his first poems in the *Fugitive* in the mid-1920s until his death on September 15, 1989, Warren was an extraordinarily productive writer of verse, fiction, literary criticism, autobiography, and meditations on American history. Turning out an average of nearly a book a year for over fifty years, he was an abiding presence in our culture. As such, he was greatly honored, often misunderstood, and finally taken for granted. Only in his absence can we begin to measure the extent of our loss. (3)

As the following essays attest, the sheer pleasure of Warren's company was no small part of that loss.

Notes

1. The Nobel laureate whose work they rejected was the Norwegian fiction writer Sigrid Undset. The college sophomore they published was a Cajun boy named Louis Moreau.
2. Most critics agree that the transitional volume for Warren was *Promises: Poems, 1954-56* (1957). In *Life Studies* (1959), Lowell abandoned the elliptical and ironic style for a poetry of direct (at times, confessional) statement, which often resembled prose broken into lines.
3. The simplistic puritanical faith of the Louisiana Cajuns was a far cry from the intellectual tradition represented by the Catholic writers Cal had been reading. (Robert Heilman once quipped that Father Shexnayder himself had probably forbidden more books than he had read.) Nevertheless, the Roman Church offered Cal the sense of order and discipline he sorely needed at this point in his life. And, like so many artists before and since, he found in the ritual of the mass an aesthetic gratification not to be had in his dour Protestant upbringing.
4. The feminist critic Elaine Showalter has tried to use this telegram as evidence that Cleanth Brooks, along with Cal Lowell and Stafford's father, constituted a patriarchal troika that hampered Jean's literary ambitions. At the end of a review of two Stafford biographies, Showalter writes: "Stafford may have mutilated herself to get back at [Lowell] or at her father or at Cleanth Brooks for that matter" (15). Elaine Showalter, "I wish she'd been a dog," *London Review of Books* 7 February 1991: 14-15.
5. The Catholic Worker Movement was a group of Catholic social activists who lived and worked among the poor in the slums of New York City. Their isolationism, mentioned by Stafford, was due to categorical pacifism rather than pro-Nazi sympathies. Although the bulk of Stafford's papers are at the University of Colorado, this letter is contained in the Beinecke Library at Yale.
6. Leslie Fiedler was one of the first critics to comment on Warren's ability to cross the culture gap. Consider, for example, *All the King's Men*, a novel of undeniable artistic achievement, which became a bestseller, won

the Pulitzer Prize, and was the basis for an Academy Award-winning movie. "For a work of real merit to win any of these doubtful distinctions is highly improbable," Fiedler notes; "and the compounded improbability of its winning all three is staggering." Leslie Fiedler, *The Collected Essays of Leslie Fiedler*, Vol. 1 (New York: Stein & Day, 1971), 339.

Works Cited

Dickey, James. *Babel to Byzantium: Poets and Poetry Now*. New York: Farrar, Straus & Giroux, 1968.
Donald, David Herbert. *Look Homeward: A Life of Thomas Wolfe*. Boston: Little, Brown, 1987.
Goodman, Charlotte Margolis. *Jean Stafford: The Savage Heart*. Austin: U of Texas P, 1990.
Hamilton, Ian. *Robert Lowell: A Biography*. New York: Random House, 1982.
Harding, Vincent. "You've Taken My Nat and Gone." In John H. Clarke, ed. *William Styron's "Nat Turner": Ten Black Writers Respond*. Boston: Beacon, 1968.
McAlexander, Hubert H., ed. *Conversations with Peter Taylor*. Jackson: UP of Mississippi, 1987.
Podhoretz, Norman. *Doings and Undoings: The Fifties and After in American Writing*. New York: Farrar, Straus, & Giroux, 1964.
Salinger, J. D. *The Catcher in the Rye* 1951, Rpt. New York: Bantam, 1964.
Stafford, Jean, "Some Letters to Peter and Eleanor Taylor." *Shenandoah* 30 (Spring 1979): 27-55.
Winchell, Mark Royden. "A Long Way from Home." *South Carolina Review* 23 (Fall 1990): 3-4.

Strange Caterwauling: Singing in the Wilderness with Boone & Audubon, Elizabeth Madox Roberts & Robert Penn Warren

by H. R. Stoneback

I

"That light's at the Jarvis place, ain't it?" [Emily Roberts] said.
Robert Penn Warren "Goodbye, Jake"

This essay is concerned with influences and intertextualities in the work of Elizabeth Madox Roberts and Robert Penn Warren; given the chronology, of course, the influences flow from Roberts to Warren, and the confluence, the merging, of their streams of artistic concerns—the Matter of Kentucky, Daniel Boone, Audubon, folk life and language, narrative and poetic style, and so forth—indicates rich sources and connections that have not yet been divined.[1] All Roberts scholars—there *are* a few of us in captivity—know that the finest short critical study of her landmark 1926 novel, *The Time of Man*, was written by Warren. That essay, "Elizabeth Madox Roberts: Life Is From Within," appeared first in the *Saturday Review*, earning cover billing together with a portrait of Miss Roberts in the March 2, 1963, issue. Shortly thereafter, with no substantive revision, the essay was reprinted as the introduction to the 1963 edition of *The Time of Man* that reintroduced Roberts to a new generation in need of, as Warren put it, "some small medicine against the special sickness and dehumanizing distortions of the 1960s" (38).

I would suggest that it is neither accidental nor incidental that Warren's essay on Roberts appeared in March 1963, a few months before his meditation on Kentucky history, "The World of Daniel Boone," was published in the December, 1963, issue of *Holiday* magazine. Perhaps Warren, typically, was hoping for double-duty from his Boone essay, as an introduction to a possible reissue of Roberts's Boone Trace saga, *The Great Meadow*. In any case, both Roberts and Warren scholars have been content—if they have noticed the matter at all—to regard his essay on *The Time of Man* as the only significant point of contact between the authors. However, I would argue that Roberts is a *seminal* influence for Warren, and thus, I hope to illuminate here the intriguing and hitherto neglected record of Roberts-Warren connections.

About that word "neglected"—it is the academic fashion to claim that every subject that we have the scholarly perseverance or critical acuity to discover has been neglected by those who came before us, so I might note that of the *twenty-four* critical studies of Warren that are in the wheelchair accessible part of my personal library not one—not one of the twenty-four books on Warren—makes any mention of Roberts. I call that *neglect*. Likewise, the sparse critical studies of Roberts have made no effort to establish a Roberts-Warren linkage; it may well seem curious that Roberts and Warren, widely considered to be Kentucky's two greatest writers, have not yet received the kind of intertextual attention their work so clearly demands.

For the Nashville Fugitives and Agrarians in the 1920s and 1930s, for Warren's teachers and colleagues at Vanderbilt, Roberts was the exemplary Southern writer. As Allen Tate wrote to Donald Davidson in 1929: "Our true Southern novelist at present is Elizabeth Roberts, who does not write as a Southerner or as anything else;" she does not purvey sociological theses, she "sticks to concrete experience," and she has "that sense of a stable world, of a total sufficiency of character, which we miss in modern life" (Fain and Young 245). Roberts continued to be held in high esteem at Vanderbilt long after she was nearly forgotten in the rest of the country; in the 1960s, when I did my doctoral work at Vanderbilt, I heard nothing but the highest praise for Roberts from the likes of Cleanth Brooks, Donald Davidson, Andrew Lytle, Allen Tate, and T. D. Young. I had an ongoing conversation about Roberts with Andrew Lytle, who in a 1977 letter to me proclaimed: "*The Time of Man* is one of the great books." He added: "I know the Tates admire her. I was with them once in Kentucky when they drove by her house and went in for a short visit. I staid in the car, which means they were meeting for the first time" (Lytle-Stoneback 8 July1977; see Stoneback, "Andrew Lytle on Roberts and Warren"). James Still and Jesse Stuart, two important Kentucky writers who did graduate work at Vanderbilt in the early 1930s (and were later friends of Roberts), also recalled the towering reputation of Roberts in Vanderbilt circles (see Stoneback, "Rivers of Earth" and "Roberts, Still, Stuart & Warren").

Warren certainly agreed with his Vanderbilt colleagues about Roberts. "By 1930," Warren recalled in his 1963 *Saturday Review* essay, "with the appearance of *The Great Meadow*, the fourth novel, it was impossible to discuss American fiction without reference to Elizabeth Madox Roberts" (20). And by 1931, the twenty-six-year-old Warren was teaching Roberts at Vanderbilt, not just as the quintessential *Southern* novelist but also as one of the most important *American* writers. Indeed, there is anecdotal evidence that Warren taught Roberts in almost every one of his Vanderbilt courses, regardless of period and topic. For a short-hand version of how I first discovered Warren's passion for Roberts when I found in 1967 a well-stocked Vanderbilt library shelf with multiple copies of Roberts's works, I will quote from my recent volume, a long poem entitled *Homage: A Letter to Robert Penn Warren*:

> [This] is about Elizabeth Madox Roberts
> whose novels you were teaching then (in *all* classes
> they said)—and how I met her in the midnight
> library stacks (I had my own key;
> my duties included Vandy departmental bibliography)
> and I held and read all night that old edition I found
> with all the marginal annotations
> by the magical incantations of place, earth, and land
> scrawled in what I knew to be your eccentric hand—
> and I knew that dawn,
> walking home through Centennial Park
> past the concrete Parthenon in the West End dark,
> what we had both learned from *The Time of Man*. (31)

Warren's first published critical commentary on Roberts appeared in his 1932 review-essay, "Not Local Color," in the *Virginia Quarterly Review*. His review deals with six recent volumes of southern fiction, including Caroline Gordon's *Penhally*, William Faulkner's *These Thirteen*, and Roberts's *A Buried Treasure*, but his most sustained attention is focused on Roberts, who exemplifies his critical point that the best Southern fiction is *not* mere local color, *not* possessed by the "abstract bad temper" of a quasi-regionalist such as Sinclair Lewis, *not* concerned with judging "a situation or society, abstractly conceived, by an abstract set of values" (154). Warren praises the "beautiful modulation and cunning grace" of Roberts's storytelling, her "flexible" poetic style "founded on, and controlled by, the sturdy idiom of the people about whom [she] writes"; and he celebrates her "rich texture of perception," her "delicate rapport" with place and community, characters and values, all of these qualities issuing naturally from the fact that she is a writer who is "comfortable within her tradition" (154-56).

Roberts, then, is Warren's textbook example of the true regionalist, the antidote for the picnic regionalism of the local colorists who clumsily destroy tradition by discovering and promulgating the merely "quaint." This bedrock principle of Vanderbilt Agrarianism remains constant for Warren, and Roberts remains his touchstone, even when her work is the *unstated* benchmark as it is, for example, in his important 1936 essay, "Some Don'ts for Literary Regionalists."

Moreover, Roberts serves Warren as an exemplar in the writing of his own fiction. In one of his earliest short stories, "Goodbye, Jake" (written in 1931 but published for the first time in 2006), the influence of Roberts is plainly visible, in some ways all too obvious: for example, Warren's protagonist is a country girl named Emily *Roberts*, who begs her lover Jake not to go away and leave her, to leave behind the family farm, as she points at the light in the valley at the *Jarvis* place, the farm next to Jake's place. Berk *Jarvis* is the name of one of Roberts's principal characters in *The Great Meadow*, the best-seller that came out the year before Warren wrote "Goodbye Jake." (And Roberts's Jarvis does go away, leaves his farm.) Those echoes are the tributes of apprentice fiction.

More important is the way that Roberts's use of agrarian motifs and concerns reverberates in Warren's fiction—from "Goodbye Jake" (and *Prime Leaf*) and throughout his work. Yet perhaps the most telling influence may be discerned in matters of style, and in Roberts's remarkable skill in rendering landscape that Warren echoes in "Goodbye, Jake" and perfects in his later fiction. Clearly, in "Goodbye, Jake," Warren writes as a fully engaged apprentice to Roberts's art of landscape. For Roberts, landscape is almost always symbolic, *paysage moralisè*, and the most extraordinary thing about her landscapes is the way they serve as objective correlatives for the inner states of being and feeling of her characters, usually young women with an intense sacramental sense of connection with the land. Roberts composes landscapes that become inscapes. The greatest risk Warren takes in "Goodbye, Jake," the challenge that he sets for himself, is to anchor the story in Emily's sensibility—he doesn't seem much interested in Jake—and to render her state of being in terms of the landscape. At this, he succeeds admirably, thanks to the example of Roberts.

But there are moments in Roberts where the land stands for itself, where *terra* (the earth), as Roberts inscribes it in *A Buried Treasure*, is simultaneously oracular and sufficient unto itself, beyond simile and metaphor, beyond symbol, in a perfectly modernist, post-symbolist mode of being (that Roberts probably learned from her study of Ezra Pound and his treatment of landscape, and Warren probably learned from both of them). *Terra*, the earth intensely observed and rendered with the exactitude that transforms the "ordinary" into the "miraculous," to *epifaneia*, the epiphany, as Czeslaw Milosz has it, of simultaneous "dread and reverence" written through the poet's "exceptional sensitivity to the rich materiality of things" (383-87)—this is another aspect of the art of landscape that Warren learns from Roberts. As a twenty-six year old book reviewer and apprentice writer of fiction he noted Roberts's use of "the fleeting word: *terra*" ("Not Local Color" 155) and sought to render the Robertsean *terra* in "Goodbye, Jake." Still, as a novelist in his seventies, he would play variations on his Roberts-derived notions of *terra* in his last novel, *A Place to Come To* (233-34 and *passim*).

Roberts never really left Kentucky, vacations and her student years at the University of Chicago aside. (Why have we always missed the allusion to Roberts in the fact that Warren's last fictional protagonist, Jed Tewksbury in *A Place to Come To*, is first a student, then a professor at the University of Chicago?) Warren did leave Kentucky, in his early twenties, never to live there again. Thus Warren negotiates and interrogates his agrarianism(s) and regionalism(s) from the non-Robertsean stance of exile—nearly a half-century in the North. If he sometimes seems like an undocumented alien wary of borders and identity in the terrain, the *terroir*, of his fiction and poetry written in exile from the South, he always has a place to come to in his creative imagination and spirit, the place called Kentucky, the place he had first seen truly and adequately rendered in the fiction of Elizabeth Madox Roberts.

Roberts's agrarian themes and her Kentucky motifs, her poetic style (anchored in folk idiom) and her mode of creation echo not just in such Warren characters as Willie Proudfit (*Night Rider*) and Ashby Wyndham (*At Heaven's Gate*) but throughout the Warren oeuvre. Early on in his exile from Kentucky, Warren planned a major Southern writers conference at Louisiana State University in 1935. Writing to his friend Allen Tate (who knew Roberts personally) about his desire to have Roberts attend (as one of the few fully reimbursed conference participants), Warren repeatedly pleads with Tate: "Urge her to come" (Clark 24-25).[2]

II

"That I should have been the recipient, on behalf of the Library [of Congress], of the Roberts Collection, has given me greater satisfaction than any other incident of my tenure of this office."
Allen Tate, Consultant in Poetry, Library of Congress 1944-45

Further compelling evidence for Roberts-Warren connections and influences may be discovered in the Roberts Papers at the Library of Congress. Allen Tate was instrumental in the library's acquisition of the Roberts Papers, which, after her death in 1941, were accessioned under the aegis of Tate as the Chair or Consultant in Poetry at the Library of Congress. In the Fall 1943 issue of the Library's *Quarterly Journal of Current Acquisitions,* Tate published a descriptive article entitled "The Elizabeth Madox Roberts Papers." He begins by thanking the Roberts family for the gift of the "literary remains" of "one of the best novelists the South has produced and the author of a modern classic, *The Time of Man.*" The Roberts Collection, Tate asserts, is with the Whitman Collection "one of the two most important literary sources for textual and critical study" in the Library's Division of Manuscripts. He notes that the papers are restricted, which limits his ability to give a full account in print of the treasures of the Roberts papers, although he does give a two-page synopsis of the manuscripts; they offer, he says, "material for the **re**creation of the imaginative process unequalled by any other similar papers in contemporary American letters."

Tate adds that he finds it "peculiarly moving; for to admiration of her writings I brought the affection of a friend; and along with these feelings I was aware…of the special sympathy, felt among writers everywhere, that comes of a common local history" (31; see also McGuire 78-79). When Tate takes leave of his Library of Congress position, which he turns over to Warren in July 1944, another Kentuckian, another Roberts aficionado, continues oversight of the cataloguing of Roberts's manuscripts.

It is one of those esoteric and fragile raptures of scholarship: to sit in the Library of Congress manuscript room and handle Roberts's deteriorating manuscripts (they have *not* made copies)—the very originals handled by Tate, then Warren. What did Warren see there? My list here must be brief, although I suggest that anyone looking for a book-or-dissertation project could expand these hints for several hundred pages. Consider these items:

(1) Extensive notes and files on the history of Kentucky, the opening and settling of the Kentucky frontier, the character of the settlers, their language and lore—some of this material, but not all of it, being notes toward the making of *The Great Meadow*;
(2) Manuscript materials for Roberts's unfinished epic on Daniel Boone, with indications that the title would be either "Daniel Boone and the Long Hunters," or simply "The Long Hunters." The material includes unpublished poems that stress such themes and images as Boone the "apostle to chaos" and Boone singing alone in the wilderness. There are scraps and notes linking Boone and Jefferson, Boone and Audubon, all against the Kentucky background. These poetic meditations on Boone, together with Roberts's extensive outline of the historical incidents, read like an outline for Warren's essay "The World of Daniel Boone" and everything he needed to write that essay is in Roberts's Boone file;
(3) Manuscript and related materials for her unfinished novel about the Ohio River flood of 1937, left unfinished at her death and bearing a title familiar to Warren aficionados—*Flood*. (Warren's 1964 novel *Flood* deals with a different river, but reverberates in many ways with Roberts's unfinished *Flood*.)

Among a host of omens and avatars of Warren's later productions is Roberts's five-page typed portrait entitled "Audubon." If these facts have not yet convinced the reader of the crucial importance of the Roberts-Warren influences and connections, then I recommend a pilgrimage to the Library of Congress, where one might sift through the Roberts Collection, handle her papers, those touchstones of intertextuality first studied by Tate and Warren.

The reader who cannot get to the Library of Congress might cheerfully settle for and study carefully Roberts-Warren resonances discernible in *The Time of Man* (1926), especially its sense of Kentucky place and folk-speech and the identity-quest of the hero, Ellen Chesser, who comes very close to saying (like Amantha Starr in Warren's *Band of Angels*): "Oh who am I?" Or study Roberts's next novel, *My Heart and My Flesh* (1927) with its ur-Faulknerian and Warrenesque themes of miscegenation, identity, and the tangled burden of Southern and family history; or her next novel *Jingling in the Wind* (1928), her satire on 1920s pseudo-sophistication, which, though widely regarded as her most flawed work, leaves the reader with a powerful core image, such as the haunting metaphor of the Spider Web that pervades her tale from the first to the last page and is tellingly echoed years later in *All the King's Men.*

Roberts's next novel, *The Great Meadow* (1930), is certainly an important source for much of Warren's southern-history-infused writing, his treatment of the Matter of Kentucky-Tennessee, in novels ranging from *Night Rider* through *At Heaven's Gate* and on beyond *The Cave* and *Flood*. Even if Warren's 1932 essay "Not Local Color," which delivers brief judgments on four Roberts novels, does note in passing the weakness of *The Great Meadow*, because its tenuous sense of reality is almost "lost in a pervasive lyricism," that very observation may be a key to Warren's later demythicizing approach to the same subjects that were dealt with in a more conventional myth-making mode by Roberts (154).

And even Roberts's last novel, her pastoral love-song with a contemporary setting, *Black is My Truelove's Hair* (1938), somehow reverberates in Warren's late fiction. In ways that have thus far shimmered only in fleeting glimpses, intuitions sensed most when I leaf through Warren's personal copy of this novel (a much dog-eared volume that is in my possession), this most contemporaneous of Roberts novels seems to be the buried subtext for Warren's penultimate novel, *Meet Me in the Green Glen*. For those who prefer concrete details and subscribe to the notion that the best writers must steal from the most obscure sources, consider Roberts's 1931 publication of what she called a children's poem, "The Legend of Munn", about the mythical Land of Munn ruled by Choo, his son Choo Choo, and grandson Choo Choo Choo, and the perilous sea-threatened existence and identity of *Munn*—and then think of the opening of *Night Rider*, with Percy *Munn* and his perilous lack of identity in that sea of humanity on that—dare I say choochoo train? (*Wings* 11).

A neglected and ephemeral item, to be sure, this children's poem that appeared in a monthly pamphlet of the Literary Guild in 1931—that year in which Warren wrote his first Robertsean fiction, "Goodbye, Jake," and also the year of his first critical essay on Roberts's work. The little booklet mailed to Literary Guild members was an essentially throwaway item of popular culture that nevertheless devoted much of its space to a striking portrait and biographical sketch of Roberts, of Kentucky frontier scenes, and a review of her new novel, *A Buried Treasure*, by the well-known literary figure, Carl Van Doren—a review that Warren probably echoed in a contrarian fashion a few months later in his review of *A Buried Treasure*. Holding my grandmother's copy of this pamphlet in my hand reminds me that in 1931 nearly everyone knew who Roberts was, even if most of us have forgotten now. My grandmother knew. Robert Penn Warren knew (See Stoneback, "Time's Wingèd Chariot").

In the 1960s when I first heard of Roberts and discovered her work on my own, I sometimes argued with my colleagues and teachers that Roberts must have been a seminal influence on Faulkner. I praised the *terroir* of her fiction, her profoundly organic sense of place and community, and cleverly explained—with little supporting evidence—the force of her effect on Faulkner's Yoknapatawpha chronicle. Just look at Lena Grove in *Light in August*, I proclaimed repeatedly: without Ellen Chesser of *The Time of Man* there would be no Lena Grove. And yet, though the evidence was all around me, I never suspected that Roberts was a far greater influence on Warren, I never fully recognized her most devout disciple until years later.

III

"Toward sunset they were struck by a strange caterwauling…"
Robert Penn Warren, "The World of Daniel Boone"

Yet it is not influence that concerns me most, but the profound intertextuality, the meditative and poetic reverberations that echo from Roberts to Warren when they write of the same subjects. Take Boone, for example. Although he is not a major character in *The Great Meadow*, Boone is the novel's presiding eminence, the Deus Loci, the Spirit of Place in the Edenic Kentucky wilderness. From the opening pages, characters talk about Boone, they follow Boone's Trace into Kentucky, they pass the place where Boone mourned the death of his son murdered by the Indians—the "red white-trash" as one character calls them. Before he makes his cameo appearance well past the halfway mark of the novel, his mythic identity is well-established. As Roberts put it in her manuscript notes to the novel: "In Boone alone we had a symbol of man leaping apart from men, thrusting forward to a lonely and hazardous freedom among the natural and chaotic things of the unmapped earth." Or this, also from her manuscript notes: Diony, the novel's central character, "represents ordered life…the mind life. She is not of the Boone kind. She feels lost in an indefinite universe. She wants ordered ways. She wants beauty and dignity and ceremony and the reasons of all things. Berk represents art. Boone represents the indefinite earth, the outside of chaos, but he is an apostle to chaos to prepare it for man's order" (Roberts Papers Box 3:1). In the novel this translates into the *insistance poétique*, the repeated assertions that Boone is "never lost" (186 and *passim*); he is utterly at home in the world, in nature, in the wilderness. Diony knows, as she repeatedly says: "I'm not the Boone kind" (187); and she knows that Boone was "a messenger to the chaotic part, a herald, an envoy there, to prepare it for civil men" (338), to make possible her epiphanic vision of "the wearying infinitives of the wilderness come to an end" (209).

When Boone comes onstage, he enters the novel singing. *The Great Meadow* resounds with song; on nearly two dozen pages we find recurrent images of singing and song lyrics, of Bangum and the wild boar, traditional folksongs that reiterate communal history, evoke the dangers of the wilderness and simultaneously project an image of singing as the act that might keep at bay the terror of the wilderness. Boone appears out of the forest, "singing to make his presence known," and pronounces his most famous lines: "I never was lost. I was bewildered right bad once for as much as a week, but not lost. I never felt lost the whole enduren time" (184-186).

And then there's Warren's Boone. In his *Holiday* magazine piece, "The World of Daniel Boone," Warren ends six of his first nine paragraphs with Kentucky-as-Eden images. He recapitulates the Robertsean touchstones of the mythic Boone, the presiding Spirit of Place who was never lost, always at home in the wilderness. He sketches the same incidents in Boone's life: mourning the death of his son at the hands of the Indians, crying at his grave years later; resisting the Indian assault on the fort at Boonesborough, dwelling in captivity with the Indians in the North. (In Roberts this action is transferred to her character, Berk Jarvis, a Boone-avatar, named after both Bishop Berkeley *and* Berks County, Pennsylvania, where Boone was born and raised.) Warren also has Boone speak his most famous one-liner, in a slightly different version from Roberts: "I can't say as ever I was lost, but I was *bewildered* once for three days" (176). And he ends his essay with a striking image of Boone singing in the wilderness, echoing Roberts's repeated images in fiction (and in her poetry) of Boone the wilderness–singer. But there are differences of detail and emphasis. One detail Warren includes that is not found in Roberts's published work on Boone (although it *is* in her manuscripts) is a brief reference to Boone's meeting with Audubon. (More on that in a moment.) The overall design of Warren's portrait of Boone is both more complex and realistic than is Roberts's straightforward presentation of the mythic Boone. Warren, characteristically, demythicizes Boone in order to reclaim the historical figure and in some sense remythicize him. We recall Warren's complaint (cited above) about the "pervasive lyricism" of Roberts's Boone-world, and the attenuated "sense of reality" he detected in *The Great Meadow* ("Not Local Color" 154). Making his alignments to bring the mythic Boone closer to reality, Warren points out, for example, that Boone the wilderness mystic was also "a prosperous innkeeper, fur buyer, occasional slave dealer, merchant and supplier of the militia"; and a land speculator, even if his claims to 100,000 acres of Kentucky's Eden were carelessly filed and ended in bankruptcy and debt (174). The best detailed discussion of this unfortunately neglected essay is in Jonathan Cullick's *Making History*, which stresses that, for Warren, the "killing of myths permits the survival of history, a more 'usable past'"; and Cullick clarifies Warren's stance as "an ambivalent realist, trying to renegotiate romanticized notions of the past while expressing nostalgia for those very notions" (19, 74).

This point is perfectly illustrated by the closing paragraph of Warren's essay, the "tale" —as Warren calls it—of how Boone was once discovered alone, singing in the wilderness. I first read this essay in the lobby of a hotel in Montego Bay, Jamaica, in 1963, when the magazine came out—a hotel, incidentally, where I was paid to sing (or caterwaul) in the nightclub, a wilderness of sorts. Until recently, I had not reread Warren's hard-to-find Boone essay, but the main thing I remembered all these decades was Warren's powerful closing image of Boone singing. It goes like this: Some "Long Hunters" are in the Kentucky wilderness; "One day," Warren writes, "toward sunset they were struck by a strange caterwauling...[a] scout went to investigate this new beast. Warily he made his way to the source of the hideous sound. It was only Daniel Boone—never famous for good voice or delicate ear—lying on a deerskin, alone in the wilderness, singing to the sunset out of his joyous heart" (177).

Like Roberts, Warren stresses Boone's joyous singing; Roberts, however, offers no qualitative description of how Boone sings, or why he sings, while Warren evokes the strange hideous sound, the joyous caterwauling of "this new beast." Boone's song is the objective correlative for everything Warren wants us to feel about Boone. It is that song, and only that song, that I remembered and was haunted by for the forty years that elapsed between my first and second reading of this essay. And it is that song that stays with Warren, too, until he revisits Boone in one of his last published poems: "Was It One of the Long Hunters of Kentucky Who Discovered Boone at Sunset?" The speaker of the poem feels the "ambiguity" of the "great wheel" of the seasons as he feels his age, but he still feels the "mystic reality / In loam's cool touch." When he loses himself in the woods (unlike Boone who was "never lost") he feels his "heart swell to a new delight." In spite of the "years that grow grimly older," he finds in the poem's final quatrain the consolation and joy of Boone's old song:

> But I think how once in his long, lone wilderness walk
> Across Kentucky—alone, sun low, arms crossed to prop his
> Face up, they found Boone singing in his tuneless crow-squawk,
> In joy just because the world is the way it is. (*Collected Poems* 611)

The title of the poem asks a question—*was* it one of the Long Hunters who found Boone in joyous song—and it leaves the historical question unanswered; the real answer to the question is that Warren, the poet as Long Hunter, has discovered Boone's joy, the "mystic reality" that takes Boone *and* Warren ever deeper *into* nature, the strange and hideous beastlike caterwauling squawking joy of walking in the world that *is*.

IV

The world declares itself. That voice
Is vaulted in—oh, arch on arch—redundancy of joy...
Robert Penn Warren, Audubon: A Vision

Before concluding, I want to say a few words about Audubon. In her unpublished manuscript notes on him, Roberts says Audubon was "an ornithologist who was...an artist, an artist who was incidentally an ornithologist." Then she brings in Audubon's hero: "Boone said of himself that he was never lost, that he was bewildered once...but never lost. Audubon knew Boone and admired him very much...visited him in the backwoods of Missouri and is thought to have painted one of the Boone portraits. Like Boone he delighted to spy out the panorama of the wilderness, to find new ways and fresh vistas." Roberts stresses Audubon's "passion to know the birds, to represent and interpret the wing in its relation to the sky and the bough," his need to follow the "insistence of design;" he is, for Roberts, the woodsman-pioneer as artist, the artist as pioneer-woodsman. She also notes Audubon's musical talents (Roberts Papers Box 8:6).

Although his *Audubon: A Vision* did not appear until 1969, Warren had written about Audubon as early as the summer of 1944, and perhaps he took a cue from Roberts's unpublished portrait of Audubon when he saw it at the Library of Congress in 1944. In any case, what matters most about Warren's *Audubon* is that it was, for many in my generation of poets, the great poem of its day and time. When it first came out in late November 1969, a poet-friend called me after midnight and read the whole poem to me over the phone. It was one of the great poetry readings, just the three of us—Jack Daniels, and the rapt disembodied voice chanting through the telephone.

It is somehow very much to the point that we shared a passion not just for Warren's work, but for the myth of Boone and the frontier, for neo-agrarian dreams of building cabins in the wilderness, and we were both working our way through our Vanderbilt PhDs by *singing* in Nashville nightclubs. We both detested the horrific Daniel Boone television series that was so popular in the 1960s; and, as fellow songwriters, we could even sing or caterwaul with withering ironic contempt (and unprintable lyric variations), the hideous unsingable theme song of the Dan'l Boone show:

> Daniel Boone was a man!
> Yes, a big man!
> With a dream of a country that'd
> Always forever be free!
> What a Boone! what a do-er!
> What a dream-come-er-true-er was he!

Possibly the worst song ever written. Indeed pop culture in the 1960s was busy relentlessly sucking the soul out of the Boone myth. Aside from the TV show, there were the popular outdoor dramas dealing with Boone, including the Fort Harrod production of "Daniel Boone—The Man and the Legend" that I almost auditioned for long ago in Harrodsburg, Kentucky. There were Daniel Boone Days and Festivals all over Kentucky (*and* Pennsylvania, Virginia, and Missouri). And it's not over yet—google Daniel Boone now and you'll get 125,152 hits, including the current "Boone My Hero Project" whose motto is: "I have never been lost, but I will admit to being confused for several weeks." And one of the first listed items will be about the winner of the Louisville regional Hooter's bikini competition, described as a "mesmerizing migrant" who demonstrates that beauty queens are like Boone, for she was headed west to make a new life in Hollywood. Of course, Hollywood has been making a mockery of Boone at least since the disastrous movie of the early 1930s based on Roberts's *The Great Meadow*. But Boone had been an American pop-culture icon long before that, since before the United States existed.

One of the early great players in the Boone outdoor drama school of entertainment was John James Audubon. By all accounts, Audubon was something of a dandy when he moved from France to the United States at the age of eighteen in 1803. At his father's southeastern Pennsylvania farm, hunting, fishing, drawing, and music were his preoccupations. Living not far from the Daniel Boone Homestead in Berks County, Audubon fell in love with the same countryside Boone had known, the woods and caves and animals; he became a passionate and skilled hunter, learning his sharpshooting skills on the same Lancaster County long rifles that Boone had used. At first, it is said, Audubon went into the woods wearing satin breeches and silk stockings. But this would not last long. After his residence in the Pennsylvania countryside and in Kentucky settlements, and his travels the length and breadth of the country in passionate pursuit of birds and art, he went to the art and publishing capital of Philadelphia in 1824 to promote his bird book, dressed in buckskins, his shoulder-length hair slicked with bear grease, calling himself the "American Woodsman." It didn't work in Philly, but they bought it in London.

Warren knows all this, even if he puts very little of it in his vision of Audubon. It is there, explicitly, once when Warren writes of Audubon: "He dreamed of hunting with Boone, from imagination painted his portrait" (*Collected Poems* 263). Implicitly, however, Boone is everywhere in the poem, the great shadowy presence, the subtext of Audubon's quest. The poem *is* a portrait, a *vision*, not a history. Its subtitle could be: "Warren dreams Audubon's dream of Boone and paints Audubon's portrait from imagination." Consider the great lines about joy, about walking in the world, about love as knowledge, and think of Boone. Consider Warren's core image of Audubon: "After sunset, / Alone, he played his flute in the forest" (262) and think of Boone's strange lonesome caterwauling in the forest. Consider these great lines:

> The world declares itself. That voice
> is vaulted in—oh, arch on arch—redundancy of joy (263)

And then hear "That voice" as not just Audubon's (and Boone's) song in the forest, but the boar grumbling in his ivy-slick, the great geese hooting northward, all the birdcalls and Audubon's whistling of them in stately halls of Europe, and hear all the voices as a song of meditation on the mystic osmosis of being. Hugh Ruppersburg has it right when he points to the "untranslatable phenomena" and the "religious exaltation" of nature, and the triumph of art and imagination in *Audubon* (93-94, 98). But Warren's "joy," his "mystic reality," is more than that.

From the American wilderness, then, Warren seizes first as a token the audible Boone, his strange caterwauling, then later extends the metaphor and song into some deeper magic of art and more passionate realms of the imagination when he creates a curious composite figure, a kind of *Auduboone*, the American Woodsman-as-Artist who, in Warren's Audubon, frames a new definition of joy, of the love that is knowledge. In Elizabeth Madox Roberts's Idea of Order in Kentucky, Boone and Audubon sing beyond the genius of the wilderness, as heralds to chaos. In Warren's Idea of Order in Kentucky, Boone and Audubon sing the joy and love and knowledge of how things are, and how the birds make ambiguous undulations as they *sing*, downward to darkness, on extended wings.

One final word: I think of Boone in Pennsylvania, next door to where my ancestors lived, and Kentucky where I lived in Boone's shadow; I think of Audubon in Pennsylvania, near Boone's homestead and my family's 1700 roots; I see Audubon in Kentucky, New Orleans, France, in Camden and on the Jersey Shore, and contemplate his last days on the Hudson River. There he knew my Hudson Valley neighbor James K. Paulding, who taught James Fenimore Cooper how to write about Boone and asked his friend Audubon to paint the famous portrait of Boone; and I remember how I wrote about Paulding while I lived in a pioneer dogtrot log cabin tilted above Boone's Cumberland River twenty miles outside Nashville, to end up living now across the Hudson River from where Audubon's portrait of Boone hung for years in the Paulding home; and how a distant relative of Paulding's told me some years ago that the ultimate American Artist was Audubon, whose first edition of *Birds of America* had just sold on the auction block at Christies for more than three million dollars; I think of how this *Auduboone* presence followed me long, long ago to the Alabama wilderness where I built a log-cabin after dropping out of college and getting out of the Marine Corps at age twenty-one.

Or maybe it was just Warren who followed me there, the Warren who worked on his *Audubon* by chanting, shouting it out loud as he drove to New Haven in his Land Rover—what a strange crow-squawking caterwauling that must have been. And I remember when I drove my battered '58 Chevy to the end of the rutted red-clay road and walked every morning at birdcall sunrise the two miles into the forest where my clearing and my cabin were, how I sang at the top of my voice, maybe intended in part to ward off lonesomeness or rattlesnakes. Yet it was a Boone-song that drew a great black snake to rise to meet me at the same point in the trail every morning, to lead the way sliding as I went singing down to the creek that ran through my clearing under the hawk-slanting sky. I now know, because Roberts and Warren sang their songs, that my strange caterwauling was an incarnational song of joy in the beingness of the world's body. And once we truly sing that song, we are never lost—maybe bewildered for a few days, but never lost.

Notes

1. This essay is a conflation of a paper presented at the 2005 Conference of the Robert Penn Warren Circle and a keynote address delivered at the 2005 Conference of the Elizabeth Madox Roberts Society.

2. Clark notes that *The Great Meadow* is Roberts's "best-known book" (25). This misleading observation may be taken as a sign of the general neglect of Roberts and disregard of Roberts-Warren connections among even the best of Warren scholars. *The Time of Man*, of course, is her "best-known book," a landmark work of the Southern literary renascence *and* American literature, celebrated since its 1926 publication by everyone from Sherwood Anderson to Ford Madox Ford, William Faulkner to Donald Davidson, Andrew Lytle, and Allen Tate. And from all available evidence, especially since he was still writing about it in 1963, *The Time of Man* was Warren's favorite Roberts work. In the early 1930s, at least, Warren regarded *The Great Meadow* as "a much weaker piece of work" than *The Time of Man* and other Roberts novels ("Not Local Color" 154).

Works Cited

Clark, William Bedford, ed. *Selected Letters of Robert Penn Warren. Volume Two: The "Southern Review" Years 1935-1942.* Baton Rouge: Louisiana State UP, 2001.

Cullick. Jonathan S. *Making History: The Biographical Narratives of Robert Penn Warren.* Baton Rouge: Louisiana State UP, 2000.

Fain, John Tyree, and T. D. Young, eds., *The Literary Correspondence of Donald Davidson and Allen Tate.* Athens: U of Georgia P 1974.

McGuire, William. *Poetry's Catbird Seat: The Consultantship in Poetry in the English Language at the Library of Congress, 1937-1987.* Washington: Library of Congress, 1988.

Milosz, Czeslaw. *To Begin Where I Am: Selected Essays.* New York: Farrar, Straus and Giroux, 2001.

Roberts, Elizabeth Madox. *The Great Meadow.* New York: Viking, 1930.

———. *Papers of Elizabeth Madox Roberts.* Washington: Library of Congress Manuscript Division. 1943-44.

Ruppersburg, Hugh. *Robert Penn Warren and the American Imagination.* Athens: U of Georgia P, 1990.

Stoneback, H. R. "Andrew Lytle on Roberts and Warren." *Elizabeth Madox Roberts Society Newsletter.* No. 6 (February 2005): 1, 5.

———. "An Introduction to 'Goodbye, Jake.'" *Shawangunk Review* 17 (Spring 2006): 96-99.

———. *Homage: A Letter to Robert Penn Warren.* New Orleans: Portals Press, 2005.

———. "Rivers of Earth and Troublesome Creeks: The Agrarianism of James Still." *The Kentucky Review.* 10 (Autumn 1990): 3-26.

———. "Roberts, Still, Stuart & Warren." *Kentucky Humanities.* 2001 No. 1 & 2: 27-37.

———. "Time's Wingèd Chariot: Images of Roberts." *Elizabeth Madox Roberts Society Newsletter.* March 2006: 2, 5.

Tate, Allen. "The Elizabeth Madox Roberts Papers." *Library of Congress Quarterly Journal of Current Acquisitions* 1 (1943): 29-31.

Warren, Robert Penn. *A Place to Come To.* New York: Random House, 1977.

———. "Elizabeth Madox Roberts: Life Is From Within." *Saturday Review* March 2, 1963: 20-21, 38.

———. "Goodbye, Jake." *Shawangunk Review.* 17 (Spring 2006): 100-10.

———. "Not Local Color." *Virginia Quarterly Review.* 8 (April 1932): 153-60.

———. "Some Don'ts for Literary Regionalists." *The American Review.* 8 (November 1936): 142-50.

———. *The Collected Poems of Robert Penn Warren.* Ed. John Burt. Baton Rouge: Louisiana State UP, 1998.

———. "The World of Daniel Boone." *Holiday.* December 1963: 162-77.

Robert Penn Warren, Thomas Wolfe, and the Problem of Autobiography

by Patricia L. Bradley

If Robert Penn Warren's career had ended when he was thirty-seven, as had Thomas Wolfe's with his death in 1938, our impressions of Warren and the canon we associate with him today would no doubt be very different. The works for which we remember Warren would have been limited to a biography of abolitionist John Brown (1929), "The Briar Patch," which was his essay contribution to *I'll Take My Stand* (1930), his *Thirty-Six Poems* (1935), *Understanding Poetry* (1938), which he co-edited with Cleanth Brooks, two novels, *Night Rider* (1939) and *At Heaven's Gate* (1943), his *Eleven Poems on the Same Theme* (1942), a smattering of short stories, a number of critical articles and reviews, and finally *Understanding Fiction* (1943), which he again co-edited with Cleanth Brooks. As even this necessarily brief listing indicates, by 1943 Warren had already written substantially across several genres: biography, essay, poetry, novel, and criticism. Still, if that body of work alone had defined our literary encounters with Warren, how understandably limited our present appreciation of him would be. Without the temperings of the mid- to late-life "revisions" of his canon permitted to the long-lived Warren, he would be ill-remembered by this present time of his centennial as an intransigent New Critic, as an avowed segregationist at best or at worst a likely racist, and as a youthful prodigy who joined the numerous ranks of poetic imitators of T. S. Eliot.

We can attribute some of the surface similarities between Kentuckian Robert Penn Warren and North Carolinian Thomas Wolfe to the universal experiences of youth and adolescence known to any young person of their day and time; other deeper similarities could speak to the special circumstances of artistic young men of the South in the early third of the twentieth century. Both were from small Southern towns—not the deep South, but similarly along its fringe—towns with identities rendered slightly more cosmopolitan than most through their connections with railroads. As a boy, Warren was awed by the frequent evidences of places and ideas beyond Guthrie, Kentucky, brought his way by the Louisville and Nashville Railroad, a connection that had even supplied his hometown with its name (Millichap 62). As part of a thriving resort community, Wolfe also understood how the fortunes of its inhabitants were directly related to train access, though in Asheville's case, it was the Southern Railroad line that provided that crucial link to the outside world. In a way, as with Warren's Guthrie, the railroad helped to create Wolfe's childhood setting: Asheville quadrupled in size after the advent of the railroad in the 1880s.

The mature Warren would dismiss Guthrie as only "a place to be 'from'" (qtd in Blotner 26), but as a boy he was awed by evidences even in Guthrie of an intellectual world practically within his reach—publications such as the *Nation*, the *New Republic*, *Poetry*, and the *Dial*—all for sale at the hotel newsstand near the railroad station (*Then & Now* 32). To the novelist Wolfe, the far-off sound of the train's whistle would serve as a recurring symbol for the world beyond Asheville, North Carolina. Until he could leave for that world on the train, it brought to his very doorstep hints of what he might find in it when he got there in the form of rich and elegant outsiders attracted to the recreational possibilities of the nearby Smoky Mountains, but also in the form of the grim and disparate "lungers" who populated his mother's boarding house in their search for respite from tuberculosis in the clear mountain air.

Warren's and Wolfe's mutual desires to leave home at the earliest occasions possible were equally strong, although probably for different reasons. Both Warren, the oldest child in his family, and Wolfe, the youngest in his, were pampered as prodigies by parents who alternately hovered over and distanced themselves from their offspring. In Warren's case, the hovering was primarily on his mother's part while his father, whose loving paternal commitment Warren never doubted, nevertheless remained a "man of mystery" (*Portrait* 7) to his son before and long after the senior Warren's death. In Wolfe's case, both parents took turns smothering and ignoring their youngest son, swapping him about from one household to another, seeing in his love for reading more oddity than not, but willing in sometimes grudging and often self-serving ways to groom the Wolfe family's one hope for intellectual distinction.

Each boy developed a love of poetry from his father. W. O. Wolfe, for example, could dramatically recite great hunks of poetry, especially Shakespeare, which his son later learned to read for himself. Robert Franklin Warren gave his son his first lesson in the art of poetry-writing and encouraged his passion for Milton when, in the completion of a high school literature assignment, the boy "simply fell in love" with the poem "Lycidas" and tried to learn everything he could about it (Blotner 27). The senior Warren and his wife Anna Ruth saw carefully to their son's education, applauding his voracious home reading and facilitating his early graduation from the high school in Guthrie; correspondingly, Wolfe's father paid for his card at the library that stood near his business, and young Tom used it assiduously. Still a year too young at fifteen to head off to college, Warren was enrolled by his parents for an extra year of high school in nearby Clarksville, Tennessee, where he boarded and lived away from home for the first time. Wolfe's parents finally broke down and paid to send their son to the North State Fitting School, a private high school, overcoming their own parsimonious reluctance and accusations of favoritism from their other children (Donald 23).

Antithetical to the paternally-fostered love for poetry, however, was the fear of failure that Warren and Wolfe each derived from his father. Young Tom, conceived at a time when a forty-nine year old father was considered "old," knew his primarily in terms of age, illness, and emasculating self-pity. Even though the initial portraits of W. O. Gant in *Look Homeward, Angel* are of a character larger than life, the repository of all that is vital and life-giving during Eugene Gant's childhood, W. O. Wolfe's failures prompted what Wolfe's biographer identifies as the son's "central theme": "a man's quest for his father" (Donald 15). Robert Franklin Warren's failures were two-fold—intellectually he had been a failed poet and economically a bankrupt. These complementary lapses, the one creative and the other practical, resulted in his son's distinctively bifurcated personality and may explain Warren's success in more than one publication genre: short stories, novels, and pedagogical nonfiction, which "paid," and his true love, poetry, which did not.

Perhaps their fears of following in their fathers' failed footsteps explains why both Warren and Wolfe differed with their fathers on the crucial decision of where to study for their undergraduate degrees. When Warren set his sights on Annapolis and chemical engineering, his father swallowed his disappointment—he having methodically but quietly steered his son for years toward Vanderbilt and a law degree—and helped him obtain the necessary paperwork to apply for a naval academy appointment. Warren's future identity as one of the original Fugitive-Agrarians was assured, however, by an accident that cost him the use of one eye along with his Naval Academy prospects. Wolfe had held out for Princeton, and if not there, the University of Virginia at Charlottesville. Strange to think that Wolfe, known for his contrarieties of literary philosophy with such Vanderbilt faculty and alumni as John Crowe Ransom, Allen Tate, Donald Davidson, and Warren, had, according to his biographer, once yearned toward UVA, "a dwelling place of culture, the last and greatest academy of the old aristocracy, an American Oxford" (qtd in Donald 30), and surely a corollary to Nashville's Vanderbilt in Old South social conservatism.

Instead, of course, Wolfe ended up at the University of North Carolina at Chapel Hill, and in his turn part of a more casually realized band than the Fugitive-Agrarians, including progressives such as Jonathan Daniels, Paul Green, Frederick Koch, and Frank P. Graham. They, according to Floyd Watkins, "could have written a *Fugitive*" if they hadn't been "fleeing the Old South" the Vanderbilt Fugitive-Agrarians were hoping to salvage (411). Watkins further notes that Wolfe's visibility after his publications of *Look Homeward, Angel* (1929) and *Of Time and the River* (1935), reinforced by his Chapel Hill connections, may have made him the perfect whipping boy for the Fugitive-Agrarians and their later new critical counterparts, most of whom "have at some time had something to say of Wolfe's art and ideas" ("Thomas Wolfe" 411). Watkins numbers among Wolfe's critics Donald Davidson, Allen Tate, John Peale Bishop, John Donald Wade, John Crowe Ransom, and Robert Penn Warren (412-13).

Not all they had to say was negative. Upon publication of *Of Time and the River*, Warren, for example, and John Donald Wade, a fellow Agrarian with whom Warren taught briefly at Vanderbilt, publicly recognized Wolfe's writing talent, the former in a 1935 review for *American Review*, and the latter in an essay entitled "Prodigal" that appeared in the *Southern Review*, also in 1935. Notwithstanding, both essays proceeded as well to fault Wolfe for limiting himself to recording, in Wade's words, merely "his own passage through the world" (194) and, in Warren's words, writing autobiography so transparent as scarcely to maintain the "pretense of fiction" (206). Warren's most famous line from his essay—"it may be well to recollect that Shakespeare merely wrote *Hamlet*; he was *not* Hamlet"—resounds with Fugitive-Agrarian, if not New Critical, dismissiveness of Wolfe's distinctive use of autobiographical materials. In fact, just the next spring Wade similarly invokes Shakespeare as literary exemplar in yet another review, adopting Warren's earlier locution in the process. Writing of Southern stereotypes such as "Jeeter Lester and his kind" in Erskine Caldwell's *Tobacco Road*, Wade cautions: "Shakespeare . . . made his Caliban, but *The Tempest* is not *filled* with Calibans" (455).

Not unreasonably, we can assume that the shared critical recoil from barely fictionalized autobiography reflected in Warren's and Wade's commentaries on Wolfe may have had its source in the Fugitive-Agrarian culture that had been generally present at Vanderbilt for over a decade as well as in the earliest New Critical views of John Crowe Ransom, in particular. In 1933 Ransom would dismiss Milton's "Lycidas," for example—the work that had fired Warren's schoolboy imagination and prompted his first yearnings toward creating his own poetry, not to mention its having provided Thomas Wolfe with the title of his first, autobiographical, novel. Ransom's critique of Milton's elegiac poem contains, in part, one of the same critical principles mustered by his former student Warren and then colleague Wade in their readings of Wolfe: the author's too ready use of autobiographical references. As Thomas Underwood observes, in "A Poem Nearly Anonymous," Ransom's well-known commentary on "Lycidas," the critic delineates "the risks Milton had taken in allowing a portion of his personality to infiltrate and slightly alter the classical form of his poetry" (36). Ransom's stance on Milton's autobiographical tendencies in "Lycidas" may explain a subsequent critical jibe at Cleanth Brooks's *Modern Poetry and the Tradition* in 1939. Reading into Brooks's new critical thesis the threatened loss of previously canonical texts, Stuart Gerry Brown observed for the *Sewanee Review* that "it is surely not a very penetrating criticism which would by implication exclude 'Lycidas'" (qtd in Winchell 171).

By 1939, however, Wolfe was lost to the world, and Warren was left to realize for his own part the role autobiography could play in the creative process—i.e., the literary effects of the "Lycidas" factor, which was clearly a mere diminished thing in modernist poetics. Critically, he remained firm in his assertions that a too ready reliance upon autobiography weakened a text. We have no better examples of Warren's defense of a sound creative distance from the incursions of self and Wolfe's subsequent but reluctant acceptance of that artistic fact of life than juxtaposed passages from the writings of each author. The first comes from Warren's 1943 essay "Pure and Impure Poetry," a logical extension of his "Note on the Hamlet of Thomas Wolfe." In this essay, the critic warns of necessary presences such as his own ironic intertextual voice that would logically challenge an author's too willing inclusion of autobiography, if that inclusion led to the author's claiming an "unearned vision that is tested by a more experientially minded readership" (Bradley 49). Once again, Warren cites Shakespeare, as he had in the earlier review of *Of Time and the River*, hearing the critic's ironic voice in Mercutio's outside the garden wall as Romeo rashly and unrealistically swears his undying love under Juliet's balcony. As with Romeo—as with Wolfe—:

> Poetry wants to be pure, but poems do not. . . . They mar themselves with cacophonies, jagged rhythms, ugly words and ugly thoughts, colloquialisms, clichés, sterile technical terms, headwork and argument, self-contradictions, cleverness, irony, realism—all things which call us back to the world of prose and imperfection.
> Sometimes a poet will reflect on this state of affairs and grieve.
> ("Pure and Impure Poetry" 174)

Wolfe as author conceded this point in his fiction that followed *Of Time and the River* by effecting as deliberate and resolute a turn from autobiography as he was capable. His decision to do so is implicitly and more personally confirmed in a letter to his mother, the anguished tone of which echoes the certainty tinged with pathos of Warren's critical pronouncement: "[Y]ou can't go home again. . . . I found that out through exile, through storm and stress, perplexity and dark confusion. I found it out with blood and sweat and agony, and for a long time I grieved" (*Letters*).

The certainty of Warren the critic, however, often outstripped that of Warren the novelist. When Warren's novel *World Enough and Time* was published in 1950, John Crowe Ransom privately disparaged it to Allen Tate for its Wolfeian qualities of "phony style," "bad rhetoric," and "pseudo-philosophy" (qtd in Underwood 36). Some years afterward, Warren was in the position of having his own critical words used against him when interviewer Marshall Walker questioned whether the novels *Wilderness* (1961) and *Band of Angels* (1955) could each have benefited from his more effective use of the ironic "Mercutio in the underbrush" (160). To his credit, Warren accepts the criticism and offers the self-criticism that the central character of *Wilderness* and the narrator in *Band of Angels* were limited by his authorial failure to inject sufficient "richness and depth" into their fictive life experiences (Marshall 162).

More contemporary with his formulation of Shakespeare's Mercutio as critical metaphor, however, was Warren's publication of his second novel, *At Heaven's Gate*, in 1942. Its working title, *And Pastures New*, like the title of Thomas Wolfe's novice work, had been borrowed from Milton's "Lycidas." Its plot, similar to those of many of Warren's novels, follows the career of young Jerry Calhoun, who abandons the teachings of his own father to find success, betrayal, and harsh epiphany, all in short order, through the mentorship of a false father. Warren's theme of the search for the true father—a form of covert autobiography, I might add—becomes more and more overtly stated in his work as he begins to gain an appreciation for the value of the autobiographical impulse to his own art. This developing appreciation is inseparable from his growing regard for his own true father,— the failed artist Robert Franklin Warren, whose initiatory lessons in writing poetry had encouraged his son to consider Milton's "Lycidas" a model for form (elegy) and substance (veiled autobiography),— and located in the poem, in those qualities more artistically satisfying than the New Critical fathers, who had later displaced him, would be willing to accept.

ଔ

Warren scholars frequently debate the significance of the long poetic drought with which he was afflicted through most of the decade of the forties and into the early fifties. Some point to this decade as the period of the painful culmination of his difficult marriage to Emma Cinina Brescia, from whom Warren was finally divorced in 1951. Others point to his need for financial stability and the greater economic certainty to be had through writing fiction and co-editing textbooks; certainly, his subsequent marriage to Eleanor Clark and his becoming a father for the first time validate that argument. Still others recognize that when Warren did resume his love affair with lyric poetry in the late 1950s—some of which was inspired by that growing family—he was working his way toward writing poetry of a different sort than he had written before. These critics cite Warren's poetry from the mid-career *Brother to Dragons* (1953), in which Warren's own father and Warren himself as "R.P.W." make significant appearances, to the late-life poetry, often dubbed "confessional," and to which, in the collection of poems entitled *Being Here* (1980), Warren himself cautiously attributes a "shadowy autobiography" (*Collected Poems* 441).

In the same way that Warren began the process of poetic self-revision in the 1950s, and probably in a way integral to that process, he also began a period of critical self-revision during the late 1960s and early 1970s. These years in particular mark a period during which Warren, in collaboration with Cleanth Brooks and R.W.B. Lewis, was writing a series of introductions to authors and literary periods preparatory to publishing their massive, two-volume anthology entitled *American Literature: The Makers and the Making* (1973). And if, in the course of what collaborator Lewis called "Warren's Long Visit to American Literature," he didn't revisit the work of Thomas Wolfe *per se* (Cleanth Brooks drew this assignment although Wolfe's first two novels bear the co-editors' imprimatur as works with which "the student should have more than a passing acquaintance" [Brooks, Warren, and Lewis xviii]), Warren did revisit both implicitly and explicitly some of his earlier critical pronouncements on the significant role played by autobiography in important American fiction. Indeed, as Lewis would later record in his reminiscence about this rich collaboration for the *Yale Review*, "Warren's visit to American literature . . . was a visit to himself" (574). To put the case in more specific terms, several of Warren's author introductions are very revealing in the extent to which they engage not only the plain biographical detail basic to an anthology introduction but also in the extent to which they function as a kind of veiled autobiography as Warren writes out some of his conclusions about his own life and work during this crucial period.

Lewis, like others who witnessed firsthand Warren's incredible energy for throwing himself into a project, seems retrospectively stunned by "the sheer magnitude of these commentaries" (571) written for inclusion in the anthology. In fact, several of Warren's author introductions for *The Makers and the Making* were substantial enough to merit individual publication elsewhere. Four of them in particular served the occasion not only for "Warren's visit to American literature," but also for his revisiting elements of his own autobiography as they were revealed through his affinities with the biographies, personal and artistic, of each of four figures: Herman Melville, John Greenleaf Whittier, Nathaniel Hawthorne, and Theodore Dreiser.

Warren's biographer Joseph Blotner also observes the general trend toward the critic's interweaving of his own autobiographic consciousness into the introductions written for *American Literature: The Makers and the Making*. Thus, in a reading of Warren's anthology introduction to Herman Melville, which had earlier been published in amplified form in the volume *Selected Poems of Herman Melville* (1970), Blotner indicates "some affinity of loss" between Warren and his subject—the two had been similarly aware of their fathers' failures and would similarly find refuge in poetry when faced with a public unsympathetic with their efforts in fiction (390-91). Blotner finds additional affinities between author and subject in Warren's *John Greenleaf Whittier's Poetry* (1971), which again appears in a somewhat different form as one of the anthology's author introductions. Of this analysis, Blotner observes how Warren, who often spoke of his closeness to his own parents and two siblings, is in this regard much like the self-described Whittier of "Snow-bound." To Blotner, Whittier in his turn presents his "Snow-bound" family in "loving portraits, . . . in the context of one of Warren's own obsessive subjects: time, especially loved ones perceived over time" (Blotner 392).

Blotner and Lewis are equally struck by Warren's autobiographical affinities with the biographical details he attributes to Nathaniel Hawthorne's life. Blotner comments, "[o]nce again, [Warren's] treatment of the writer's background and subject matter, skills and obsessions, suggests his own" (393). In my own analysis of the Warren and Hawthorne affinity in the essay "Nathaniel Hawthorne in the Attic: Robert Penn Warren's 'The Circus in the Attic' and Critical (Auto)Biography," I approach another convoluted affinity that Warren shares with Hawthorne, and that is their equal reluctance to own and develop the autobiographical elements of their art. Ironically, for Warren, especially given his strongly stated views on the literary weaknesses that can result from such elements, his Hawthorne introduction becomes a cautionary tale in which the nineteenth-century master shrinks from the possibilities for self-knowledge that a less distanced perspective—an autobiographical perspective, for example—would permit. For Warren, Hawthorne's evasive use of symbol and resolute literary focus on the safe expanse of history provide the ultimate insurance for his authorial comfort with himself and his materials. Hawthorne consistently turns from the self-awareness autobiographical elements in his fiction would confer; Warren, as critical observer of the phenomenon, seems poised to learn from the omissions of this literary father.

Warren's Dreiser study was also "recycled," a longer version having appeared in 1971 as *Homage to Theodore Dreiser* in recognition of the centennial of its subject's birth. It came at a time when Dreiser's literary reputation as a novelist was hardly on the upswing, a detail that, according to Blotner, posited still another affinity between Warren and his topic. Other affinities noted by Blotner include their shared balancing of lyricism and naturalism in their novels, their common experiences of "tremendous ambition and drive for success," and similar identities as "yearners," Dreiser for professional and intellectual status and Warren for some enriching force of life in which to place his faith (Blotner 401). Most telling for Blotner, however, is Warren's recognition in *Homage* that "the secret drama of Dreiser's [work] is the rejection of a father who, after failure, lived" (qtd in Blotner 401). This factor alone creates an intriguing triangularity among Warren, his current subject Dreiser, and his former subject Wolfe.

Finally, however, *Homage to Theodore Dreiser* is the study wherein we see most clearly how Warren's "long visit to American literature" was also his opportunity to revisit some of the critical pronouncements he had made in such essays as "The Hamlet of Thomas Wolfe" and "Pure and Impure Poetry." In this book-length essay, we see him struggling to come to terms with Dreiser's dependence upon autobiography as a foundation for what Warren asserts as "art"; thus, it is not entirely coincidental, perhaps, that this defense and promotion of the Dreiserian canon implicitly and explicitly identifies the many biographical details and artistic methods shared by Dreiser and Thomas Wolfe.

For example, Warren's citation of Dreiser's mantra, "No common man am I" (14), his focus on Dreiser's "yearnings for wealth, display, . . . power," and his recognition of his "deep social resentments" (16) are replicated in Wolfe's well-documented narcissism. Wolfe, as his biographer states, was absorbed with "grandiose fantasies of unlimited success, power, brilliance, and endless love" (Donald 15). Indeed, some of the coarse biographical details Warren includes about Dreiser are as integral to the formation of his literary character as they are to Wolfe's. Warren quotes Dreiser's description of himself as "blazing with sex" and records that he was "a ferocious masturbator" (16), descriptions that match the commentary on Wolfe's sexual proclivities in David Donald's biography. Even Dreiser's predisposition for voicing the most personal details of his life to others has a counterpart in Wolfe's social behavior. Warren observes:

> [T]he same kind of compulsive veracity (so strangely mixed with his compulsive lying) that made [Dreiser] record such details of his own life as masturbation . . . , made him struggle to convert into fiction the substances of experience at both the personal and social levels. (34)

"Compulsive veracity" is an equally fitting term for the quality Wolfe exhibited in the company of Warren and several others of the Fugitive-Agrarians to whom he affirmed the inauthenticity of the brothel in which portions of Faulkner's *Sanctuary* are set. Wolfe attributed this knowledge to his having "intimate acquaintance with whore houses in many places" (qtd in Donald 361). "Compulsive veracity" is also a term appropriate to the types of revelations that appear in as personal a novel as *Look Homeward, Angel*, as well as, Warren argues, to the entire scope of Dreiser's canon. It is possible that even Wolfe himself intuited his personal and literary affinities with Dreiser when he recognized him as a "gigantically thorough realist" (qtd in Donald 145).

From these psychic and grossly physical similarities, however, we turn to the matter of fiction intermingled with autobiography, the topic on which Warren expends a great deal of critical energy over his lengthy career, first as a youthful reader and writer in "A Note on the Hamlet of Thomas Wolfe" and finally as a seasoned critic and novelist in *Homage to Theodore Dreiser*. Where the younger Warren reveals himself as a wary reader of Thomas Wolfe's two most autobiographical works, *Look Homeward, Angel* and *Of Time and the River*, in the passage of thirty years and with his rereading of Theodore Dreiser's canon, Warren writes a qualified validation of his autobiographical impulses in 1969, even claiming Dreiser as "second to none" among his literary preferences (qtd in Blotner 399).

Significantly in his *Homage*, the Dreiser novel that Warren finds least critically satisfying is the one with the most resemblances to Wolfe's first two novels: *The "Genius"* (1915). Warren speaks positively of Dreiser's theme; because he wrote about "the self-consciousness of the artist in the modern world," Warren places him in the ranks of such authors as "Flaubert and Melville . . . Proust, Mann, Hemingway, Wolfe, and Camus" (53). Warren adds that "Thomas Wolfe's *Of Time and the River* is in many ways similar to *The 'Genius,'* even in the name of the hero" (148), Eugene Witla, whose first name means "the 'wellborn'" (*Homage* 53), a fact about Eugene Gant that Thomas Wolfe also shares with his reader in *Look Homeward, Angel*, although he makes the important distinction between "wellborn" and "well bred." In a negative vein, Warren's comment that "*The 'Genius'* was a thinly disguised version of Dreiser's ambitious career, his marriage, his promiscuous love affairs" (49) would seem to echo his earlier estimation of Wolfe's first two novels as making "thin and slovenly" gestures toward fiction, and his reference to the "appalling bulk of the manuscript," which Dreiser at the time regarded as "his finest novel" (51) hearkens to the many literary anecdotes recounting Thomas Wolfe's own authorial capacity for infinite self-expression and self-delusion.

Warren's overall defense of Dreiser's autobiographical tendencies in his fiction is immediate and bluntly-spoken. More than once, Warren claims for himself the privilege "to turn autobiographical" in his critical viewpoints (72), and thus he first addresses his personal temptation to downplay Dreiser's achievements, "to think of [Dreiser] as a kind of uninspired recorder blundering along in a dreary effort to transcribe actuality . . . [or] .

. . to think that what is good is good by the accident of the actuality that he happened to live into—not by any power that he, as artist, might have achieved" (*Homage* 9). The critical view Warren now renounces sounds much like the Warren of thirty years earlier who denigrates *Look Homeward, Angel* and *Of Time and the River* as "essentially two parts of an autobiography" in which "the pretense of fiction is . . . thin and slovenly" ("The Hamlet" 206). True, Warren admits, "Dreiser did write voluminously in the form of straight biography about himself and his work"; equally true is that "these autobiographical writings are scarcely distinguishable from his fiction" (*Homage* 9). But Warren tempers these observations with a realization won from a lifetime of his own writing, both critical and creative: "What is wrong with this way of thinking is, of course, that it does not account for the fact that, in one sense, art is the artist's way of understanding—of creating even—the actuality that he lives" (*Homage* 9).

Or, in Warren's case, the artful rendering of autobiographical materials was his way of understanding—of creating even—the actuality that he had lived and sought at the end of his life to understand more fully. Warren's long visit to American literature for *The Makers and the Making*—Warren's long visit to himself that entailed visits to writers such as Theodore Dreiser—and Warren's long preoccupation with autobiography that had begun with his earliest critical pronouncements on Thomas Wolfe—all speak to a blending of autobiographical and creative impulses that will come to remarkable confluence in final works both personal and poetic. In Warren's *Portrait of a Father* (1988), ostensibly a reminiscence about Robert Franklin Warren, but in reality as close to straightforward autobiography as we have from the pen of Robert Penn Warren, the son lovingly acknowledges the father with whom and in whom he had studied Milton's "Lycidas" as elegy informed by autobiography. This prose work, however, is only the culmination of what is, according to Harold Bloom, the great and defining poetry of Warren's last major phase, that period after 1965, the year he turned sixty. Warren, granted by virtue of his long life a period of poetic self-revision, gave himself over then to "a great contest with time, with cultural and family history, and above all, with himself. . . . Warren wrestled with the angel of the poetic sublime and carried away the victory of a new name" (Bloom xxiii).

Works Cited

Blotner, Joseph. *Robert Penn Warren: A Biography*. New York: Random House, 1997.
Bradley, Patricia L. "Nathaniel Hawthorne in the Attic: Robert Penn Warren's 'The Circus in the Attic' and Critical (Auto)Biography." *Nathaniel Hawthorne Review* 29.2 (Fall 2003): 38-49.
———. *Robert Penn Warren's Circus Aesthetic and the Southern Renaissance*. Knoxville: U of Tennessee P, 2004.
Brooks, Cleanth, Robert Penn Warren, and R.W.B. Lewis. Letter to the Reader. *American Literature: The Makers and the Making*. New York: St. Martin's Press, 1973. xi-xx.
Donald, David Herbert. *Look Homeward: A Life of Thomas Wolfe*. Boston: Little, Brown, 1987.
Lewis, R.W.B. "Warren's Long Visit to American Literature." *Yale Review* 70.4 (Summer 1981): 568-91.
Millichap, Joseph R. *Dixie Limited: Railroads, Culture, and the Southern Renaissance*. Lexington: UP of Kentucky, 2002.
Underwood, Thomas. "Autobiography and Ideology in the South: Thomas Wolfe and the Vanderbilt Agrarians." *American Literature* 61.1 (March 1989): 31-45.
Wade, John Donald. "Sweet Are the Uses of Degeneracy." *Southern Review* 1 (1935/36): 449-66.
Walker, Marshall. "Robert Penn Warren: An Interview." *Talking with Robert Penn Warren*. Ed. Floyd Watkins, John T. Hiers, and Mary Louise Weaks. Athens: U of Georgia P, 1990. 147-69.
Warren, Robert Penn. *The Collected Poems of Robert Penn Warren*. Ed. John Burt. Baton Rouge: Louisiana State

UP, 1998.
———. *Homage to Theodore Dreiser*. New York: Random House, 1971.
———. "A Note on the Hamlet of Thomas Wolfe." *Thomas Wolfe: Three Decades of Criticism*. Ed. Leslie A. Field. New York: New York UP, 1968. 205-16.
———. *Portrait of a Father*. Lexington: UP of Kentucky, 1988.
———. "Pure and Impure Poetry." *A Robert Penn Warren Reader*. New York: Random House, 1987. 173-95.
Watkins, Floyd. *Then & Now: The Personal Past in the Poetry of Robert Penn Warren*. Lexington: UP of Kentucky, 1982.
———. "Thomas Wolfe and the Nashville Agrarians." *The Georgia Review* 4 (Winter 1953): 410-423.
Winchell, Mark Royden. *Cleanth Brooks and the Rise of Modern Criticism*. Charlottesville: UP of Virginia, 1996.
Wolfe, Thomas. *The Letters of Thomas Wolfe*. Ed. Elizabeth Nowell. New York: Scribner's, 1956.

Cleanth Brooks and Robert Penn Warren:
A Beautiful Friendship

by Mark Royden Winchell

The story of their first meeting has been told so many times that it has become part of the folklore of modern Southern literature. One day, during the fall of 1924, Robert Penn Warren stopped by Kissam Hall on the Vanderbilt campus to visit his friend and classmate Saville Clark. With Clark was his new roommate, a freshman named Cleanth Brooks. Although only a year and a half older than Brooks, the precocious Warren was already a senior and an important member of the group of poets that called themselves "Fugitives." Despite his local eminence, Red Warren took enough of an interest in his new acquaintance to look at one of Cleanth's freshman themes and to compliment him on his "natural style." As Humphrey Bogart said to Claude Rains at the end of *Casablanca*, it was the beginning of a beautiful friendship.[1]

That friendship continued for the next sixty-five years, ending only with Warren's death on September 14, 1989. For most of this time, the two men were in close proximity to one another. When Brooks arrived at Oxford as a Rhodes Scholar in October 1929, Warren had already been there a year and left a note in Cleanth's room welcoming him to campus. Then, from 1934-42, they were colleagues in the English department at Louisiana State University. During the last seven of those years, they edited the original series of the *Southern Review*. By 1947, Brooks was teaching at Yale, where he was joined by Warren in 1950; they would be neighbors in Connecticut for the next four decades.

For several reason, the friendship of Brooks and Warren did not flourish during their undergraduate days. Not only was Cleanth less advanced in intellect and less committed to the literary life, he also possessed a very different temperament from Red. At eighteen, Cleanth Brooks was a preacher's kid (son of the Reverend Cleanth Brooks, Sr., of the Methodist Episcopal Church, South) who had experienced no adolescent rebellion to speak of. His years at a small Tennessee prep school were spent in an environment morally consistent with everything he learned in his father's home. Although not sinful in themselves, dancing and card playing were considered dangerously frivolous. Frowned upon at any time, drinking was strictly forbidden now that Prohibition was the law of the land. Courtship was permitted but sexual liberties were not. (The boys at prep school even had to take an oath not to leave campus after dark.) Had Cleanth chafed under any of these restrictions, the more open atmosphere at Vanderbilt would have been an invitation to bacchanalian revels. In fact, he neither participated in such revels nor condemned them. He simply seemed interested in other things.

In contrast, Red Warren was a creature of the Jazz Age, whose nocturnal exploits read like something out of a Scott Fitzgerald short story set on a small Southern campus. Warren's frequent companion in these exploits was a student of French named Bill Bandy. As Warren recalls, Bandy "had the only Stutz Bearcat on the campus. About three o'clock one morning, with several of us as passengers, he undertook to climb the great story-high stone flight of entrance steps to Wesley Hall in the Bearcat. He succeeded, and then made a hair-raising descent, bouncing back step by step in reverse as astonished theological heads popped out of the upper windows of the building. Bandy leveled off at the bottom and sped away. The culprits were never identified" ("Reminiscence 208). On another night Red Warren, so drunk on bootleg liquor that he could not make it back to his own lodging, appeared at Kissam Hall and collapsed in bed with Cleanth Brooks.

It was not until their time at Oxford that the friendship of Brooks and Warren matured socially and intellectually. Their academic work differed, as Red was pursuing a B.Litt degree while Cleanth was enrolled in the Hours B. A. program, but they spent many an after-hours session either in Red's lodgings in Wellington Square or among friends in Exeter College. Cleanth recalls a night at Exeter when a group of young men (some Rebels, some Yankees, some British) began discussing the War Between the States: "It was a matter of intense interest to Red and he promised to lay out before us then and there precisely what had gone on at the Battle of Gettysburg and particularly what had gone awry for the Confederate side.... Unfortunately, just before the batteries opened up on Cemetery Ridge in preparation for Pickett's Charge, the college bell began its hideous racket, warning that one had to be in his rooms before 12:15. So Pickett's Charge was over before it began, Red was out of the room in a trice, his scholar's gown fluttering behind him as he fled" ("Brooks on Warren" 20).

The B.Litt program Red was finishing was for an advanced research degree similar to a Ph.D. in an American university. He was also writing poetry noticeably influenced by the extravagant and baroque imagery one finds in the plays of Shakespeare and his contemporaries. Unlike Donne, who was better known for the logical development of a controlling metaphor, Warren sought psychological unity through an accumulation of striking, often violent, images rendered in archaic diction. (He had already developed an interest in Elizabethan drama, which would become one of his primary teaching areas during his later academic career.) At the same time, Red never got so absorbed in the literature of another age and another land that he lost his American roots. (On many an evening at Oxford, he enjoyed hearing Cleanth's angelic rendition of "Frankie and Johnny," an American folk song about a homicidal woman and the man who "done her wrong.") His year in England had also made Red more of a Southerner than he had been back in Tennessee. His book *John Brown: The Making of a Martyr* came out in 1929, and his participation in the Agrarian manifesto *I'll Take My Stand* (1930) kept the fate of Southern culture on his mind.

Unlike the English department at Vanderbilt, the program at Oxford was not hospitable to new developments in literary criticism. The nearby University of Cambridge, however, was a different matter. Like Vanderbilt, Cambridge in the twenties produced what George Core calls a "fifth column" of young writers and critics who were challenging the old orthodoxy (Core 23). If there was a difference (other than the greater distinction of the English university), it was that Cambridge criticism was more fully integrated into the official curriculum. In 1921, a young Cambridge graduate named Ivor Armstrong Richards joined the faculty of his alma mater as a lecturer in English and Moral Science. By the end of the decade, he was giving lectures that were so popular that some had to be held in the streets—the first time that had happened at Cambridge since the Middle Ages.

When Cleanth and Red were at Oxford in the late twenties, the former Fugitives had, as yet, published little criticism. Although their poetry had inspired an interest in contextual analysis and close reading, their critical insights tended to be random and untheoretical. Cleanth, in particular, believed that Richards was raising some of the questions inchoate in the Fugitive approach to poetry.

In 1929, Richards published a book called *Practical Criticism*, which was based on a series of classroom experiments conducted among honours students at Cambridge between 1925 and 1928. Richards gave out a total of thirteen unidentified poems to those students and asked for their response. When judged by commonly accepted literary standards, five of the thirteen poems would have been considered bad; six good to great; and two borderline. Richards's students, confronting the text without the benefit of history or biography, not only varied widely in their judgments but also fell prey to every conceivable form of misreading. Although it would have been easy enough for Richards to give them the "right" answers, his concern was with nurturing the sort of critical intelligence that would enable his students to come up with those answers on their own.

Like the textbooks that Brooks and Warren would later edit, *Practical Criticism* was, at heart, an exercise in pedagogy. Whatever else it may be, applied criticism is also a form of remedial reading.[2] In letting his students make mistakes, Richards played the role of a diagnostician, who observes a problem in order to discover its causes. The problems he found included an inability to discern the plain sense of a poem, a failure to apprehend its rhythm and movement, difficulties in visualizing its imagery; irrelevant associations from the reader's personal life, stock responses to the poem's theme, an excess of sentiment (sentimentality), a deficiency of sentiment (hardness of heart); doctrinal prejudices (usually political or religious), technical preconceptions, and other critical expectations. In identifying these deficiencies, Richards indirectly defined a positive approach to criticism. As Brooks himself observed, "if one is able to point out a sufficiency of errors made by others, he has at least implied the general lineaments of a sound reading" ("I. A. Richards and Practical Criticism" 38).

I

After he finished his degree at Oxford, Cleanth Brooks was hired to teach English at Louisiana State University in Baton Rouge. (At the time, the Dean of the Graduate School, Charles W. Pipkin, was actively recruiting promising faculty in all departments.) During his first four years at LSU (1930-34), Cleanth had little direct contact with Red Warren. Although he recalled seeing a picture of a dark-haired California girl on Red's dresser at Oxford, he did not realize that Red was already secretly married to Emma Brescia, who was called "Cinina" by her friends. The new bride, with whom Red began to live on his return to the Untied States, had been born in Ecuador of Italian parents (her father later became a music professor at Mills College in Oakland, California) and spoke several languages fluently. It was as a young married man that Red had to decide whether to pursue a safe career as a scholar or to take his chances with poetry, fiction, and criticism. Deciding for the latter, he turned down a fellowship to complete his doctorate at Yale and vowed never to contribute an article to a scholarly journal (Bohner 25).

With a new wife to support and his years as a best-selling author still in the future, Red accepted a one-year appointment to teach English at Southwestern College, an exclusive liberal arts school in Memphis. In 1931, he left there to take a temporary position at Vanderbilt. Returning to the scene of his past triumphs, Red might well have thought that he had entered a time warp. Although the Fugitive group had disbanded, two of it founding members, John Crowe Ransom and Donald Davidson, were still on the scene, still writing poetry and criticism. At the same time, their activities on behalf of the socially conservative Agrarian movement were gaining them the sort of publicity that the New South liberals who ran Vanderbilt found embarrassing. The English department chairman Edwin Mims, in particular, considered *I'll Take My Stand* an attack on the progressive values he had championed in his own writing. If Ransom and Davidson were well-established members of the department, Warren was little more than an upstart, and it is a small wonder that Mims agreed to hire him at all. The year Warren graduated from Vanderbilt, Mims resigned from a position teaching night school at the Watkins Institute in Nashville, but when he learned that Red had applied for the job and would be his successor, Mims rescinded his resignation out of pure spite.

At the end of the 1933-34 school year, Warren's contract was not renewed. (Years later, John Ransom wrote to Cleanth: "The letting go of Warren, who asked so little as a reward for staying, is the most nearly criminal thing in the Vanderbilt record"; Ransom *Letters* 277). Once again, Charles Pipkin came to the rescue, inviting Red to the LSU campus for a lecture and hoping that the English department chairman, W. A. Reed, would do the rest. Given Red's greater prominence in the literary world, his appointment to the LSU faculty was more nearly a foregone conclusion than it had been for Cleanth. Brooks and Warren were now together for the third time in their careers and ready to embark on a collaboration that would alter the literary history of our time.

The event that set all of this in motion occurred on an otherwise unremarkable Sunday afternoon in February 1935. LSU president James Monroe Smith drove his black Cadillac limousine up to the cottage Warren was renting on Park Drive in south Baton Rouge. Smith invited Red, his wife Cinina, and their boarder Albert Erskine for a drive in the country—an unusual courtesy for a university president to extend to an assistant professor who had yet to complete his first year on the faculty. Smith, however, had concluded that LSU needed a literary quarterly, and he wanted Warren's advice on how to bring this dream to fruition. Red advised the president that the project could be accomplished for approximately $10,000 a year, "if you paid a fair rate for contributions, gave writers decent company between the covers, and concentrated editorial authority sufficiently for the magazine to have its own distinctive character and quality" (Brooks and Warren *Anthology* xi). At Smith's urging, Warren and Erskine joined forces with Cleanth and Charles Pipkin to draw up a plan for the magazine; and, the next day, Smith officially authorized the project. The first issue of the *Southern Review* appeared five months later.

The beginnings of the review were so hectic that the magazine tended to define itself along the way. Although the presence of Pipkin as nominal editor assured that the journal would give some space to social and political issues, Brooks and Warren were the young workhorses who soon determined the character of the publication. Red Warren, in particular, seemed to be either directly or indirectly acquainted with most of the important contemporary writers in the English-speaking world. Although many early solicitations fell on barren ground, enough were answered to produce a choice crop of contributors. With strong financial backing, the *Southern Review* was able to pay a cent and a half per word for prose contributions and thirty-five cents a line for poetry. What was even more important to writers who could command higher fees from commercial magazines was the select company they kept in the *Southern Review*.

In addition to putting up with the daily nuisances of running a magazine, Cleanth Brooks read ninety manuscripts a week, taught three classes, did his own writing, served on university committees, and maintained a multigenerational household in the depths of the Great Depression. Although he received no additional summer compensation, he was also the person most responsible for keeping the magazine functioning twelve months a year. (Without such vigilance, a quarterly simply cannot exist.) With Red frequently gone from campus (spending a guest semester at another university or the summer in Italy), the day-to-day operations of the magazine fell increasingly to Cleanth and the review's business manager, Albert Erskine.

It was on the *Southern Review* that the legendary collaboration of Brooks and Warren began taking shape. In editorial conferences occurring as often as two or three times a week, they fashioned a literary quarterly that would set the standard for all such magazines in the future. According to Albert Erskine's successor John Palmer, Red and Cleanth resembled agreeable colleagues less than they did two different parts of the same person. Red Warren was a creative genius, who filled any room that he entered with his expansive gestures, staccato brogue, and inimitable Kentucky horse laugh. For him, criticism was not a sullen and lonely art but a social act—the meeting of kindred spirits to talk about books. The circle of friends might be as intimate as himself and one other person, as dynamic as a group of poets calling themselves Fugitives, as recalcitrant as a typical class of university sophomores, or as amorphous as the reading public itself. When Robert Penn Warren was at work, the surrounding area would soon become a godawful mess. He would jot an idea or an image down on a piece of paper, wad that paper up, and start over with a fresh sheet. Very few of the wads ever made their way to the wastebasket.

In contrast, Cleanth kept a tidier desk and a more orderly mind. If Red's light could be as blinding and diffuse as the sun itself, Cleanth's was more like a laser beam—less primal but more focused. Typically, Red would originate an idea to which Cleanth, with his penetrating logic and encyclopedic knowledge of literature, gave structure and substance. But, as with many generalizations, the reverse could be true. Cleanth (certainly one of the most original critics of the age) was sometimes the source of insight, to which Red (the maker of too many completed works to be a man of inspiration only) supplied shape and closure.

When they collaborated on a textbook, their personalities would blend; when they edited the *Southern Review*, those personalities were submerged. At least since the Renaissance, artists have generally signed their names to their works—both literally and figuratively. The editorial art, however, is almost medieval in nature. It is the destiny of the editor to be anonymous; he lives to make others look good, while rendering himself invisible. (For Cleanth, this meant reworking, and rewriting, the syntax of many of the articles submitted by Pipkin's friends in the social sciences—John Dewey among them.) Like a gothic cathedral or a well-made movie, a magazine is a group effort. The editor is not only an architect but one of the bricklayers; he is both director and cameraman. He also has to be something of a public relations expert. The public with whom he deals can include everyone from the local printer to the university bursar, not to mention legions of contributors and would-be contributors. They send manuscripts and queries in every mail and sometimes even call on the telephone or show up in person. John Palmer remembers when the secretary of the *Southern Review*, Jean Stafford, came into his office to inform him that Henry Miller was out in the waiting room. The notorious expatriate, whose writings were banned in this country, was trying to sell enough of his work to finance his way west to Taos, New Mexico.[3]

If the general academic progress of LSU during the political reign of Huey Long seemed an anomaly to the outside world, the existence of the *Southern Review* in Long's Louisiana was even more remarkable. It is certain that James Monroe Smith would never have proposed a literary quarterly to Red Warren had he thought that the Long would have disapproved. In a perverse bit of argumentation, Robert Gorham Davis suggested years later in the *New York Times* that Huey needed the *Southern Review* to give him respectability and provide cover for his political venality. Long partisans argue just as implausibly that Huey was actually a misunderstood patron of art and literature. William Faulkner was probably nearer the truth when, in "Knight's Gambit," he has Gavin Stevens tell his nephew Chick Mallison that "Huey Long in Louisiana had made himself the founder owner and supporter of…one of the best literary magazines anywhere, without ever looking inside it probably nor even caring what the people who wrote and edited it thought of him" (229-30).

II

Back in the mid-thirties, while they were doing the writing and editing that would make them world famous in the profession of letters, Cleanth Brooks and Robert Penn Warren were earning their keep primarily as college teachers of English. As Brooks recalled the situation forty years later: "Our students, many of them bright enough and certainly amiable and charming enough, had no notion how to read a literary text. Many of them approached a Shakespeare sonnet or Keats's 'Ode to a Nightingale' or Pope's *Rape of the Lock* much as they would approach an ad in a Sears-Roebuck catalogue or an editorial in their local newspaper." A student to whom Red was teaching *King Lear* mournfully shook his head and muttered: "I just don't like to read about bad people" (Brooks, "Forty Years," 5). The practical question Cleanth and Red faced was a more acute version of the one that I. A. Richards had faced at Cambridge a decade earlier—how to teach literature (particularly works of some difficulty and sophistication) to such students.

The available textbooks were of little help. James Dow McCallum's *The College Omnibus*, published by Harcourt Brace in 1933, was the standard anthology, both at LSU and elsewhere. One could obviously criticize this text on historical grounds. With none of its selections written before 1800, it gave its readers no sense of the development of English literature prior to the Romantic era. From the standpoint of criticism, it was even more deficient. Anyone teaching Keats's "Ode to a Nightingale" would have to be content with a short biographical introduction and a dollop of impressionistic response. ("The song of the nightingale brings sadness and exhilaration to the poet and makes him long to be lifted up and away from the limitations of life. The seventh stanza is particularly beautiful"; McCallum 670).

A reasonably competent English teacher might be expected to know when Keats lived and to have a vague emotional response to the poem already. What he might not have was an effective means of explaining to a class full of college sophomores (most of whom have probably never been "half in love with easeful death") what this poem has to say that would be of any interest to them. Reading the poem with dramatic emphasis (the Edwin

Mims approach) might heighten appreciation but not understanding. For a conscientious teacher, it was simply not enough to say what Louis Armstrong said about jazz: "If you have to ask what it is, you wouldn't understand if I told you."

Fortunately, many students, then as now, had dirty minds; so the poems with double entendres, such as *The Rape of the Lock,* were easier to teach. In fact, the sort of analytical skills necessary to discern Pope's hidden meanings were precisely what students needed to read poetry in general. If McCallum's *Omnibus* and the other existing textbooks were not teaching such skills, Warren argued that he and Brooks would simply need to provide their own text. Consequently, at the suggestion of W. A. Read, Warren prepared a thirty-page mimeographed booklet on metrics and imagery. This class handout was first used by Brooks, Warren, and a graduate student named John T. Purser in the spring semester of 1935. By the fall of 1936, the three had published a critical anthology of poetry, fiction, drama, and expository prose under the title *An Approach to Literature.*

As Thomas W. Cutrer has pointed out, the depth of the Depression was not a propitious time to bring out a new textbook, especially with the McCallum anthology being so recent and so widely accepted. Nevertheless, Marcus Wilkerson, director of the new LSU Press, approved of the idea, and President Smith promised financial backing. (The enthusiastic young Purser had to be dissuaded from seeking the political influence of his friend O. K. Allen, who had succeeded Huey Long as governor; see Cutrer 181). Perhaps because the book represented such a radical departure from the McCallum approach, it was not greeted with universal approval, even in Baton Rouge. When threatened traditionalists started referring to it as "The *Re*proach to Literature," Brooks and Warren picked up on the joke and began calling it that in their private correspondence.

Not only was the *Approach* short on biographical and historical information but—horror of horrors—it included a generous selection of Southern writers, where McCallum had none. Many of these were either Agrarian allies of Brooks and Warren or contributors to the *Southern Review.* Even if this could be seen as cronyism, the cronies of Brooks and Warren included some of the finest writers of the day. Thomas W. Cutrer believes that "Brooks and Warren were making an attempt to remove their native region from the educational imperialism which had been its lot since *McGuffey's Reader, Webster's Dictionary,* and the Yankee schoolmarm invaded the South in the nineteen century" (182). It is therefore ironic that among the first schools to adopt the new book were the universities of Maine and New Hampshire.

It could be argued that, in treating literature as a series of technical problems, this text takes some of the magic out of the reading experience. Brooks and Warren were, in fact, accused of being "cold-blooded analysts who found no pleasure, certainly no joy—in literature." Even if this were true, which it is not, their pedagogical approach made literature an accessible mode of discourse rather than a forbidding mystery that could be admired but never known. Moreover, they were intent on making it accessible *as literature*, not as an adjunct to sociology. As Brooks recalled over forty years later, "We were trying to apply the grease to the wheel that squeaked the loudest. Besides, the typical instructor, product as he was of the graduate schools of that day, had been thoroughly trained in literary history, or so we assumed" (*Community* 82).

The success of *An Approach to Literature* was such that, by 1939, most major textbook companies were trying to buy the copyright from the LSU Press. (Brooks and Warren had not even offered the book to a commercial house in 1935.) F. S. Crofts (later Appleton-Century-Crofts) won out and acquired both the plates and the rights for two per cent of future royalties. In 1975, forty years after its original publication, the book went into its fifth edition. Had Brooks and Warren never published another textbook, the longevity of *An Approach to Literature* would have earned them a niche in the history of modern English pedagogy. Far from complacent with what they had done, Cleanth and Red were soon at work on a book that would revolutionize the teaching of literature for more than a generation.

The first edition of that book, *Understanding Poetry*, appeared in 1938 with no grandiose ambitions, even if the title itself claimed more than Brooks and Warren had originally intended. They had simply wanted to call the book *Reading Poems*; however, the marketing division of their publisher, Henry Holt, convinced them that that title was too modest. (It is interesting to note that when Wright Thomas and Stuart Gerry Brown called their textbook *Reading Poems*, Leslie Fiedler accused them of a nominalistic rejection of the very concept of poetry.) In fact, the phrase "understanding poetry" is a perfect statement of the book's purpose—its end is critical *understanding* rather than vague appreciation, and the object of that understanding is *poetry*, not literary history or biography.

Nearly fifty years later, Warren observed that his labors with Brooks were "quite literally...collaborative":

> We sat down and argued out general notions and general plans for the book—only to find as work developed that we were constantly being thrown back to revise original ideas. But very early Cleanth had made a fundamental suggestion. After an introductory section of general discussion, we would get down to individual poems and start with narrative, including folk ballads. Folk poetry has one great pedagogical advantage. It springs from a nonliterary world and some event that has some special appeal to the imagination of that world.... Our whole effort was to show how the non-bookish poetry could lead straight to the bookish: that is to a narrative poem by, say, Frost. ("Brooks and Warren" 2)

Among the folk poems included was the old favorite of their Oxford days—"Frankie and Johnny."

Part of the excitement generated by *Understanding Poetry* lay in its being a genuinely *critical* text, which did not hesitate to attack canonical writers, including that favorite whipping boy of literary modernists Percy Bysshe Shelley. Although the book includes nine of Shelley's poems, the only one analyzed is "The Indian Serenade." Brooks and Warren correctly note that one's response to this poem is predicated on one's reaction to its speaker (the question of ethos). What makes both the speaker and his message suspect is Shelley's failure to demonstrate or dramatize the emotions the speaker expresses. The famously egregious line "I die! I faint! I fail!" (which seems like a reversal of the normal sequence of actions) might be a statement of emotion genuinely earned, or it might be the hysterical utterance of a self-indulgent adolescent. There is nothing *in the poem* to convince us which it is.

Even before *Understanding Poetry* began making its impact in the classroom, it was hailed by the critics as the first wave of a pedagogical revolution. In the inaugural issue of the *Kenyon Review*, John Crowe Ransom wrote: "Mr. Brooks has established his place among the subtler critics, while he keeps to himself his own versifying, and Mr. Warren is one of the really superlative poets of our time" ("Teaching" 82). Ransom goes on to note that "the analyses [of *Understanding Poetry*] are as much of the old poems as of the new poems, and those of the old are as fresh and illuminating as those of the new; or at least, nearly. What can this mean but that criticism as it is now practiced is a new thing?... Probably we need the new critics for the sake of understanding our classics even more, and much more than we need them for securing our possession of the strange moderns" (83)[4]

Although Brooks and Warren are now gone, the pedagogical revolution they effected has become so fully absorbed that what was once known as the New Criticism has long since become accepted practice. In a letter to me dated December 6, 1993, the poet and critic Dana Gioia wrote: "The three best selling college poetry textbooks of the past thirty years were probably *How Does a Poem Mean?* by John Ciardi, *Sound and Sense* by Laurence Perrine, and (probably the best selling of all) *An Introduction to Poetry* by X. J. Kennedy. All three are strikingly New Critical as are the legions of their imitators. These are the books that are used by millions of students and tens of thousands of teachers in the classroom. New Criticism, even if it doesn't go by that name, remains virtually unchallenged as the method of choice in college classrooms."[5]

III

In 1942, a new administration at LSU suspended the *Southern Review*, ostensibly in the interest of war-time austerity. This final indignity prompted Red Warren to take a position at the University of Minnesota. Although Cleanth Brooks also had several opportunities to better himself, he remained at LSU until Yale offered him a full professorship in 1947. In the fall of 1950 Thornton Wilder, who was a longtime fellow of one of Yale's undergraduate colleges and a good friend of Cleanth, suggested that the university might revitalize its School of Drama by hiring more creative writers to teach playwrighting. At that point, Red Warren had left Minnesota and was teaching part time in the Yale English department while living in New York. Because Marc Connolly was leaving the School of Drama, there was a permanent opening in that program. A. Whitney Griswold, the new president of Yale, called Red to his office one Saturday afternoon and invited Cleanth to come along. Although he would be officially listed as Professor of Playwrighting, Red was promised another course in the English department. Thus, for the fourth time in their careers, the same campus was home to Brooks and Warren.

When the Yale registrar called Cleanth in late April 1951, hoping to locate Red, who had not turned in his grades, Cleanth discovered that his friend was in Reno ending his long and troubled marriage with Cinina. The following year, Red and Eleanor Clark were married at Eleanor's mother's home in the Connecticut countryside. It was a small private ceremony with Albert Erskine as best man and Albert's former wife, Katherine Anne Porter, as matron of honor. On the way over, Cleanth had to stop to let his dog Pompey relieve himself. Pompey, with a mind of his own and energy to match, tried to run away, pulling Cleanth against a barbed wire fence. By the time the Brooks contingent arrived at the wedding, Cleanth's shirt was soaked with blood, and he had to borrow a clean one from Red. Despite this slapstick beginning, the marriage turned out to be a spectacular success. Red was happy, perhaps for the first time in his life.

During the time they were separated in the 1940s, Brooks and Warren published two more textbooks—*Understanding Fiction* (1943) and *Modern Rhetoric* (1947). By the 1960s, when they were both teaching at Yale, they were contemplating an anthology of American literature. This project was delayed, however, when Cleanth went to London to serve a two-year stint as cultural attaché at the American embassy. After Cleanth's return to Yale in 1966, he and Red immersed themselves in what would become a magisterial tome called *American Literature: The Makers and the Making*, which was published by St. Martin's Press in 1973.

Because the book required more historical commentary than either Cleanth or Red felt comfortable with, they asked their colleague R. W. B. Lewis to join them as a third collaborator. Lewis recalls convening for two or three days at a time at the Warren homes in Fairfield, Connecticut, and Brattleboro, Vermont, at the Brooks estate in Northford, Connecticut, and at his own master's living quarters at Yale's Calhoun College. At those sessions, they would discuss and criticize each other's individual contributions and work on parts of the book that were genuinely collaborative. Lewis describes how one of these parts, the "Letter to the Reader," was composed:

> We were at the Warrens' Vermont place during a summer week, and in between swimming in the mountain pool and striding along the country roads, between chatty meals on the screened porch and leisurely drink-times on the terrace, we met in a small cabin across the lawn from the main house and worked away. Warren sat at a rustic table with a typewriter in front of him; Brooks and I shifted and prowled about. Warren, an erratic typist at best, would listen to different tentative formulations of this sentence or that, and when the right one struck him he would tap it out haphazardly on the page. The resulting script, full of x-ed out lines and proximate spellings, was turned over to Brooks, who took it back home and rewrote it in his own style. That version was then amended, separately, by Warren and me, and Brooks thereafter gave it a final run-through. (569)

This experience convinced Lewis of "an irreducible subsurface regionalism in American literary folk." In fact, as the three colleagues began discussing the mid-nineteenth century, Lewis got "the eerie but enlivening sensation that we were, between us, reenacting the Civil War." Brooks and Warren seemed to him to become increasingly Southern. "To my ear their very accents thickened," Lewis recalls; "and though I am in fact Chicago-born, I felt myself becoming more and more northern and even, like Emily Dickinson, beginning to see 'New Englandly.' When Warren presented me with his selection of Melville's war poems, I remarked that to judge from this lot—all of them springing from northern defeats and disasters—one would be in doubt as to which side had actually 'won' the war" (570).

The book that was actually produced by this collaboration ran to two million words, a fourth of which consisted of commentary. Lewis figures that he, Brooks, and Warren each wrote around five hundred typescript pages each. The result was not just a standard classroom anthology but also a critical history of American literature from the seventeenth century to the present. In fact, the book was so good that it never won the wide acceptance it deserved. Since the 1930s, students had gotten either less capable or less willing to learn.

IV

When the *Southern Review* was suspended in 1942, Cleanth Brooks and Red Warren knew that for them life in Louisiana would never be the same again. Even though both eventually left for better jobs in the North, the memory of Baton Rouge went with them. Years later, Red observed that "after Louisiana nothing has been real" (see Simpson "Continuity" 8). What even the author of *All the King's Men* might have found surprising was the degree to which the Louisiana he once knew had remained the same, although Huey Long had been dead since 1935, his son had been in the Senate for half his life. Waves of reform had periodically swept through the state over the ensuing fifty years, but the reformers committed the cardinal sin of being uninteresting. In 1985 the state was ruled by a populist demagogue who might have taught Huey a thing or two. Edwin Edwards was a flamboyant womanizer who went on gambling sprees to Las Vegas several times a year; his administration was riddled with graft, and he considered a federal indictment to be a rite of passage. He once remarked that the only way he could be defeated for election was if he were found in bed with a dead girl or a live boy.

What *had* changed in Louisiana was the attitude of LSU toward the *Southern Review*. The magazine had been revived in 1965 and by 1985 had been in existence for nearly three times as long as the original series. When the university prepared to celebrate the 125th year of its own founding, the emphasis was on events that had taken place in its seventy-fifth year—principally the establishment of the literary magazine that James Monroe Smith had hoped would put LSU on the map. On October 9-11, 1985, the Baton Rouge campus commemorated twenty years of the new *Southern Review* and honored those who had started the original magazine half a century earlier. The occasion was also a kind of personal homage to the two men who had played the tired old role of prophets without honor. As so many of the literary giants of 1935 had faded into obscurity, Brooks and Warren had grown in stature. They had also grown old.

Earlier that year, Red had marked his sixty-second year as a professional writer by publishing *New and Selected Poems: 1923-1985*. Because his reputation will almost surely rest on the poems published since 1954, they constitute the bulk of the volume (287 of 322 pages); and because the poems are printed in reverse chronological order, the more recent work enjoys pride of place. Moreover, the sheer length of Red's career was a wonder in itself. As Louis Rubin has pointed out, when Warren published his first poems in 1923, Thomas Hardy, Joseph Conrad, Anatole France, Henri Bergson, and George Washington Cable were still alive. "Nobody much had ever heard of William Faulkner, Thomas Wolfe, or Hart Crane. *The Great Gatsby* would not be published for another two years, [and] Eudora Welty was a thirteen-year-old in Jackson, Mississippi" (137). The standing ovation that Warren received in 1985 was a particularly bittersweet tribute. The obscurantists who had let him go so many years earlier were themselves gone. In contrast, at least one high-ranking member of the current university administration was at every session of the 1985 conference. By living long and well, Red Warren had achieved the best revenge.

If Red was the star of the occasion, second billing would almost certainly have gone to Eudora Welty. The Southern literary community was pretty much agreed that, with Faulkner gone, Warren and Welty were the two most prominent writers in the South. The general populace, which usually did not read poetry or criticism, knew Warren and Welty as popular fiction writers—even if that knowledge did not extend beyond *All the*

King's Men and "Why I Live at the P. O." Although no celebrity, Cleanth was far from unknown. Many prominent Louisianans now in their fifties and sixties still remembered having their eyes opened to the complexities of poetry in Brooks's sophomore literature class.[6] The Brooks and Warren textbooks and Cleanth's own best known critical book *The Well Wrought Urn* had long since become standard references for the specialist and non-specialist alike. If literary fashion had passed the New Critics by, no one would have suspected it that weekend at LSU.

Other participants in the conference included Ernest J. Gaines, Gloria Naylor, Houston Baker, Henry Louis Gates, Robert B. Heilman, Charles East, James W. Applewhite, Walter Sullivan, Elizabeth Spencer, William C. Havard, Louis D. Rubin, Jr., George Core, Ronald Schuchard, Denis Donaghue, and Walker Percy. One virtually unknown participant was the young filmmaker Ken Burns, who recreated the ambience of 1935 with a documentary film on Huey Long. A few years later, Burns produced a popular documentary series on the "Civil War" for PBS—a project suggested by Red Warren, who had been featured prominently in the Huey Long film.

Only Red's family and friends realized what an ordeal the trip to Baton Rouge had been for him. He had been in failing health and showed every one of his eighty years. (In contrast, Cleanth possessed the energy of a man half his age.) As the conference wore on, Red spent more and more time in his room at the faculty club, drinking bourbon and swapping stories with Cleanth, Cleanth's wife Tinkum, and Eudora Welty. His single public performance (a poetry reading) was interrupted by a fit of coughing so serious that *Southern Review* editor James Olney had to finish for him. The one question that cast a shadow over the festivities was whether Red was simply under the weather or seriously ill. His prolific output of poetry caused some to think that he was ageless. But he was making fewer public appearances and even canceling invitations he had accepted. His brogue seemed to grow thicker, so that his comments in radio and television interviews were frequently indecipherable. Then, in the summer of 1985, he was diagnosed with inoperable bone cancer. Walter Sullivan recalls asking the Brookses what was wrong with Red that final night in Baton Rouge. Ever the diplomat, Cleanth said: "He's not feeling well." The more plainspoken Tinkum replied: "He's doomed."[7]

V

On September 26, 1983, nearly two years before the discovery of his terminal illness, Red had written to Cleanth about what their friendship had meant to his work:

> You can't imagine how much I owe you about poetry—on two counts. Our long collaborations always brought something new and eye-opening to me, seminal notions for me, often couched in some seemingly incidental or casual remark. One of the happiest recollections I have is that of the long sessions of work on *UP* [*Understanding Poetry*]—not to mention earlier and later conversations. The other count has to do with the confidence you gave me about my own efforts. I'm sure that you were over-generous, but even allowing for that, it still meant something fundamental to me. I have often wanted to say something like this to you, but I know that you'd give me an embarrassed shrug and disclaimer. Anyway I can say it now without your interruption.[8]

During the four years that it took for Red to die, he continued to be lionized by a public unaware of his illness. (As George Garrett has noted, Warren received so many honorary degrees and medals "that some anonymous wag called him the General Pinochet of American Literature in honor of his politics not at all, but rather the top-heavy tinkling appearance of over-decorated Latin American leaders"; 50-51). In the spring of 1986, Congress found a new way to honor the country's greatest living poet by naming him America's first poet laureate. The job was actually poetry consultant to the Library of Congress (a position that Red had held more than forty years earlier), but the title was new and impressive. It came perilously close to being a posthumous honor.

During the last year of his life, Red was virtually unable to speak. Toward the end, Albert Erskine told Red's daughter Rosanna to read her father one of his oldest poems, "Bearded Oaks." Upon hearing the poem's final lines—"We live in time so little time / And we learn all so painfully, / That we may spare this hour's term / To practice for eternity"—Red gave a smile of recognition and, with difficulty, spoke the name "Albert." He slipped back into a coma and never uttered another word.[9] On September 15, 1989, he was gone.

Red's burial near the family's summer home in West Wardsboro, Vemont, seemed to come right out of a movie script. Although it was still fairly early in the fall, snow and sleet were already on the ground. The funeral prosession made its way from an old church down the long gravel path to the graveyard. Tinkum Brooks's nephew Carver Blanchard sang that wonderful old Scottish hymn "Abide with Me." When Red was laid to rest, it was the first time in a hundred years that this old Vermont burying ground had been disturbed. Pondering the final ritual, Louis P. Simpson writes: "We may fancy that this act expressed the last vision of a place to come to by a poet for whom the mystery of his identity was deeply fused with the mystery of place; for a poet who was an unmovable nonbeliever but who said repeatedly that he yearned to believe; for a poet who was southern to the bone—knew that he would never be at home save in the South—and yet knew as deeply that, because of his very nature as a southerner, he was an exile who could never come home again" ("Warren and the South" 11).

It remained only for Vanderbilt to pay its last respects to its most distinguished graduate. A memorial service was held on campus in November, as the friends and admirers of Red Warren gathered to measure the extent of their loss, while cherishing all that was vouchsafed them in art and memory. After the public speeches in the Vanderbilt chapel, a few of Red's family members and closest friends gathered in a private dining room in the administration building, Kirkland Hall. After dinner, they swapped stories and reminiscences about the man they had known.

When it came Cleanth's turn, he spoke of Red's love of popular music and his amusement whenever he heard the inimitable Brooks rendition of America's great folk songs. Pretty soon, the entire table was urging a reluctant Cleanth to perform as he had at Oxford sixty years earlier. Finally, Eleanor Warren said: "Do it for Red." Cleanth pushed his chair back from the table and sat straight, without even touching his back to the back of the chair. He then began to sing in the most proper angelic voice: "Frankie and Johnny were lovers..."[10]

Notes

1. Except where indicated, the personal information in this essay was gleaned from a series of interviews I

conducted with Cleanth Brooks between 1990 and 1993.
2. In an attempt to ridicule what was starting to be called the New Criticism, the historical scholar Douglas Bush dismissed it as "an advanced course in remedial reading." See Douglas Bush, "The New Criticism: Some Old Fashioned Queries," *PMLA* 64, supp., pt. 2 (March 1949), 13.
3. Interview with John Palmer on June 21, 1993.
4. The close reading exemplified by Richards and the Vanderbilt critics came to be called the New Criticism largely because John Crowe Ransom published a book by that title in 1941. Ransom's intention was not so much to give a name to a particular school of criticism as it was to call attention to the fact that the professional study of literature (even in the academy) was becoming more critical and less traditionally philological or scholarly. The term caught on, even as the "new" criticism gradually became the reigning orthodoxy in literary studies.
5. Personal correspondence with Dana Gioia, dated December 6, 1993.
6. Consider the example of Harold McSween. A native of Alexandria, Louisiana (who was baptized by Cleanth Brooks, Sr.), McSween took Cleanth's class in sophomore literature and later enjoyed a successful career as a lawyer, businessman, and U. S. congressman. After losing congressional races to a dying Earl Long and to Earl's cousin Gillis Long, McSween retired from politics. He later became a widely published writer, contributing fiction, poetry, and criticism to the *Sewanee*, *Southern*, and *Virginia Quarterly* reviews.
7. Interview with Walter Sullivan, April 21, 1992.
8. The original text of this letter is contained in the Beinecke Rare Book and Manuscript Library at Yale University.
9. Interview with Carver Blanchard, June 19, 1993.
10. Interview with Walter Sullivan, April 21, 1993.

Works Cited

Bohner, Charles. *Robert Penn Warren*. Rev. ed. Boston: Twayne, 1981.
Brooks, Cleanth. "Brooks on Warren." *Four Quarters* 21 (May 1972): 19-22.
———. *Community, Religion, and Literature*. Columbia: U of Missouri P, 1995.
———. "Forty Years of *Understanding Poetry*." *College English Association Forum* 10 (April 1980): 5-12.
———. "I. A. Richards and *Practical Criticism*." In George Core, ed. *The Critics Who Made Us: Essays from the Sewanee Review*. Columbia: U of Missouri P, 1993. 35-46.
Brooks, Cleanth and Robert Penn Warren, eds. *An Anthology of Stories from the Southern Review*. Baton Rouge: Louisiana State UP, 1953.
Core, George. "Vanderbilt English and the Rise of the New Criticism." In Mark Royden Winchell, ed. *The Vanderbilt Tradition: Essays in Honor of Thomas Daniel Young*. Baton Rouge: Louisiana State UP, 1991. 19-35.
Cutrer, Thomas W. *Parnassus on the Mississippi: The Southern Review and the Baton Rouge Literary Community, 1935-1942*. Baton Rouge: Louisiana State UP, 1984.
Faulkner, William. *Knight's Gambit and Other Stories*. New York: Random House, 1950.
Garrett, George. "Warren's Poetry: Some Things We Ought to Be Thinking About." *South Carolina Review* 23 (Fall 1990): 49-57.
Lewis, R. W. B. "Warren's Long Visit to American Literature." *Yale Review* 70 (July 1981): 568-91.
McCallum, James Dow, ed. *The College Omnibus*. New York: Harcourt Brace, 1933.
Ransom, John Crowe. *Selected Letters of John Crowe Ransom*. Ed. Thomas Daniel Young and George Core. Baton Rouge: Louisiana State UP, 1985.
———. "The Teaching of Poetry." *Kenyon Review* 1 (1939): 81-83.
Rubin, Louis D., Jr. "RPW, 1905-1989." In *The Mockingbird in the Gum Tree: A Literary Gallimaufry*. Baton Rouge: Louisiana State UP, 1991. 137-45.
Simpson, Lewis P. "A Certain Continuity." In Lewis P. Simpson et al. eds. *The Southern Review and Modern Literature: 1935-1985*. Baton Rouge: Louisiana State UP, 1988. 1-18.
———. "Robert Penn Warren and the South." *Southern Review*, n.s., 26 (Winter 1990): 7-12.
Warren, Robert Penn. "A Reminiscence." In John Edgerton, ed. *Nashville: The Faces of Two Centuries, 1780-1980*. Nashville: PlusMedia, 1979. 205-20.
———. "Brooks and Warren." *Humanities*, April 1985, 1-3.

Robert Penn Warren and Albert Russell Erskine, Jr.: A Sixty-Year Friendship

by James A. Grimshaw, Jr.

A seemingly ordinary event occurred in the fall of 1930 at Southwestern College in Memphis (now Rhodes College) when a twenty-five-year-old adjunct faculty member—a tall, red-headed, freckle-faced young man—asked a six-foot-four-inch junior economics major to play chess. Robert Penn Warren, just back from a Rhodes Scholarship and receiving his B.Litt. from Oxford University, and Albert Russell Erskine, Jr., the nineteen-year-old undergraduate, became friends who would also be professionally connected, for sixty years.[1] Their relationship is nowhere better recorded to date than in their letters, which reveal the give-and-take of ideas involving their strong commitment to literature, their travels, their work, and their professional dealings as writer and editor. The letters that follow are selected from the 1930s and '40s as early examples of their extraordinary friendship.

Warren left Southwestern College the following year (1931) and joined the faculty at Vanderbilt University. According to his account in the "Editor's Note" to *A Robert Penn Warren Reader*, Erskine changed his major to English and began his graduate studies at Vanderbilt with the encouragement of Warren. Erskine completed his M.A. in 1933 under Donald Davidson (Blotner 142). In 1934 Warren joined his friend Cleanth Brooks, whom he had met at Vanderbilt during his undergraduate days, at Louisiana State University; and together they arranged a graduate assistantship for Erskine in Baton Rouge. Erskine observed that "This made three places where during the thirties I was a student and Red was teaching, yet I never took one of his courses, though I knew many others were profiting from them, but I know I learned more from his conversation than I ever did from formal instruction" ("Editor's Note" x).

Warren and Erskine's first year at LSU proved quite eventful. Southern Methodist University published the *Southwest Review*, edited by John McGinnis and assisted by Henry Nash Smith. Because of financial difficulties, SMU agreed to LSU's offer of a merger. Brooks, who had joined the LSU faculty two years before Warren, had been named as an editor; and Warren was appointed to the LSU board of editors in 1934. Based on Mark Royden Winchell's assessment in *Cleanth Brooks and the Rise of Modern Criticism*, Erskine's review of Stark Young's novel *So Red the Rose* for the *Southwest Review* exacerbated existing tensions between the two editorial camps:

> It is doubtful that Robert Penn Warren had an ideological ax to grind when he asked his young Baton Rouge associate Albert Erskine to review *So Red the Rose*. Had Erskine simply praised the novel as literature, his review probably would have passed muster in Dallas. Instead, he endorsed Young's reactionary social vision and declared the paternalistic slave owners of the Old South morally superior to the capitalist employers of our own time. (This position, which has been articulated by figures as diverse as William Grayson and Eugene Genovese,

was also held by Edmund Wilson.) When he read the review, Smith wrote to Warren that its thesis seemed to be "I know this isn't a great novel, but I dare any (liberal) white trash to say so." After Erskine agreed to some minor changes, the Dallas editors grudgingly accepted the review for the spring 1935 issue of their magazine. It would be the last issue published in collaboration with Baton Rouge. LSU had already announced the Southern Literary Conference at which it would launch its own new magazine. (91)

That spring Brooks and Warren, who had been named managing editors of the newly conceived *Southern Review*, asked Erskine to be the business manager.[2] Erskine's undergraduate major in economics, his penchant for business, and his love of literature enabled him to be an active participant in the editorial sessions and proved to be beneficial for Warren throughout their friendship. The *Southern Review* fulfilled its objective of being an internationally recognized journal. While Warren traveled on fellowships and pursued his creative writing during the second half of the 1930s, he nonetheless continued to carry his part of the editing load via mail. Clearly, though, both Brooks and Warren relied on Erskine who began doing some preliminary editing and sorting of submissions as well as handling the business end of the journal. For example, Warren wrote Erskine on July 16, 1937:

> By the way, tell Cleanth that in the bundle of manuscripts to be returned he will find [Pier M.] Pasinetti's story. It is rather long, but not so long as Katherine Anne Porter's piece, and it probably could be cut a little. Some of the translating needs a little retouching, but that will be an easy matter. I am very anxious to have you read the piece. I have just heard from Pier. He has seen the Houghton Mifflin people; he did not get a contract, but they are very favorably disposed, saying that they wanted to see a little more of the particular novel in question (he showed them about forty pages translated) before settling the matter definitely.
>
> One shock we have received on returning this afternoon to Oakland comes from the fact that checks given here *after* receiving your note (written July 5) have been returned. One of the returned checks was given here on July 7, and so probably didn't reach Baton Rouge until, say, July 11. Apparently, the money was never deposited. The thing may have been sidetracked into Alumni Hall. Will you take a look there, if the bank has not received the deposit? And if it is not there, will you again, please sir, beard Mrs. Heidelberg? She told me in June that she would definitely attend to the matter of the advance the first of July. I saw her make a note of the matter in her book, and naturally assumed that the thing was all settled. I can think of no explanation, except, as I said, a sidetracking of the check into Alumni Hall.
>
> And if the money has not been deposited, will you please give $24.48 out of the enclosed check for $25.00 to Horace G. Porter of the Campus Credit Union. I sent him a monthly payment some days ago, and he writes me that it bounced—as it wouldn't have done if my salary check had been in. I wired him to cash it again—yesterday, in fact—but that was before I had discovered the fact that the

salary had not been deposited. If my salary is already deposited when you receive this letter, will you simply ask Porter if the check has gone through and tell him that I had a salary check wandering around, for I wrote him yesterday that the salary check had been deposited. This is urgent, and I shall be eternally grateful to you for taking care of this as soon as you receive the letter.[3]

Erskine's involvement with manuscripts was also a harbinger of his career in editing at Doubleday Doran and at Reynal & Hitchcock before moving to Random House in 1947. In 1950 Random House published Warren's fourth novel, *World Enough and Time*, and the relationship between Erskine as editor and Warren as writer was secured.

Warren had secretly married Cinina Brescia in Sacramento, California, in 1929 while he was still a student at Oxford; then on September 12, 1930, they were openly married in Marion, Arkansas. Erskine, a true friend to Warren, befriended Cinina, and over the years she would ask him to do favors for her. While she and Red were traveling in 1937, Cinina wrote Albert several times to thank him for attending to her "various annoying errands" regarding the acquisition of some property in Baton Rouge and other personal business. Occasionally she projected an authoritative air in her letters. When Warren became involved in the personal business, the discussion became more pragmatic and sensitive to Albert's feelings, as reflected in this letter from some time in 1938:

> You mention the electrical equipment at your house, and ask whether we would want to take it over. That is highly probable. But there is one catch. I don't see how our new place could be ready for occupancy before February, since the final plans will not be made until after we return from California. Then the blueprints have to be sent to Washington for approval. That, apparently, is a formality, but it will take time. This delay would mean that we would be paying monthly installments on the equipment for six months without receiving any return use. Would the savings in price, say on the stove and water heater, warrant those proceedings? Do you know what the original costs are, down payments (if any), and the total balance due on each piece? And there is another matter which we talked about: the housing question. Would you be interested in taking an apartment together until, say, February? I know, of course, that it would be difficult to get a place on a short lease or on a month-to-month arrangement. And I know that you said you probably would not want to come out to our place to live in February because of the car problem. That proposition is still open if you care to consider it. But there is another which might be of more interest to you. I shall outline it briefly. Say we get an apartment for about thirty to forty dollars a month, something like Cleanth's or the Daspit's. We pay all the rent until we leave, and you pay simply a share on light and water and send your laundry out (for Mamie has all of that she can handle, apparently). If you care to have meals with us, we could simply divide the food bill three ways. But we would pay all of Mamie's wages. This arrangement would throw the full rent off on you in February or March, but the fact of no rent for the first four or five months would make that up, probably. If this arrangement suits you, you might ask Heidel to start looking. A location near the campus would probably suit us better on account of

the car savings, but that wouldn't be absolutely essential. If we got an apartment that did not have a stove or water heater, we could simply take your equipment on over, but the unfurnished apartments probably have both of those things. *Now, if such an arrangement does not suit you, please say so without any hesitation.* But since we have to make some positive decision almost immediately, will you let us know your own decision, by air mail, at the earliest possible moment?

Warren's correspondence to Erskine during the 1930s suggested a growing professional relationship as well. In relation to his own writing, Warren wrote to Albert on August 1, 1938: "It has recently occurred to me that I might be able to persuade my colleagues, Mr. Brooks and Mr. Erskine, to glance at a little story called 'How Willie Proudfit Came Home,' with the view of publishing it in the *Southern Review*. I think that I have managed to give it a frame that will enable it to stand alone—but I'm not sure, and I want you all to deal frankly with me. Since the novel publication has been postponed until at least January, that would give, perhaps, enough time in between. But, again, if the local situation seems to you all to be against using the piece, please say so. And Cleanth, will you mention the matter to Pip? That is, unless you all think better not to use the story."[4]

In 1937 Erskine met his first-wife-to-be, Katherine Anne Porter, at Benfolly, Allen Tate and Carolyn Gordon's house in Clarksville, Tennessee. Erskine had read the short stories Porter submitted to the *Southern Review* and was enchanted by her writing. According to Porter's biographer, Joan Givner, "Erskine had been enthusiastic about Porter's work from the time it first came to the review, and when one story was read at an editorial conference he had been so enthralled he read it over and over" (304-05). Porter got along well with Warren and Brooks, who were genuinely interested in her stories for the *Southern Review*; and she visited Baton Rouge, where she and Erskine became better acquainted. Their relationship led to marriage by a notary on April 19, 1938 (the day after his twenty-seventh birthday), in New Orleans, with the Warrens as witnesses; Erskine's bride was forty-six. The marriage, which was a disaster, ended in a separation in 1940 and divorce in 1942, the year Albert married his second wife, Peggy Anthony. The Erskine portrayed in Porter's letters is not the Erskine revealed in the correspondence between Warren and himself. Though Warren was sympathetic to Erskine's psychological pain, he remained a friend to both Porter and Erskine; and business at the review went on as normal.

Their growing friendship was often garnished with requests for other favors. While in Italy, Warren wrote the following request on January 22, 1940: "P.S. Albert, will you do me a favor? I am sending a copy of the poem to Charles Pearce at the *New Yorker*, who has asked me for a poem. If he sends it back to you, as I have asked him to do in case of rejection, will you send it to John Berryman, who is managing the poetry for *Nation*, and who has asked me for a poem?[5] I'd greatly appreciate it, for it would save me a lot of time. Thanks." During this time, Warren was also writing to Katherine Anne Porter without any reference to the marital difficulties Albert and she were having.

With the outbreak of WWII in 1939, transportation across the Atlantic was often delayed and sometimes canceled. The delay in Italy must have been extremely frustrating for the Warrens. Mail was not getting through to them, and a common chorus in Warren's letters to Erskine was "no news." Warren asked constantly about what was happening at LSU; whether Albert had heard from John Crowe Ransom and others about the status of a poem or another piece he had submitted. When Warren finally returned, he settled in to work with Francis Fergusson, professor of drama at Bennington College, on a play called *Proud Flesh*. On June 12, 1940, then, Warren wrote Albert and Katherine Anne about his experiences abroad:

> The last few weeks in Rome we tried to get down to a long full letter in answer to your letters, but the circumstances were not very conducive to long full letters during those last days, and besides, scarcely anything we had to say would have gone out through the Italian censors. We had felt pretty secure because of the information which we had had through Pier and one or two other people, except for a few days—the time when we sent the cable to the office to stop mail, the time when the war settled down to earnest in the West. Before that Pier was working on his permit to leave the country, and through that and through his magazine work was in pretty close contact with some of the big bastards, such as Bottai and Pavolini. They kept promising him a passport but told him that he would have to be back in August, for Italy would move in August, that preparations would not be complete before that time. He intended to come over here and then skip and try to take out American citizenship. In late April they told him he could definitely have the permit to sail on May 14. Meanwhile I had seen the immigration people in Naples and had worked out the procedure from the US end of things; and I had had some talks with the Consul in Rome. It would have worked, all right, it seems, if he could have managed to get out. He was, for a few days, sure that everything was set. He was even getting his stuff together to leave. Then the bombshell broke. They called him in and told him that Italy would go in on June 8. He promptly brought us the news, and said that the time had come to beat it. His news reached us the day before the big outburst of anti-British manifestoes etc., but the next day was Sunday, and we could take no steps about leaving. Monday morning I tried to get my passage moved up from June, but after some telephoning to Genoa learned that all space was taken. Then we decided to go to Genoa and make a personal effort to get passage. We pulled out of Rome on very short notice—we had kept our small affairs in such a condition that we could move quickly—and went to Genoa. There, after some twenty-four hours or so—we got places on the *Washington*. Cots. But after a day or so we had regular beds—at the expense, I imagine, of some refugees. But we had separate cabins, for they were putting women in some cabins and men in others to save space. The boat was crawling with refugees—Norwegians (and, God, they were a sick and bitter lot!), Germans (Jew and Gentile), French, Italians (one of my room-mates was an Italian boy, American citizen, born in Brooklyn, who had managed to escape by the barest; and his brother, an American citizen, had been seized for the army), and Americans from all over Europe. We spent most of our time listening to horror stories, which, on the whole, were pretty horrible, and sometimes funny. For instance, the story of the American woman in Rome who went to Germany to save refugee dogs. A Mrs. Comfort, whose husband runs one of the Quaker refugee organizations, told that tale. Her husband, she said, hadn't been able to get into Germany to save a few human beings, but this wom-

an had managed to get in to save some dogs. The Norwegians had some pretty tales of treachery, and some good accounts of the bombing of Oslo, which they saw. It seems, to judge by their account, that the report in *Life* had some glaring inaccuracies—the report by Leland Stowe, who said that the Norwegians didn't mind. By the way, it may be of some slight cheer to hear that the British bombing of Oslo was a marvel of accuracy, every bomb on the airports and docks, and not a one on the city itself. And outside the city they got the villa in which the German staff was quartered—got it at night and didn't touch a thing else in the neighborhood. But people here, of course, had a lot of news we hadn't been able to get in the last few days when the Vatican paper was driven off the stands in Rome (that was the only paper which gave any decent news); so we have spent a lot of time recently in trying to catch up on what has happened. Meanwhile it sure looks like we are in for it, sooner or later, and, I imagine, sooner rather than later. The only encouraging thing I know is that there simply aren't any Fascists in Italy. We met two during the entire year, and we must have talked to hundreds of people—everybody. And everybody would talk without encouragement. And everybody was against the war, against Germany, and against the Party; and almost everybody was pro-Ally. The talk was very public, too. We went to a restaurant just before leaving Genoa and heard the owner give hell to a Fascist officer:

Officer: What, you won't fight? Aren't you proud and strong?
Owner: I am no longer proud and I am very weak.
Officer: You wouldn't fight for the Empire?
Owner: What's it done for me? They promised me gold and diamonds, but I haven't seen any.
Officer: What makes you think you ought to have them?
Owner: I don't think so. I don't want them. It wasn't my idea. It was theirs.
Officer: We'll close down your restaurant.
Owner: All right. Close me down. I began working with my hands when I was fifteen, and I made this restaurant. I can work again. Then, when you are finished, I'll open up again. And remember this, you can't fight without us old ones, and I'm not by myself. I fought in the last war, and we old ones won't fight with you in this one.

Then he called over one of his waiters, a scrawny little fellow, and struck him a backhand, lightly, across the chest. The waiter staggered about five feet.

Owner: There's one of your proud and strong young Fascists for you!

Everybody in the restaurant—and everybody was listening—burst out laughing. Including an officer of aviation.

Owner: And my father-in-law doesn't agree with me either about the war. So the last time he came I told him not to come back till the war was over. And I shut the door in his face.

That night the officer didn't come to dinner, and we figured he wouldn't come back and would probably close down the restaurant. But he came back the next day for lunch. The owner went over to his table and said: "So I see you came back!"

Everybody says that there will be a revolution if the war lasts any time at all. And from what we heard and saw, we are certainly prepared to believe it. We went to a couple of meetings of the gang Pier belongs to. There's a very definite and organized movement among the young men to get hold of every post possible in the Party and grab the works at the first opportunity. They say there's not a chance to attack from the outside, that the opportunity was missed a long time back. But they say that now the whole organization of the Party is honeycombed (that's the word you are supposed to use in such connections, isn't it?) with people "belonging to us"—even high army people and high people in the Party. One of the gang, secretary of the Fascist organization dealing with universities, told us that not more than thirty percent of the students are now Fascists, but he said you'd have to add a number of pure opportunists to that figure. But everybody says that there will not be an open break at the beginning of the war, that they will "march, but with our own tanks at our backs."

By 1941, when Erskine was "connected" with the *Saturday Review,* Warren asked for Katherine Anne's address. Warren was teaching a semester at the Iowa Writer's Workshop but still conducting *Southern Review* business via mail. He asked Albert to steer some good material to Baton Rouge. The LSU administration was undergoing a shakeup, from which Albert was free and Warren remained distant. After buying a house in Baton Rouge, Red and Cinina traveled to Mexico in the fall. During that time he wrote an essay on Katherine Anne Porter, which John Crowe Ransom subsequently published in the *Kenyon Review.* In a September 1, 1941, letter Warren wrote Albert: "The only sizable flaw in our summer was an auto wreck a month ago. One night, coming back from Guadalajara, we met a cow on the road, got into a skid from wet brakes—we'd just forded a stream which had swollen over the road—and turned over two or three times, and wound up in a ditch, the car on its side. The doors, or rather, the upper door, was jammed, but I managed to force it (it never would close again, so it was pretty well jammed) and we got out and stood in the rain for an hour or so. Cinina got a wrenched back which laid her up for a few days, but I, and a friend with us, escaped, unhurt. The body of the car was in a mess, but the motor and running gear were unhurt. Insurance covered everything but what happened, of course, upset. The Mexican insurance, that is; why I didn't have that, I don't know; and the U.S. insurance doesn't apply here. So it cost me a nice figure. But we were damned lucky, and I have no complaint. And the garage here did a beautiful job on body-work; you can't tell a trace now without a microscope."

Erskine, now associated with New Directions, advised Warren on his second volume of poetry, *Eleven Poems on the Same Theme,* which appeared in 1942, and whose title Erskine had suggested in lieu of "Bearded Oaks and Other Poems on the Same Theme." Warren also left the order of the eleven poems up to his friend, though he recommended that it start with "Bearded Oaks." When Warren wrote Albert on January 30, 1942, he said that a story in *Time* about the LSU president had broken the day before and that he did not know when he and Brooks would be fired as editors of the *Southern Review*. The spring 1942 issue was the last publication of the original series of the magazine.

By October 19, 1942, Warren wrote in sympathy when the *Saturday Review* position did not work out for Albert, and he mentioned Peggy, Erskine's second wife. That fall Erskine went with another publisher (Reynal & Hitchcock) and was busily trying to drum up authors. In support of Albert's decision, Warren responded on December 15, 1942:

> It's fine about the new job. It sounds like exactly the sort of thing you wanted, and I know that you will knock the spots off at it. As for undermining my relations with my publishers, maybe they wouldn't mind a bit. I sent in the finished MS of the new novel more than [a] month ago, and didn't hear a word until yesterday, when I got a blank from the promotions department asking for some biographical information for a "forthcoming publication." Well, if they're in trouble, they asked for, and read the damned thing before they made me an offer for it. But it's a hell of a time to publish novels, anyway—and especially a novel like this one. (By the way, speaking of novels, I received a royalty statement the other day on *Night Rider*. I had received about thirty bucks from the previous one, and so opened this one with the most languid interest. Well, a check for several hundred dollars fell out. It seems that a book club in England has bought it, and the check was what I had left of, I presume, the advance, after the British Government and Houghton had taken their cuts. But it was damned lucky, anyway.)
>
> You may say that you are supposed to drum up authors. Well, Peter Taylor is still not signed up. Houghton got cold feet on him at the last, it appears. If you want to get in touch with him, you can do so through his father—Hillsman Taylor, Stonewall Avenue, Memphis. But you probably know that anyway.

After Warren moved to Minneapolis to teach at the University of Minnesota, he mentioned several times the prospect of their being drafted into the military, though he felt Albert would not pass the physical because of his "bum leg." Warren, and Brooks for that matter, were both prepared to serve. None of them qualified physically.

Humor occasionally encroached in their day-to-day transactions. On Reynal & Hitchcock letterhead, dated January 3, 1947, Erskine wrote Red:

> We were delighted to receive from you a very pretty book, which—judging from its outer wrappings and label—seems to have been intended for us, but which within bears the inscription "To Wallace Fowlie, etc." Now I do not know what Mr. Fowlie received instead of this book, and since I do not know where he is, I don't know how to go about retrieving it—but maybe this will all work itself out in the end.
>
> I was glad to hear that you liked [Malcom Lowry's] *Under the Volcano* well enough at the halfway mark to be interested in the execution of the second part. Since I find the second half even more exciting than the first, I am not filled with fear at your final judgment; but I am still burning with curiosity to get your letter.
>
> Here is the review which will appear in the *Times Book Review* section next

Sunday. It is better by far, in spite of one or two dubious notes, than I would have dared hope for in that journal. You probably saw the *New Yorker* one, which was at least content with your part of the book. I don't suppose we could have hoped for any more space from them, but I wish they hadn't been quite so offhand about it. I will send along any others I see, or, failing that, tell you where they can be found.

By March 1947 Warren gave Albert encouragement about his break with Reynal & Hitchcock. Warren had been helping his friend contact authors and had been reading early manuscripts of prospects. After Erskine, and his associate Frank Taylor left R&H, Warren did continue his relation with the firm. In April Warren heard that Albert was joining Bennett Cerf and Donald Klopfer at Random House. Erskine had also been in the running for the directorship of the University of North Carolina Press. Warren's letters reflected his increasing trust in Erskine's critical acumen, as he continued to send him manuscripts and to give him updates on transactions arranged through his agent, Helen Strauss at the William A. Morris Agency. By 1947, Warren was well aware of the difficulty in his own marriage; however, even to his close friends, Cleanth and Albert, he did not discuss the assorted details in his letters. Cinina's psychological well-being continued to decline, and she became more abusive in words and actions; yet Warren closed his letters to include Cinina, as in his April 15, 1947, letter to Albert: "Do let me know how things go in your new spot. I'm very anxious for word. Cinina joins me in love to you both. As ever, Red."

On the same day, April 15, Erskine wrote Red to explain his silence:

> Just a hurried and overdue word: for the past two weeks, Frank and I have been negotiating with Random House, and for the most of that period it has been 99% settled that we should join their editorial department. I wanted, however, to say that it had all been settled, and the papers signed, before I said anything at all. But somehow the news leaked out and has been in the papers here, though no papers are signed yet (we are to have a sort of contract, if things work out); they should be, though, within the next day or two, unless something happens.
>
> I have already taken up with them the business of the scouting, and damn it, they claim they have too many commitments of that kind already, much as they would like, etc. Well, I hope I can break that down in time, but it will surely take time, because if I go there at all it is on the comparatively small-fry basis; and it's a big place. So I can't ask you not to go ahead and make whatever similar arrangement might be offered elsewhere. Needless to say, I regret it, and I hope that maybe in a year I can change it.
>
> Am I in any way gumming up any plans by holding the novelette so long? I in fact read it within a few days of its arrival, but wanted to read it again before attempting to say anything about it (I liked it tremendously, but there were one or two points not quite clear to me and I wanted to investigate them further in what I hoped would be a less distracted state of mind, which unfortunately has not yet arrived ...). It came just about the time that trouble at Reynal & Hitchcock began to come out in the open: i.e., when Reynal began to discuss firing all the staff that Frank and I had collected—an operation which by the middle

of February was just about completed. So that for six weeks before leaving there I spent all my time either discussing or (worse) brooding about what to do. We decided that leaving was best, even though we had not settled on our next step; and now for another six weeks we've been trying to get back to work again. In short, it hasn't, as you can imagine, been smooth and unperplext.

But maybe it will work out now, and as soon as anything does I'll wire you, so that you'll not be left hanging by these vaguenesses. Meantime, if you need back that copy of the story, please say so; otherwise I want to read it again with what I hope will be a clearer head.

Erskine had a wonderful sense of humor, dry and often subtle, though not so subtle in his May 16, 1947, letter concerning the phenomenal success of Warren's recent novel *All the King's Men*. The last paragraph captured, too, his self-effacing tendency:

> Jesus, what a quandary to find oneself in! Shall I spend the summer on the West Coast on account of Hollywood, or must I be near the Atlantic and Broadway? If I were you I would select a nice place in the very center between the two cities (with a private airfield, of course) so that you can take off at need or at will in other directions. All this and Guggenheim too, to say nothing of Pulitzer and Book of the Month Club.... No doubt you are getting a more intimate feeling about that needle's eye problem that you learned in your youth. I hope that the injury to your wrist is not serious. From the legibility of the handwritten part of your letter, I take it that it must be your right wrist that you hurt, and that you are now writing with your uncorrupted left.
>
> I hope that it will turn out that the demands of Broadway are more immediate than those of the West, and that you will indeed be able to spend some time here. In any event, I am glad that you will be here for a few days in June.
>
> I hope that the waggishness of my telegram did not seem to indicate to you that I wasn't happy about the more intangible aspects of the Pulitzer Prize, which henceforth will be something of an honor as well as something of an emolument. Seriously, I am pleased as hell about all of these things. Your cup is indeed running over, and it is fun to sit in the saucer.

Erskine continued to assist Warren by depositing his checks (from Random House, Yale, etc.) when the need seemed immediate. They spent some time in Westport that summer and later that fall, Warren asked for another favor regarding transportation to Europe—destination Italy. Albert's letter on July 20th referred to Peggy's being in New York and something "new and different" as a result. Peggy received a scholarship from the Belgian government to study in her field of art history.

Erskine, eager to bring Warren to Random House, helped coordinate contracts for the transition—possibly "the longest contract on record" he wrote Warren on February 27, 1948—and for RH to acquire rights to Warren's first novel *Night Rider*, which they completed successfully. It was reissued in 1948. His concluding line, after requesting that Warren respond to several questions, was not exaggerated: "I look forward to all these 'duties' (related to the reissue of *Night Rider*) with considerable pleasure." In his March 18th reply, Warren expressed his gratitude for Albert's help, especially for sending him, by air, two cartons of John Alden cigarettes in Taormina, Sicily. Albert was smoking Sano pipe tobacco at the time. (His pipe smoking was partial cause of his cancer about forty years later.) While in Italy, Warren was writing his fourth novel, *World Enough and Time*, which Random House published in 1950. He sent the first two chapters to Erskine on April 12th, 1948, for comment. In his letters to his friend and soon-to-be-editor, he explained what he was attempting to accomplish.

> Here is the first of the novel, two chapters, running about 40,000 words, or near it. One scene is missing, as you will see, from Chapter II, but I have written in a note to give the continuity, and toward the end of Chapter II a paragraph is missing as a kind of summary of what Jeremiah reads aloud from Plato. I haven't yet decided which of two passages to use from Plato, and I'll wait till I can get a translation of the proper epoch. Naturally, you are not to take this as a final draft, but I hope that this is close enough to a final draft so that you can get some notion of the drift of things. There are, of course, some lags. For instance, the wife of Colonel Fort should be introduced early and some indication made of his family life. But aside from such mechanical things, I am anxious to get your criticism and suggestion. When you all come to stay with us at Sirmione, or elsewhere, you and I can do some close work on it, and then I hope to have as much more for your inspection. But meanwhile I should be very glad to have some remarks and impressions. I am at the stage when I begin to feel the need of a reaction.
>
> Things are going pretty fast with the writing, as you can see. For one thing, I don't have any other central occupation, and can put in about as many hours a day as the traffic and the backbone will bear. I hope to be able to beat the deadline by quite a bit, and if I get in a good summer, I may be able to give you the manuscript in January 1949. But there are always unexpected difficulties.
>
> If Mr. Cerf is interested at this stage, you have my full permission to show the thing to him. If he does read it, I should of course like to have his comments.

Erskine's response is a measure of his friendship and professionalism. Within two weeks' time, he sent the following "preliminary" critique, dated April 30th:

> Though I've not quite finished my second reading of the two chapters, I want to get off a few remarks anyway, already because of a lot of unexpected interruptions I am later with this than I intended to be.
>
> Anyway, it was a delight to read it. What I cannot possibly now have is a feeling of its proportional relation to the whole; nor can I yet weigh the assets and liabilities of the Method (though I think I can recognize a few of each). We had so little conversation about it really that either more or none at all might have been better: I almost wish none, so that I could have tested it as a reader who had no idea whatever of what was coming or what it meant, and could then see how readily one can find his way into the story, whereas now I know just enough to make that impossible and not enough to feel privy to your plans, and

I'll have to perform the pure test on other readers (which I've already done with Peggy and shall next week with Bennett, though I'm of two minds about turning people loose on partial and unfinal manuscripts).

On the day last week that the chapters arrived I happened to learn from Helen of the existence of "The Confessions of Jereboam O. Beauchamp" and to ask her for it; then the MS arrived and I decided not to read the other document, though now I am not sure whether I should or not, whether it will give me knowledge which I will then think is communicated by the MS even if it isn't. (I ran into this a little, I remember, with *Night Rider* and *AKM* [*All the King's Men*] as a result of conversations about what you intended to do and readings of the partial MSS; and it got so with *Under the Volcano* that I could hardly tell what was in the book and what I'd gotten from Lowry's letters that other readers wouldn't have access to.) But then I wonder if I'd be of any editorial use whatever (whatever that is) if I waited around until something was finished, and done in absolute secrecy for fear I might get some hint of it, and then read it for the "pure" reaction. Maybe it is better to be fully implicated, so far as that is possible, though I have no grand notions I assure you about the "help" I can be to you.

Well, I'd like to make a few tentative observations on the Method. What I remember from the brief remarks you made about it some time back runs a little like this: that it would be a combination of quotes from "documents" (all of which I understood were to be fictitious so far as their actual words were concerned) and the words of one of our contemporaries, who, given these documents, had set out on the basis of them to reconstruct, interpret, and comment on what had happened. Maybe my memory is faulty, or maybe you have altered your plan, or maybe you haven't; but I don't think I would have been able so to describe the method simply on the basis of reading this much and not having heard anything else about it. Perhaps I would, perhaps it is not too important anyway whether I (or anyone) would or not at this stage. But what I feel is this: that for passages of considerable length I seem to be reading something told from the point of view we call omniscient, so that it almost seems odd to come upon some disclaimer of knowing, some statement regretting that the record is not quite clear or complete at this point (How can we not know *this*? one might ask, when we know the last scene with such multiplicity of detail, complete with dialogue, the way things looked, felt, smelt, sounded, and all? Why don't we know everything?). Of course, I am not at all sure how important the plausibility of the method is, whether it needs to have (and to show that it has) an interior logic all its own that it doesn't violate and that cannot be questioned or doubted. Not too important, I'd guess, if its product works, which God knows in most regards it so far does. But I get interested in the method as method, and hence arise the questions. Maybe the method could stand more insisting on and pointing out: establishing clearly the fullness of the documents as the source of what we do know instead of referring only to the holes that exist in them.

Another problem in connection with the method is that of tone-of-voice. Don't we have almost the problem of a narrator (the "I" of the first sentence, which becomes thereafter, for obvious reasons of clarity, "we") and therefore the problem of consistency of tone and attitude of all portions of the writing which appear outside the quotation marks, as well as the consistency of those that appear within—and almost an attitude of the former toward the latter, which would make clear at any point why the former chooses the quoted passage in preference to his own words. I should have begun this paragraph by saying that all this is a condition that for the most part exists, rather than throwing it out as something to be attained. I don't know how important as principle this is, but it seems enough so to make it worth while watching for violations of it. Jeremiah's style is nearly all of a piece, or so it seems to me; but my doubts are raised by such quotations as "he would whip me till I bellowed like a scrub bull in a canebrake in cocklebur season" (I-14)—where I not only doubt if his father ever said it on any such occasion, but more strongly that Jeremiah would remember it if he had or choose to quote it if he did remember, and on the same page the similar metaphor about the extent of beating prompts the same dubiety. Because one of J's outstanding qualities (thus far) seems to be his absolutely total lack not only of humor but awareness of its existence, so that I feel he would be incapable of making such a remark (the second is his own) or remembering someone else's. Now maybe you have included these to show that J did not indeed lack humor (or perhaps there are other instances that have slipped my mind, or there are others coming in what follows), in which case there would need to be more evidence of it to prove it. But I also suspect by now that one of the important clues to his character is his humorlessness.

One fine thing about this device for telling, as you are doubtless thoroughly aware, is that you can use Jeremiah's kind of rhetoric for all it is worth (and it is worth a lot) without seeming to be directly responsible for it yourself, and also that you can judiciously limit the amount of it to doses one can swallow. I can see now why you couldn't let *him* tell the whole thing: there would be a ringing in the reader's ears from about page ten on. The contrasts between the two voices make a pleasing counterpoint—though occasionally there are places where the contrast is not enough marked. (Maybe I am making up too elaborate motives for the Method, maybe I misunderstand it and need more before I get it. I'm only trying at this stage to explain what I think it is and how I like it. I like it.)

It is possible that the first chapter would gain if you could save the background of Cassius Fort and either impose it by degrees, passim, or in a lump later on. There are of necessity so many backgrounds in this chapter that it tends toward sluggishness a little, especially near the end; and it seems strategically important for the first chapter to move forward into the story as much as possible instead of backward out of it. And it doesn't seem to me necessary for the reader to know all this about him even before J himself does. (Naturally, not knowing what is coming I can be only tentative in this observation. I wouldn't want to see him moved into chapter II, bodily; but I wonder if he is not important enough that his nature can emerge by degrees rather than as a preliminary summary.)

(It is now, I regret to say, Tuesday, May 4, instead of Friday—when I started this. But we had to go away for the weekend, and I was too sleepy Friday night to continue. But meantime I have finished my second reading.) I don't think there is any point taking up here any of the other small points that I'd like to bring up when I see you. I think it is going beautifully, despite the fact that what I've written above seems to stress questions and doubts (it would be pointless just now to write you a glowing account of the parts I like best and why, etc., even though they are the most of it.) ...

To go back to my original subject for a moment: I think it makes more sense for me to go ahead and read "The Confession of Jereboam." (For one thing I want to know what happens, and for another I think more and more it is silly for me to think I can arrange things so that I can read it in the manner—by *it* I mean the final product—of some outside reader who never heard a word about it.)

I've re-read *Night Rider* in the past two weeks, and it was wonderful to see how it held up after nearly ten years. I was constantly amazed both by things I did remember and by those I didn't, and also those I didn't remember until I got just on the opening of the scenes, when suddenly I would remember what was coming (e.g., I wouldn't have been able to say that Willy Proudfit had a nephew, he'd gone entirely, but as soon as I saw his name I even remembered what he would do). The Random House edition of *Night Rider* is planned for August. I don't see any reason to bother about that last paragraph, now that I've looked at it again (though I notice one of the reviews also mentioned suicide in connection with Mr. Munn's end). I found one typographical error and noted it for correction (though I won't guarantee I didn't miss any, I'm pretty sure there are no bad ones). I'm suggesting that a complete list of "Books by RPW" go in the front. Don't you think this is OK, even in an earlier book than five on the list[?] After all, this is technically different from a "third printing" by the original publisher. I think they should all be listed and I've asked Saxe [Commins], who handles such matters here, and he thinks so too.

Returned from Italy and writing from Santa Monica, California, Warren wrote on April 18, 1949:

According to Frank, who tells me that he talked with you on the phone the other night, there is some misunderstanding between us. Or perhaps I forgot to say to you that I was planning, hoping, and praying to push the novel through by early June? At least, I hope to have a draft then which you can work over. What will remain to be done after you see the draft, God knows. Anyway, since my arrival here I have been driving along at a fair pace. I had this section well developed in notes before coming, and I am now on page 85 of the eighth chapter. I shall finish within a week. This is, I say, chapter VIII. But it will really be VIII and IX in the final round-up, for I have to go back and divide it. It neatly falls into two sections about page 42. There will remain two more chapters, X and XI, by the new calculation. In God's grace, they will run about fifty pages each, about two month's work—if work goes well. But this chapter (VIII and IX) set out to be about fifty or sixty pages. You never can tell. I am a little disturbed about the scale the thing is developing. But we'll have to work on that when it is all done.

Erskine's tone in a May 6, 1949, letter came about as short as he would let show in his correspondence: "When the first draft is finished, I hope that I shall be able to have access to the original script instead of the various carbons which I have read piece-meal in the past. Sometimes the physical difficulties of reading these have been a barrier to a clear picture. Then, as you say, it may be advisable for us to get together, but at the moment I don't know whether this will be possible or not. I hope that it will be, because I am sure that we can accomplish a great deal more in much less time than we could possibly do through the mail."

Warren was willing to accommodate Albert's request for a cleaner manuscript and promised in a May 11th letter to "have the fresh copy made for you by middle or late July." Wanting to avoid unnecessary delays and to clarify his criticism, Albert responded on May 17th: "Just an extension of remarks about what I mean by a 'better manuscript.' I should say, off hand, that a complete retyping at this stage would be unnecessary, because it is not so much the interlinear corrections (though, naturally, they do slow one down) but the quality of the carbons that I have had access to. It is just that those two (or at the most, three) sheets of carbon paper that you have been using for the last year or so are beginning to get a little dim. The combination of lack of color and onion skin paper produces fatigue rather quickly. I wonder, therefore, if you had a better carbon; or failing that, if I could have the original instead of the carbon. I would especially not like to lose a month of retyping; I would even rather deal with the carbons that are in Helen's office at the moment."

During the fall of 1949, their correspondence was frequent with exchanges on the finished manuscript of *World Enough and Time*. Erskine sent detailed queries and suggestions, to which Warren responded in an October 12th letter: "I have worked through every one of your million suggestions and queries and in almost every instance have followed your ideas. I did not do so in regard to the scene between the lawyers and Jeremiah after the reading of Marlowe's letter. I prayed over it, but just didn't see it your way. I felt that I needed the distortion to point up the importance of the episode, etc. I may come to your view later. I didn't get as much reduction in Crotinthian McClardy as you no doubt wanted, but I got some. And as far as Antiope and Hippolyta are concerned, I think you will find that here there is a difference in names with reference to the same episode in the life of Theseus—and Hippolyta perhaps is more common—at least it is to me. In general I have made substantial reductions, especially in Chapter V and Chapter VIII, and I hope that I have improved the pact throughout. I have checked the chronology carefully and the dating. That ought to be straight now: I worked out a schedule from the text. The quotations have been checked for accuracy. One French idiom remains to be checked."

On October 24th, Erskine replied:

> I'd hoped to get a letter off to you by Friday, but it was not until late Friday afternoon that I finished "collating" the carbon and the original; the two MSS are now, I believe, identical with the cuts and additions all made in the carbon, and the name changed in both (changing Hawkins to Crawford is a more extensive job than one might think, and I hope I caught them all: I wish I'd thought of the name Crawley at the time we made this decision, though that might have been too much, and anyway I've now gotten used to Crawford). Other readers have now begun to read both copies, but it is too early for a report on reactions.
>
> Very little remains to be done now, I think. When I look at what you have

done, I marvel at how quickly you were able to do it. The cutting is masterful, making the pace (to me at least) just about perfect—though I shall be in a better position to judge that when I read it in galleys without all the marks, as I intend to do, to be sure there are no holes. You have cut more than I would have thought possible, much less asked; and yet I don't think you've done any harm. There are only two places of which I am doubtful, of which more below, and they are not very important.

Here, as I see it, is what remains:
We need a name for Simpson County.

> I-21   I can't make out one word in a written-in passage: "clambering rock or _____ soft-foot by the cane." Top of page
>
> II-13   I changed R's birthday from 1797 to 1798. Since month is not given, this seemed necessary to agree with statement that she is 3 yrs older than J (1801).
>
> II-53   I enclose copy of one of your inserts, where cutting seems to have bollixed up a sentence: I don't get the "resting at last in ... and rests there...." Please mark and return.
>
> V-47ff.   Rachel and the key. I liked this much better on rereading last time and wonder if it should be kept—though pace gains by its elimination. I'm on the fence.
>
> X-12   I've consistently admired the little paragraph about the autumn leaves, and I'd like to see it back in. It was only last week that I noticed that this duplicates a shorter treatment of the same thing in I-47 (McClardy section), but I'd rather cut it here and keep it in X, if that is OK with you.
>
> X-62   I altered two remaining references along here to One-eye's visit to the jail, since that scene is gone. He now refers to "Crawford's visit."
>
> I'm still not convinced that Crawford should mention Lilburn when he visits J in IX (I'm still using old chapter numbers, by the way). This ties Lilburn not only with Bumps and Jessup and the reward money, but with the missing handbill; and I think the fact that L comes in under Wilkie's auspices would then rather make J suspect Wilkie (since he has God's plenty of reasons already) than make him accept L. But it is credible that he should accept him if he does not know he has anything to do with the handbill or with Bumps and Jessup, etc. That is why I'm pleading that Crawford only mention the fact that One-eye claims to have the handbill, without reference to others involved or to circumstances, which he in fact doesn't even need to know about, and which J and the reader not only do not need at this point but shouldn't have—or so it seems to me.

Almost by return mail, Warren wrote on October 27th:

On your queries of October 24.

1. Why not let Simpson County stand? It is a real County, and the others are fictional, but nothing happens in Simpson and so, let it stand.

2. II [sic]-21. The word is "bogueing."

3. II-13. Okay about Raccee's [?] birthday.

4. V-47. All right, restore the Rache-key episode, and we'll face a final decision in proof. I'm on the fence, too, and the final decision will probably have to be yours.

5. X-12. Okay, keep the autumn leaves here, and cut that in I-47. The duplication was intentional, but then I got worried about it as being too artificial.

6. I'm still not sure about the failure to mention Lilburn in the jail visit of Crawford. Let's talk about this when I come to NY and we have the text before us.

With the promising news that the Random House partners were enthusiastic about *World Enough and Time,* Erskine wrote Warren the good news and a proposed publication date of March 3rd. Erskine went on to say in his November 17th letter:

The jacket. Nothing settled yet. McKnight Kauffer has submitted one sketch, which has been rejected. The most that could be said for it (even by me, one of his admirers) was that it was "striking"—but too starkly forbiddingly moderne. It was felt by the saleswise that it would only frighten away prospective customers. He is working on another idea, but at the same time another expert, who specializes in representational illustration, is working on still another. Not a single big illustration, but a series of little ones to extend around the jacket from the front to the back of the book, but only in the lower fifth of the space, leaving most of the area for big type. The idea behind all this is that the jacket ought to convey immediately more about the period, color, etc., of the book than can be accomplished by simply the title and abstract design. This other fellow did the jackets for several Robert Graves books that Random did some years back.

As you know, this kind of approach is contrary to both my theory and approach in the days I did jackets (*my* approach having been based partly on conviction but partly, I suspect, on the fact that I don't know how to draw). I still don't like illustration, for my own contemplation and enjoyment, that is; but I am no longer sure as I used to be that all sales managers are wrong and that the public doesn't like illustrations. What I believe now is that the public doesn't give a damn what it's wrapped in, once they've heard of a book; but that the booksellers, who have to buy it first, are so sold on illustrated jackets that they tend to resist the others. Or so I gather from things I hear.

In any event it is not yet settled. I don't want anything to be done that will be distasteful to you, but on the other hand I think it possible that the kind of typographic simplicity that we both like *would* hamper distribution. And I don't think that the quality of the book can be in any way affected by what it is wrapped in, and am therefore more or less willing to let the promoters do what they think they can do best with. But if what is submitted is too monstrous, I'll oppose it and seek your aid. And if you're definitely opposed to pictures of any size or kind, shout now and I'll take a stand.

So far I've been too uncertain in my own mind to take any kind of position. For this reason: While the book is certainly a modern book, in one sense of the word, and perhaps the most important sense, I can't help feeling that it would look funny in too modern dress. Not funny, but somehow wrong. On the other hand, most attempts at "period style" in typography and symbol end up by feeling slightly nostalgic, faintly amused, almost deprecatory. Which is why I'm willing to admit that the pictorial approach might be feasible.

Warren was reading galleys and still making minor revisions as late as the end of November 1949; Erskine was actually suggesting some of those revisions that dealt with very small points of consistency, e.g., whether Jessup has a mustache. *World Enough and Time* was finally published June 20, 1950; and through Albert's planning, came out with a pamphlet, *World Enough and Time: Background of a Novel*; in a special limited edition (numbered but not signed) for presentation to the Booksellers of America; in a Kentucky Edition of 1,000 copies signed by the author; and as a Literary Guild Selection for July 1950. The first British edition was published in 1951 by Eyre & Spottiswoode.

The Warren-Erskine relationship settled into a relatively standard but by no means boring one as they planned meeting up in Italy, continued to write and edit, and to comfort and shore up one another in times of crisis. Red and Cinina's divorce was final on June 28, 1951; Albert and Peggy also had divorced. In a May 27, 1951, letter just thirty-two days before his own divorce, Warren wrote to Albert: "I think that the situation has some tragic elements in it, for along the way it looked so natural and perfect, the relation between you and Peggy. No, until recently I had not become aware of the mounting tension, or in so far as I had been aware of it I had misread it and set it aside. In general, as the fruit of a bitter experience, I have come to the conclusion, for which I claim no great originality, that when a relation gets charged with a certain kind of ambiguity and distress it is just destruction and self-destruction to try to persist in it. But, as we all well know, what one 'wants' is never quite simple—though it can be, with luck and will, a lot simpler than some people are inclined to believe. As you said, this doesn't get anybody any forwarder. I do want you to know, however, that from the bottom of my heart I wish you both well."[6]

Warren was often a sounding board for Albert as well. Albert had shown him previously the Malcolm Lowry manuscript *Under the Volcano*, Karl Shapiro's essays, and Pier Pasinetti's manuscript of a novel. In a note dated April 7, 1952, Warren shared his impression of another author's work: "I have finished Ralph Ellison's *Invisible Man* and am grateful to you for the opportunity of reading it. He has a powerful narrative sense, he can write up to his big scenes—and some of them are really impressive—and he has a subject that is important. I don't see how the book can fail to make some kind of stir. For the moment waiving the matter of his literary abilities (which are all to the good, it seems to me), the mere fact that this book is written by a Negro gives it a special force and significance. To me it was more enlightening about one important aspect of the Negro's relation to our society than anything else I've ever read. And the treatment of the Brotherhood—which I take to be the CP—ought to be enough to put this book in the news beyond the literary news." Warren's responses were frequently accompanied by his rationale or assessment in light of current literary activity.

Erskine and Warren edited two Dell Books collections, which have remained in print continuously since their appearance: *Short Story Masterpieces* (1954) and *Six Centuries of Great Poetry* (1955). The anthologies reflect the breadth of reading they did and their keen eye for enduring literature.

The give-and-take exchange of ideas and critiques of literature continued into the

1980s, more via telephone and somewhat less via the postal system because of declining health. In 1987 Albert was diagnosed with cancer. In a handwritten, undated letter to Albert's third wife, Marisa, Warren wrote: "I have had miraculous luck in friends all my life. I don't know what would have happened without them. Luck in various basic ways. And I have had Albert as a *friend*—and I do *not* use the word loosely—since I was 25 years old. In more than one way he has been truly essential for my good fortunes. This is not a recent discovery to me. Nor is it a recent discovery that you and Sylvia [*sic*] are part of [it]." Other handwritten letters of encouragement followed. Albert continued to work and brought out *A Robert Penn Warren Reader* (1988) and *New and Selected Essays* (1989) before his friend died on September 15, 1989. Albert passed away on May 15, 1993. It was an extraordinary union of two minds in a life-long commitment to literature.

Notes

1. Robert Penn Warren (April 24, 1905-September 15, 1989) is more widely known than is Albert Russell Erskine, Jr., (April 18, 1911-May 15, 1993), who became a highly respected senior vice-president at Random House and editor of Ralph Ellison, William Faulkner, Malcolm Lowry, Cormac McCarthy, James A. Michener, John O'Hara, Jean Stafford, William Styron, and Eudora Welty, as well as Warren and others.
2. For much more detail about the founding of the *Southern Review*, see Thomas W. Cutrer, *Parnassus on the Mississippi: The* Southern Review *and the Baton Rouge Literary Community, 1935-1942* (Baton Rouge: Louisiana State UP, 1984).
3. Robert Penn Warren letters, in Albert Russell Erskine, Jr., Papers (Private Collection); Albert Russell Erskine, Jr., letters, in Robert Penn Warren Papers, Yale Collection of American Literature (MSS 51), Beinecke Rare Book and Manuscript Library, Yale University, New Haven, CT. Use of the letters in this essay are with the kind permission of Mrs. Albert R. Erskine and Ms. Silvia Erskine, and the estate of Robert Penn Warren. See also *Selected Letters of Robert Penn Warren: Triumph and Transition, 1943-1952*, ed. Randy Hendricks and James A. Perkins, vol. 3 (Baton Rouge: Louisiana State UP, 2005), which was published after this article was written and submitted, but is here acknowledged as a source for its content of other letters from Warren to Erskine. For further information on Pier Pasinetti, see the following essay by William Bedford Clark.
4. Warren's short story appeared in the *Southern Review* 4 (Autumn 1938): 299-321. It was included in the Edward J. O'Brien Best Short Story Collection for 1939. It is an excerpt from Warren's first novel, *Night Rider* (1939). Pip is Charles W. Pipkin, graduate dean at LSU, and one of the founding editors of the *Southern Review*.
5. The poem was "Crime," which appeared in *Nation* May 25, 1940: 655; and subsequently, in *Eleven Poems on the Same Theme* (Norfolk, CT: New Directions, 1942) [12-13].
6. However, "All's well that ends well": On December 7, 1952, Warren married Eleanor Clark, by whom he had two children, Rosanna and Gabriel. Albert was Red's best man, and Katherine Anne Porter was the matron of honor. And on September 24, 1959, Erskine married Marisa Bisi, by whom he had a daughter, Silvia.

Works Cited

Blotner, Joseph. "Albert Erskine Partially Seen." *Sewanee Review* 93.1 (2005): 139-61.
Erskine, Albert Russell, Jr. Letters. In Robert Penn Warren Papers. Yale Collection of American Literature (MSS 51) Beinecke Rare Book and Manuscript Library. Yale University, New Haven, CT.
Warren, Robert Penn. Letters. In Albert Russell Erskine, Jr., Papers. Private Collection.
Winchell, Mark Royden. *Cleanth Brooks and the Rise of Modern Criticism*. Charlottesville: UP of Virginia, 1996.

Warren and Pasinetti: A Study in Friendship

by William Bedford Clark

> Without friends no one would choose to live, though
> he had all other goods; even rich men and those in
> in possession of office and of dominating power are
> thought to need friends most of all; for what is the use
> of such prosperity without the opportunity of beneficence,
> which is exercised chiefly towards friends?
>
> Aristotle, *Nicomachean Ethics*, VIII, i

On December 16, 1939, scarcely three and half months after Hitler's invasion of Poland and the outbreak of the Second World War, Robert Penn Warren wrote his friends Katherine Anne Porter and Albert Erskine from Rome, where he and his wife Cinina were intent upon getting as much as possible out of their European sabbatical before Italy entered the war and they faced the possibility of being stranded for the duration. His tone was light-hearted and chatty, but his language (with an obvious eye toward the possibility of intercepted mail) was circumspect and guarded. One heavily encoded passage stands out:

> By the way our friend who is interested in family history, and on whose work we spent some time last spring doing Ms and proof, has applied for a place, any kind of a place, with [Joseph] Brewer [president of Olivet College] and with some other people. His credentials…are enormously impressive. If either, or both of you, can find it in your hearts to clarify Brewer's mind on any essential points, it would be a chore done in a very good and almost imperative cause. I leave this to your powers of divination. I wrote to Joe,… but it was not possible for me to explain certain matters which are important. (*Selected Letters* II 248)

Several weeks later, on January 11, 1940, Warren wrote his co-editor at the *Southern Review*, Cleanth Brooks, in a like manner: "you all may be seeing our friend who is interested in family history much sooner than you ever suspected, and for an indefinite period. He is…making desperate efforts to change his whole plan of life…[out of] motives with which you would have the deepest sympathy." Warren concluded: "I hear that he simply can't take any more of what he has been taking" (*Selected Letters* II 254).

The mysterious "friend who is interested in family history" was P. M. (Pier Maria) Pasinetti, whose story "Family History" had appeared in the Summer 1939 *Southern Review* and whose anti-German and anti-Fascist sentiments had placed him in a precarious position. In a subsequent letter to Porter (February 20, 1940), Pasinetti's identity is even more deeply encoded. He is now "Amos," and Warren assures Porter than "Amos" is not only free of whatever questionable opinions he might have voiced as a twenty-two-year-old graduate student at Louisiana State University, but that "The change has been complete, violent, and I am convinced, irrevocable.... As for the violence of the change which [I] mention above, I have, at times, found myself in a position of trying to restrain public manifestations" (*Selected Letters* II 266). Once he and Cinina were safely back in the States, thanks in part to a timely tip from Pasinetti that Mussolini was at last ready to drop the pretense of neutrality and join Hitler in war against the Allies, Warren was free to speak openly, and he did so in a June 8, 1940, letter to Brooks:

> Poor Pier Pasinetti had finally managed to wrangle his permit to come to America, after working all winter on the proposition. He is the saddest and bitterest man you ever saw, and if he doesn't learn a little self-control he will shortly end in a concentration camp or with a busted head. He says anything and says it anywhere, in a voice like a fog-horn. The only chance he has for survival is that a lot of other people do the same thing and I don't suppose they can arrest everybody. ...[A] few days before he was supposed to sail, they revoked his permit. He was planning to come here and take out American citizenship. (*Selected Letters* II 278)

Pasinetti would eventually return to the United States, where he would go on to earn dual distinction as an academic and a novelist, but only after the war was over—and only after intense and protracted efforts by Robert Penn Warren on his behalf. A look at Warren's relationship with this brilliant young Italian, son of a prominent Venetian family, reveals much about what it meant to be a friend of "Red" and testifies in a dramatic way to the loyalty and responsibility Warren showed toward those in his circle whose promise he recognized and whose talent he admired.

I

After studying at Oxford and taking his degree from the University of Padua, Pier Maria Pasinetti arrived in Baton Rouge in September 1935 to assume a graduate fellowship awarded by the Italian Foreign Ministry and Institute for International Education.[1] When his bus pulled in, Robert Penn Warren was there to meet it, and—Pasinetti's accommodations at the French House on the Louisiana State University campus being temporarily unavailable—the Warrens proceeded to take him in as a houseguest (Interview). This unanticipated courtesy no doubt had something to do with the fact that Cinina Warren (the former Emma Brescia) was teaching courses in Italian at LSU and had been instrumental in organizing a university event honoring the Italian ambassador during the previous term.[2] The powers-that-be likely regarded her and her amenable husband as ideal contacts for the newly arrived exchange student, but whatever the case this early intimacy proved fortuitous. One is tempted to say providential. Pasinetti soon became a valued member of the Warrens' social set (they were remarkably gregarious), and among the friendships he struck up was one with the energetic and discerning Albert Erskine, only two years his senior, who, under the modest designation of "business manager," was playing an indispensable role in launching the *Southern Review*.[3] Decades later, he would serve as Pasinetti's editor at Random House.[4]

During his year at LSU, Pasinetti produced a quite creditable master's thesis on "The Tragic Elements in Hawthorne's Works"—in retrospect a telling choice of topic given his dynamic awareness of the interplay between past and present and the characteristic preoccupation with inter-generational relationships that was to inform much of his fiction.[5] (The thesis was nominally directed by Earl R. Bradshear, no particular friend of Robert Penn Warren, but Cleanth Brooks was on the examining committee—as was the venerable department head W. A. "Corky" Read.).[6] Academic credentialing was important, of course, but Pasinetti was already committed to creative writing, and when he left Baton Rouge for further study at the University of California he could boast of an additional feather in his cap. His story "Home-coming" was included in the Spring 1936 issue of the *Review*. Considerably less ambitious than "Family History," the second (and last) of his *Southern Review* pieces, it nonetheless warrants reading as a striking vignette, somewhat cinematic in conception and execution, in which the vacuity and wilful isolation of a powerful, ostensibly successful, man (perhaps a Fascist official) are made woefully evident. For Pasinetti, as for Hawthorne and Warren, the loss of self in a deracinated world would prove a perennial and fruitful subject. (By contrast, the narcissistic and much bedeviled protagonist of "Family History" ultimately *defines* himself out of his private inferno when he intuits and accepts the purgatorial dimension of unrelenting blood ties—shorthand for communal responsibility—and commits himself to the problematic survival of a new generation.)

Once Pasinetti was settled in Berkeley, he wrote the Warrens (who seem to have made him a loan while he awaited a check from his father), and at least two letters from this period have survived.[7] They not only reveal the degree of intimacy that had come to characterize his relationship with the glamorous and well-connected couple during their relatively brief year together in Baton Rouge, they constitute a running self-portrait of the correspondent himself, an immensely gifted—if at times ingenuous—young man who is commendably earnest about his literary vocation and realistic about the responsibilities and prospects such a commitment entails, even as he indulges a seemingly irrepressible predisposition for satirical commentary, displaying powers of discernment and wit that are by turns genial and combative. It is little wonder that Red and Cinina found the puckish Pier such good company. A letter of September 4, 1936, written shortly after his arrival in California, is wide-ranging and representative. It opens with a comic account of the psychological profiling new students at Berkeley were expected to undergo, proceeds to recreate an amusing evening spent with Cinina's father (the composer Domenico Brescia, whose broad culture reminded Pasinetti of a Renaissance humanist), touches playfully upon Pasinetti's most recent romantic interest (a girl with regrettable tastes in poetry), and concludes with a rather aggressive caricature of a bewildered exchange student from Japan. From the second of the surviving letters from Berkeley (May 5, 1937), we can infer the extent to which Warren was already employing his considerable network of literary connections to Pasinetti's advantage. His stay at the university coming to an end, Pasinetti writes that he has received a letter from an editor at a leading publishing house, Paul Brooks, who read "Home-coming" in the *Southern Review* and would be interested in seeing a book-length manuscript when and if Pasinetti completes one. (Brooks had made a point of dropping Warren's name and was in fact his primary contact at Houghton-Mifflin, the firm that would bring out *Night Rider* in 1939.) Pasinetti asks Warren for advice on how best to proceed and in closing notes that he has recently spent time with the established

West Coast poets Howard Baker and Lincoln Fitzell—close friends of Warren from his own days as a graduate student at Berkeley. Red's interest in promoting Pasinetti's career, even at this early juncture, could not be more manifest.

Pasinetti returned to Europe when his year in California was up. The illness of his father back in Venice (it would ultimately prove fatal) seems to have been a major factor (Interview), but whatever the case, Pasinetti was in a position to welcome the Warrens when they made a hurried trip to Italy over the summer of 1938, and he reciprocated their many kindnesses by hosting their stay in Venice, to their immense "'satisfaction'" (Blotner 168-170). Little wonder. Venice was Pasinetti's city in every sense, not only his native place but the future hub of his fictive universe. It would be difficult to imagine a more informative or entertaining guide to the storied metropolis, rich in art, intrigue, and literary associations. As Blotner suggests, Warren may have made his first trip to Italy in deference to Cinina's ethnic sensibilities and at her insistence, but the journey—not least his time with Pier—marked the start of a lifelong fascination with all things Italian,[8] and Warren was eager to return on a Guggenheim fellowship in the fall of 1939. The Pier Pasinetti the Warrens met on this second occasion in Italy was a changed man. He had undergone what he would later describe as a "decisive experience,"[9] one that turned him into a vocal critic of totalitarianism and (to recall Warren's words) a likely candidate for "a concentration camp" or "busted head."

In the fall of 1938, Pasinetti was in Berlin, studying and teaching, and there he witnessed the shocking aftermath of *Kristallnacht*, the "night of shattered glass," in which synagogues and Jewish places of business, marked with the Star of David, were subjected to brutal vandalism and arson at the instigation of the Nazi regime.[10] This coordinated act of violence throughout the Reich was clearly no spontaneous pogrom, but a foretaste of the coming Holocaust, and Pasinetti would later recreate his disgust and outrage in his first novel, *Venetian Red* (1960), through the medium of Giorgio Partibon, a character modeled in part on the author. Viewing the devastation in the early morning light, Giorgio and his friends find that their "image of the world was changing that morning, was widening, like a tumor, revealing malignancy as it grew. From now on, there would be a new shadow over everything for them, the suspicion that every form of life always had the possibility of suddenly revealing itself to be coincident with death." They sense "a fracture in the world and in communal life, a declaration of anarchy, to which nothing now would ever put an end," and they watch in horror as a Jewish merchant is carried out of his shop by the mob:

> His head thrown backward, supine above that yelling crowd that had lifted him, the man's face showed such extreme pallor that it appeared absurd; a corpse would have given a plainer impression of death, but he seemed now to be even beyond death. He would occasionally move his eyes, emptied of any expression, or his hands, in a weak, useless, automatically defensive gesture, or his lips, uttering a lament that was no longer even of terror. (*Venetian Red* 334-335)

The victim's name is Gerecht (the "righteous one"), and the Christic parallels—and Pasinetti's point—are unmistakable. *Kristallnacht* represented a crucifixion of decency itself.

The year 1940 found Warren back in the United States and Pasinetti, his visa revoked, facing an increasingly problematic future as the war widened on every front. Warren's concern for his friend remained correspondingly acute, and the possibility of somehow bringing Pasinetti to America was never far from his thoughts. In a lengthy letter of August 23, 1940, filled with news, gossip, and talk of food and drink, Warren took pains to reassure the young Italian: "We talk of you often, and think of you more often, and look forward to a reunion. Which, we trust, may not be too far off" (*Selected Letters* II 289).[11] As Warren himself must have suspected, his "trust" was more rhetorical than realistic, and the path toward reunion took a disarming detour in 1941, when Pasinetti was "sent to the University of Göttingen as Italian lecturer, where because of his transparent moral and political views his situation was not without danger" (*World Authors* 584).

On April 16, 1941, Warren wrote Pasinetti with good news. Edward J. O'Brien had selected "Family History" for inclusion in his *Best Short Stories, 1940*, and a copy of that popular anthology had been set aside for him in the *Southern Review* offices at LSU. Warren, on a visiting appointment at the University of Iowa, offered Pasinetti his impressions of the painter Grant Wood, the neo-humanist Norman Foerster ("brooding over the abyss"), and the emerging critic Austin Warren (a friend of Pasinetti's onetime mentor Mario Praz), and he concluded with already familiar sentiments: "We talk of you constantly, and would give a great deal to see you. I shan't undertake to tell you how much we look forward to our next meeting" (*Selected Letters* II 31). On May 16, Pasinetti replied, hinting in a covert way that the Italians and Germans regarded America's entry into the war as a matter of not if, but when. That would make communication, even by mail, unlikely. The good times he and the Warrens had once shared now seemed to belong to some prehistoric epoch. Pasinetti was working as best he could at his own writing. The times were decidedly inauspicious, but he insisted that the writerly vocation was all the more important in light of that fact—a view Warren would have emphatically seconded.

As the seat of a great university, Göttingen was no doubt relatively idyllic compared to the Berlin Pasinetti had known earlier, but Germany was still the belly of the Beast, and Pasinetti's dream of coming to America must have seemed all but unattainable as he concentrated on his duties as *Lektor* and worked at finding time for fiction. Then things took a dramatic and positive turn in 1942. Pasinetti was offered and accepted an appointment at the University of Stockholm, which made it possible for him to assume refuge in a neutral country. A literary analogue suggests itself: In the *Commedia*, Dante had to pass through the Inferno before he could begin the long climb up Mount Purgatory. Pasinetti was delivered out of the Third Reich, but his final goal of a new life in the United States was by no means assured. Sweden's neutrality was a complicated matter, dependent upon highly nuanced diplomacy, tough-minded pragmatism, and sheer luck. At the quotidian level, Pasinetti's financial status was strained, and his chances of waiting out the war in Sweden were far from certain (PMP to RPW, 6/4/43; YCAL). Not surprisingly, he began to suffer from stress-related complications (PMP to RPW, 10/16/43; YCAL).

Warren was able to allay Pasinetti's financial worries somewhat (PMP to RPW, 8/20/43; YCAL), and he was clearly intent upon lifting his friend's spirits as best he could. His letters from Minneapolis (he was now at the University of Minnesota) are replete with comic caricature and anecdote. One example should suffice. Cinina was frequently ill, and the Warrens had hired a servant:

> She has the habit of reaching out and pinching me on the ribs to emphasize

some point and then cackling like a hen that's laid a rectangular egg. I went out to a dinner recently leaving her with Cinina. When I came home about eleven-thirty, I found her piled on the bed with her head on my pillow, cozy as could be. But at last I've discovered the source of her high spirits. I keep my liquor in a cabinet in the kitchen, and the horrible suspicion finally dawned upon me. She's a dram-snatcher.... So now I've moved the temptation into my study and have put it under lock and key. (*Selected Letters* III, 37)

(In an earlier letter [April 28, 1943], Warren, having turned thirty-eight, had shared his recipe for "a peculiarly insidious" birthday punch: "1 quart sauterne; 1 quart gin; 1 pint rum; 1 half-pint sherry; 1 pint grapefruit juice; enough pineapple juice to sweeten to taste; 1 large cake of ice." He added, "[I]t is superfluous for me to point out that it is not for the women and children" [*Selected Letters* III 22-23]).

Given the delay and probable miscarriage of mail between the United States and Sweden, Warren took to mailing his letters to Pasinetti in duplicate—sending a carbon-copy under separate cover. As they monitored the vicissitudes of war from opposite sides of the Atlantic, the two devised a code for referring to Hitler and Mussolini ("Llewellyn" and "Jones" respectively),[13] and there was constant talk of "the voyage" and their much-anticipated—but still problematic—reunion. "We'll be on the dock [when you arrive]," Warren promised (May 31, 1943 [*Selected Letters* III 31]). Meanwhile, Pasinetti did what he could to maintain his equilibrium and optimism by going about his daily routine, viewing Hollywood films, and culling through back issues of the *New Yorker* (PMP to RPW, 6/4/43; YCAL), and Warren whetted his friend's appetite for "the voyage" with high-spirited accounts of American people and places. Pasinetti sought Warren's help in placing an article on current affairs in an American magazine (PMP to RPW, 8/20/43; YCAL), and at his request Warren would go to considerable pains to assist an impoverished Italian sculptor adrift in Stockholm (see his October 29,1943, letter to Passinetti [*Selected Letters* III 48-51]). The friends often engaged in serious (and fairly technical) literary digressions, with Warren describing his various works-in-progress (such as "The Ballad of Billie Potts") and Pasinetti detailing some of the formal challenges he was facing in his own fiction. He felt free to affirm the insights set forth in Warren's new essay "Pure and Impure Poetry" in a wholly unaffected and collegial way (PMP to RPW, 1/14/43; YCAL)—which is in itself significant. Pasinetti may have been his junior by some eight years and a former student, but there is never a note of condescension in Warren's letters to him, nor does Pasinetti, for all his obvious distress, ever surrender his self-respect—or lose his saving sense of humor. This was clearly a friendship grounded on mutual admiration, a common devotion to the writer's calling, and a shared vision, not merely recollected *bonhommie*.

The most pressing common concern was, of course, making "the voyage" a reality. Pasinetti gained the ear of the American writer Frederic Prokosch, on assignment at the American legation in Stockholm, and it became clear that chances for a visa to the United States would be much enhanced if the applicant were in effect invited into the country (PMP to RPW, 11/14/43 & 2/24/44; YCAL). Warren, busy as he was with teaching and writing, went into full gear. Pasinetti was, after all, the citizen of a belligerent country, but that presented in itself no legal barriers, though bureaucratic procedures were another matter. Warren made inquiries in Washington and consulted with the head of the

Guggenheim Foundation in New York, "who was very helpful and took a lot of trouble to track down the one person in the world who knew all about the problem, play by play," and he lobbied Lewis Webster Jones, president of Bennington College, to make Pasinetti an offer (RPW to PMP, 4/8/44; *Selected Letters* III 68).

When it became clear that Pasinetti could not be in-country in time for Bennington's fall term, the project was temporarily derailed, but Warren, not to be discouraged, promoted Pasinetti's cause among his colleagues at Minnesota (unsuccessfully) and managed for a time to generate serious interest at the neighboring College of St. Thomas (RPW to PMP, 7/14/44; *Selected Letters* III 80-82). Meanwhile, the writer Allan Seager, whom Pasinetti had known at Oxford (Interview), joined Warren in co-sponsoring Pasinetti's reentry.[14] By January 22, 1945, Warren (now Consultant in Poetry at the Library of Congress) could report that Bennington was definitely prepared to hire Pasinetti (*Selected Letters* III 120-122), and to sweeten his friend's prospects he took it upon himself to negotiate a contract with the publishing firm of Reynal & Hitchcock for a novel Pasinetti had yet to write (see RPW to PMP, 5/30/45; *Selected Letters* III 140-142). It was hardly a coincidence that Albert Erskine, having left New Directions, was at this time a power-player at R&H, and Pasinetti was grateful for this act of kindness—and expression of confidence—on the part of his old friend from the halcyon days in Baton Rouge (PMP to RPW, 7/25/45; YCAL).

Warren had fulfilled all the requirements for his friend's transatlantic crossing, but the bureaucratic "red-tape" and inefficiency that had presented impediments from the beginning would frustrate the process repeatedly, and Pier was subjected to an emotional rollercoaster over the subsequent months—as a flurry of letters and cables from Stockholm attest (YCAL). It was early 1946 before the way was finally cleared and Pasinetti could book passage from Jöteborg to Philadelphia. The crossing took seventeen days—"the voyage" turned out to be a voyage indeed—but by February he was able to report at Bennington (*World Authors* 585). It is unclear if the Warrens had managed to meet his boat, but on August 12, 1946, Red wrote Edward Davison from Gambier, Ohio, where he and Cinina were guests of the John Crowe Ransoms: "Pier Pasinetti...is with us now." It must have given him particular satisfaction to add, "He has taken out his citizenship papers, thus fulfilling a project begun in 1937" (*Selected Letters* III 203).

II

To trace the subsequent course of the Pasinetti-Warren friendship in an adequate way would require an essay of at least twice the present length. Indeed, an annotated edition reprinting both sides of the surviving correspondence (which extended at least into the 1970s) would be welcome.[15] After a year of teaching at Bennington, Pasinetti entered the new doctoral program in Comparative Literature at Yale, where he wrote a prize-winning dissertation under Warren's old Iowa acquaintance, the legendary René Wellek (Interview). Warren then managed to arrange for a job offer from Robert B. Heilman at the University of Washington,[16] but Pier elected to go to the University of California-Los Angeles, where he was to have a long and distinguished career as teacher, scholar, editor, and critic—with occasional ventures into film. Pasinetti, who died in 2006, published twelve novels, four of which are available in English: *Venetian Red* (1960); *The Smile on* the *Face of the Lion* (1965); *From the Academy Bridge* (1970); and *Suddenly Tomorrow* (1972). Clearly, Warren's faith in his friend's considerable gifts and future promise was justified many times over, and his wartime investment in time, treasure, and trouble paid substantial dividends.

Notes

1. For these details, I am relying on the biographical sketch appended to Pasinetti's 1936 M.A. thesis (63).
2. For an indication of Cinina's role in welcoming the ambassador to LSU, see her letter of March 21, 1935, to the Agrarian historian Frank Lawrence Owsley, who had accepted a place on the program (*Selected Letters*, II 28-29).
3. A good brief account of the founding of the *Review* and Erskine's role can be found in the Introduction to Brooks and Warren's anthology *Stories from the* Southern Review (xi-xvi). Pasinetti's "Family History" was one of the stories they chose to reprint, an indication that their enthusiasm for it had not waned.
4. See Pasinetti's moving and informative tribute to Erskine in the *Dictionary of Literary Biography Yearbook: 1993* (277-79).
5. Apart from scattered reviews, there has been little written about Pasinetti in the United States. A notable exception is Cristina Della Coletta's perceptive entry in the *Dictionary of Literary Biography: Italian Novelists Since World War II* (247-55). Professor Coletta's treatment is rich in biographical detail and critical insight, and my sense of Pasinetti the man and artist and my reading of his work owe much to her. I wish to acknowledge a general debt here.
6. Bradshear was among those senior colleagues on the "reactionary right" who opposed the Brooks and Warren faction in the departmental wars at LSU (Cutrer 175, 232). Pasinetti has indicated that Bradshear's influence on his thesis amounted to "zero" (Interview). W.A. Read was an amputee, thus the irreverent nickname. (I owe this detail to conversations with Cleanth Brooks.)
7. The letters of Pasinetti to Warren I draw upon in this essay are located among the Robert Penn Warren Papers in the Yale Collection of American Literature at the Beinecke Rare Book and Manuscript Library, New Haven, Connecticut (hereafter YCAL). I am indebted to my collaborator on the Warren Correspondence Project, James A. Perkins, for bringing them to my attention and to Stephen C. Jones at the Beinecke for his invaluable assistance.
8. A thorough and systematic study of the influence of Italian literature, history, and culture in shaping Warren's fiction and poetry is long overdue, but this is hardly surprising. Few students of American literature (the present critic included) have the necessary equipment to take on such a subject.
9. The words are Pasinetti's. See the (third-person) autobiographical statement he provided for his entry in *World Authors, 1975-1980* (585-586).
10. In a November 21, 1938, letter to Warren and Cinina (written in Italian), Pasinetti recorded his reaction to the enormity of *Kristallnacht* (YCAL). He would never be able to forget the things he had seen, and the memory made him physically ill. (I wish to thank my colleague Giovanna del Negro for her translation.) Pasinetti was filled with foreboding and immediately grasped the signal importance of Kristallnacht as a malignant turning point in modern history, a view confirmed by another foreign observer, the correspondent (and later chronicler) William L. Shirer, whose book on the Nazi regime, though dated, has retained its status as a minor classic. See *The Rise and Fall of the Third Reich* (450-455).
11. Pier Pasinetti was a remarkably gracious man, and I am profoundly grateful to him for sharing his letters from Warren with me and making them available to the Robert Penn Warren Correspondence Project. Warren's letters to Pasinetti during this period are typically long and detailed, filled with entertaining anecdotes and asides. They occasionally resemble well-wrought set-pieces and suggest a conscious effort on Warren's part to alleviate his friend's anxiety through humor and high-spirits.
12. For an account of how Sweden managed to escape the fate of its neighbors Norway and Denmark and hang on to a tenuous neutrality under a constant German threat, see W. M. Carlgren, *Swedish Foreign Policy during the Second World War* (1977).
13. With the collapse of the Italian war effort, the political confusion and reprisals that followed in its wake, and the Germans on the defensive, Pasinetti became more detailed and candid in sharing reports from his homeland. Three letters in particular stand out (PMP to RPW, 8/20 & 10/16/43 & 9/14/44; YCAL). In a remarkable letter of October 16, 1943, his virulent contempt for the Nazis is palpable (YCAL).

14. The Pasinetti file (YCAL) contains an undated note to Warren from Seager, dictated and in his wife's hand (he was suffering from lumbago), which makes it clear he was anxious to do whatever it took to bring Pasinetti to America. Natalie Davison, wife of the writer Edward Davison and mother of the future-poet Peter Davison, was also instrumental in promoting Pasinetti's cause (Blotner 21).
15. I have in mind a volume along the lines of *Cleanth Brooks and Robert Penn Warren: A Literary Correspondence* or *Cleanth Brooks and Allen Tate: Collected Letters*, edited by James A. Grimshaw and Alphonse Vinh, respectively. Pasinetti's letters, like Warren's, are more often than not *written* in the best and fullest sense of the word.
16. See Warren's glowing recommendation of Pasinetti in a letter of January 19, 1949, to Heilman, a very close friend and former colleague at LSU (*Selected Letters* III, 324-26).

Works Cited

Aristotle, *Basic Works*. Ed. Richard McKeon. New York: Random House, 1968.
Blotner, Joseph. *Robert Penn Warren: A Biography*. New York: Random House, 1997.
Brooks, Cleanth and Robert Penn Warren eds. *Stories from the* Southern Review. Baton Rouge: Louisiana State UP, 1953.
Carlgren, W.M. *Swedish Foreign Policy during the Second World War*. Trans. Arthur Spencer. New York: St. Martin's, 1977.
Cleanth Brooks and Allen Tate: Collected Letters. Ed. Alphonse Vinh. Columbia: U of Missouri P, 1998.
Cleanth Brooks and Robert Penn Warren: A Literary Correspondence. Ed. James A. Grimshaw, Jr. Columbia: U of Missouri P, 1998.
Coletta, Cristina Della. "Pier Maria Pasinetti." *Dictionary of Literary Biography*. Vol. 177. Detroit: Gale, 1997. 247-55.
Cutrer, Thomas W. *Parnassus on the Mississippi: The* Southern Review *and the Baton Rouge Literary Community, 1935-1942*. Baton Rouge: Louisiana State UP, 1984.
Pasinetti, P.M. "Albert Erskine." *Dictionary of Literary Biography Yearbook, 1993*. Detroit: Gale, 1994. 277-79.
———. "Family History." *Southern Review* 5 (1939-40): 69-104.
———. *From the Academy Bridge*. New York: Random House, 1970.
———. "Home-coming." *Southern Review* 2 (1936-37): 736-48.
———. *Suddenly Tomorrow*. New York: Random House, 1972.
———. Telephone interview. 21 July 2005.
———. *The Smile on the Face of the Lion*. New York: Random House, 1965.
———. "The Tragic Elements in Hawthorne's Works." Thesis. Louisiana State U. 1936.
———. Unpublished correspondence. Yale Collection of American Literature, Beinecke Rare Book and Manuscript Library, New Haven.
———. *Venetian Red*. New York: Random House, 1960.
Shirer, William L. *The Rise and Fall of the Third Reich*. New York: Simon & Schuster, 1960.
Warren Robert Penn. "Pure and Impure Poetry." *Kenyon Review* 5 (1943): 228-54.
———. "The Ballad of Billie Potts." *Partisan Review* 11 (Winter 1944): 56-70.
———. *Selected Letters*, vol 2: *The* Southern Review *Years*. Ed. William Bedford Clark. Baton Rouge: Louisiana State UP, 2001.
———. *Selected Letters*, vol 3: *Triumph and Transition*. Ed. Randy Hendricks and James A. Perkins. Baton Rouge: Louisiana State UP, 2005.
World Authors, 1975-1980. New York: H.W. Wilson, 1985.

Apocalypse and Redemption: The Life and Works of Robert Penn Warren and Robert Lowell

by Tony Morris

On the first day of summer, 1940, Robert Lowell and his wife, Jean Stafford, arrived in Baton Rouge, Louisiana. Lowell, who would begin graduate work as a junior fellow at LSU, wrote to his grandmother that the city was an "inland, windless, waterless, suburban" of "crude-oil, palm-beachy trees and Huey Long's two million dollar sky-scraper capitol."[1] The Lowells moved into a three-room apartment at 1106 Chimes Street, recently vacated by Robert Penn Warren and his wife, Cinina. Once settled, they reported to the offices of the *Southern Review*, where Stafford would begin work as a secretary and Lowell would meet and begin a life-long friendship with Warren. Lowell would portray their relationship, many years later, as "an old master still engaging the dazzled disciple" (*Poems* 734). Yet, despite Lowell's master/disciple analogy, the reasons for their shared professional and personal affinities are not readily apparent—at least not from the outset. In some ways, their backgrounds and personalities could not have been more incongruous.

Lowell, who was born March 1, 1917, twelve years after Warren, had descended from an old patrician line of Boston Brahmans. His mother's family history spanned back to the *Mayflower* Winslows and to the Massachusetts Bay Colony days, when Edward Winslow (1595-1655) was thrice-elected governor of Plymouth Plantation. Arthur Winslow, Lowell's grandfather, was a stern and domineering self-made millionaire who lived on fashionable Chestnut Street, just off Beacon Street, and could count as his neighbors such notables as Edwin Booth, Julia Ward Howe, Francis Parkman, and Oliver Wendell Holmes.

On his father's side, the family could boast of famous literary personages such as James Russell and Amy Lowell and Civil War heroes such as Colonel Charles Russell Lowell, who, when already fatally wounded in the fighting around the wilderness in the fall of 1864, would have himself strapped to his horse so that he could lead a final cavalry charge against the Confederate lines. This Lowell had also married the sister of Colonel Robert Shaw, who would lead the Black Massachusetts 54th in its fatal assault on Battery Wagner, part of the network of forts protecting Charleston Harbor. After the battle, Shaw's body would be tossed into a common pit along with his soldiers. The inspiration for Lowell's famous poem "For the Union Dead" stemmed from the hypocritical and shameful response to the event by the Boston citizenry at the time of the massacre and their disingenuous attempt to erase their reprehensible actions by building a bronze commemorative monument to that day in 1897 (Mariani 27-30).

Warren's family history, while noteworthy, may have carried more of the plebian strain in it than Lowell's grandfather Arthur Winslow would have approved. In a direct line that extended back eleven generations on his mother's side came Sir William Penn the admiral and William Penn the Quaker. The American branch included Virginian, John Granville Penn, who signed the Declaration of Independence. In the same generation was Colonel Abram Penn, who led the Henry County militia against Cornwallis and was present at the surrender at Yorktown. His son, Edmund, married Mary Ferris and moved from Patrick County in southwest Virginia to Kentucky, finally settling near Murfreesboro, Tennessee, in 1836. Twenty years later, their son, Gabriel Thomas (Warren's grandfather), was born in Trenton, not far from the Mississippi River. Gabriel Penn fought for the Confederacy under Bedford Forrest, and while on leave after Forrest's victory at Fort Pillow, he married Mary Eliza Mitchell in Trenton on June 24, 1864.

Warren's great-great grandfather on his father's side, William Warren, had been wounded at the Battle of Cowpens, fought in two more battles, and then migrated to Kentucky. One of his sons, William Henry Harrison Warren, fought at Shiloh in Forrest's infantry and rose to the rank of major before being invalided out of the war. His eldest son, William Henry Harrison Warren, Jr., also a veteran of Shiloh, left the Sixth Kentucky Mounted Infantry before the war's end at the expiration of his enlistment. Robert Penn Warren's father, Robert Franklin Warren, was born four years after the surrender. The son's only historical connection to literary fame came from his father who, in 1890, had two poems published in a vanity anthology called *Local and National Poets of America, with Interesting Biographical Sketches and Choice Selections from Over One Thousand Living American Poets* (Blotner 3-15).

By the time he arrived at LSU, fresh from Kenyon, where he graduated summa cum laude with highest honors in classics under the tutelage of John Crowe Ransom, Lowell had already developed a reputation as a brilliant but difficult prodigy. His intemperate, surly, and—some would say—tyrannical ways had earned him the nickname Cal—for Caligula. And although friends such as Ransom, Allen Tate, and Peter Taylor saw in him the potential for greatness as a writer, his creative output up to this point was mostly limited to derivative, stiff verse. Ransom, after publishing two poems in the *Kenyon Review*, turned down all subsequent submissions, calling them "forbidding," "clotting," and "too ambiguous."

Like Lowell, Warren was an exceptional scholar. He graduated summa cum laude from Vanderbilt, then continued his studies at Berkley and Yale, before finally receiving a B. Litt from New College, Oxford, which he attended as a Rhodes Scholar. However, unlike Lowell, Warren's quietly intense personality earned him the reputation of a deeply serious but sociable intellectual whose gracious and practical manner could charm anyone. Lowell's portrait of Warren rightly captures this trait in a poem titled, "Louisiana State University in 1940":

> Red, you could make friends with anyone,
> criminals, or even showy writer giants
> you slaughtered in a review. . . (*Poems* 735)[2]

Finally, by 1940, Warren's famously prolific creative and scholarly output was well underway, having already included: *John Brown: The Making of a Martyr*; *Prime Leaf*, a novelette; *Thirty-Six Poems*; *An Approach to Literature* and *Understanding Poetry* (with Cleanth Brooks); and, *Night Rider*, a novel. Furthermore, he had been the co-editor of the *Southern Review* for the five previous years and had just been awarded a Guggenheim Fellowship. By the time Lowell had published his first book of poems, *Land of Unlikeness*, in 1944, Warren had published three more books of poetry (*Eleven Poems on the Same Theme*, *Selected Poems: 1923-1943*, and *The Ballad of Billie Potts*), a second novel (*At Heaven's Gate*), and had been appointed Consultant in Poetry to the Library of Congress.

Notwithstanding these differences, Warren and Lowell got along well at LSU. Although

Lowell was headstrong and had a tendency to browbeat and intimidate his friends, he held a deep reverence and respect for those with the intellectual acumen and creative energy to match his own. His desire to garner the tools he would need to develop into a strong poet led him, over the years, to cultivate several such "master / disciple" relationships--with writers such as Allen Tate, Ezra Pound and William Carlos Williams, to whom he wrote in 1958, "I have no master, only masters, you are about the first among them" (Hamilton, 308).

In Warren, Lowell found one of his earliest masters. After his arrival at LSU, he reported to his Kenyon classmate, Robie Macauley that "[Cleanth] Brooks and Warren / Brooksandwarren are excellent. Especially Warren; result: I am reading English theology" (Hamilton 75). Another result of these studies, he later tells Tate, is that he is developing a critical vocabulary of his own, including such theoretical terms as "heresy," "diabolic," and "frivolous gnosticism" (Mariani 92). In addition to his discovery of English theology, he and Warren started spending two hours a day at lunch reading Dante in the original to each other. As Warren tells it, "Cal and I locked up the doors several days a week at twelve o'clock and had a sandwich and a quick Coke and then we read Dante for two hours" (Hiers et al. 298). The experience made such an impression on Lowell that he decided to convert to Catholicism that same year.

For his part, Warren recognized, as Ransom and Tate had before him, Lowell's eager and incisive intellect and found in him an affable, if somewhat unstable, character. Speaking of those days spent with Lowell, Warren told David Farrell in a 1977 interview that, "he was always a naïf of one kind or another. And a calculated naïf, too. But he had a charm and he had great intelligence and he read widely, and he could be wonderfully good company." But Warren also sensed something unpredictable, erratic, and volatile in Lowell's personality. Moreover, his prediction that Lowell was on his way to being "really mad," unfortunately, would bear itself out in the coming years as Lowell was hospitalized thirteen times over the course of his life for manic episodes. Nevertheless, Warren enjoyed his company and praised much of the poetry Lowell would write. "I saw a lot of him and I liked his society a lot, and we saw each other out and we talked and argued a lot. I loved his poetry; it was tremendously fine" (Hiers et al. 299).

And more than anything, it was their mutual love for poetry and the process of poetic creation that cemented the relationship between these two. Although they each brought to bear distinctly different philosophical (one might even say theological) approaches to their poetry, they both believed that poetry and the life of the poet (the process of writing poetry) was vital to knowing—to gaining knowledge about the truth of one's self and, ultimately, about the reality of the world (at least in the metaphysical sense) in which one lives. And they both used the poetic process as a way of exploring the interrelationship of art and human experience.

Talking about this interrelationship at a reunion of Fugitive poets in 1956, Warren said that "[p]oetry is an exploration; the process of writing is an exploration. You may dimly envisage what a poem will be when you start it, but only as you wrangle through the process do you know your own meaning. In one way, it's a way of knowing what kind of poem you can write. And in finding that you find out yourself—I mean a lot about yourself." He continues:

> I don't mean in the way Merrill's [Moore] talking about: I mean in the sense of what you can make available, poetically, is clearly something that refers to all of your living in very indirect and complicated ways. But you know more about

yourself, not in a psychoanalytic way, but in another way of having dealt with yourself in a process. The poem is a way of knowing what kind of a person you can be, getting your reality shaped a little bit better. And it's a way of living, and not a parlor trick even in its most modest reaches; I mean, the most modest kind of effort that we make is a way of living. And I think Bill [Elliott] has something important when he insists that there is such a thing as a poetic condition, which is the willingness to approach a poem in that spirit, rather than in the spirit of a performer, when you get down to the business of writing a poem, or even thinking about poetry. (Hiers et al. 15-16)

This "poetic condition" is a philosophical approach to living that acknowledges a deeper reality, or knowing of the world through "a process of envisionments" (117), a willingness to "soak yourself in the world of the thing you're dealing with," and to experience, through such an immersion, the power in language that "drags the bottom of somebody into being." And for Warren, these revelatory moments of "envisionments" make knowing possible. "It's that stab of some kind, early," that "sense of an image that makes that thing available to you indefinitely, so you can go back to it, and always find that peephole on the other world," that "moment of contact with . . . the reality, or realness" (16-17).

Reality. Realness brought about by a process of "poetic conditioning" that produces "envisionments." These are the philosophical underpinnings of Warren's poetics—a poetics that links the meaning of the world to the vital and vivifying power of the word. In his essay, "'The Great Mirage': Conrad and *Nostromo*," Warren writes that the philosophical poet is one "for whom the image strives to rise to symbol, for whom images always fall into a dialectical configuration, for whom the urgency of experience, no matter how vividly and strongly experience may enchant, is the urgency to know the meaning of experience" (*Essays* 160). For Warren, the work of the poet is no less than the work of finding meaning in the human experience—and not just at the psychological level, but at the philosophical and spiritual level, where one can find "that peephole to the other world" and connect with reality.

This "urgency to know the meaning of experience" is no less vital to the work of Lowell. As Steven Axelrod points out in his study, *Robert Lowell: Life and Art*, "all of Lowell's subsequent work after *Life Studies* [1959] is centered around his quest for the craft and inspiration to bring even more experience into his art, and his related quest to account for the place art makes in experience" (6). Like Warren, Lowell sees the poetic condition as one that inextricably connects writing and the poetry it produces with the life of the poet—what he calls "one life, one writing." Under such a condition, the poet can more truly "feel" and therefore know the meaning of his experiences. And he sees in this process not only a means of proving existence, but also a means of creating identity (Lowell *Poems* 375).

Lowell told Frederick Seidel in a 1961 interview for the *Paris Review* that, "Almost the whole problem of writing poetry is to bring it back to what you really feel, and that takes an awful lot of maneuvering. . . . A lot of poetry seems to me very good in the tradition but just doesn't move me very much because it doesn't have personal vibrance to it" (41). According to Lowell, writing a poem which contains "personal vibrance," is achieved only after the poet has developed a deep sympathy with and a keen observation of people and things. Once this connection is made (what Warren calls the "moment of contact") the poet experiences a glimmer of truth where the vivid focus of the image reveals some meaning of the experience:

> Some little image, some detail you've noticed—you're writing about a little country shop, just describing it, and your poem ends up with an existentialist account of your experience. But it's the shop that started it off. You didn't know why it meant a lot to you. Often images and often the sense of the beginning and end of a poem are all you have—some journey to be gone through between those things; you know that, but you don't know the details. And that's marvelous; then you feel the poem will come out. It's a terrible struggle, because what you really feel hasn't got the form, it's not what you can put down in a poem. And the poem you're equipped to write concerns nothing that you care very much about or have much to say on. Then the great moment comes when there's enough resolution of your technical equipment, your way of constructing things, and what you can make a poem out of, to hit something you really want to say. You may not know you have it to say. (40-1)

To experience that "great moment" and finally "hit something you really want to say" is central to Lowell's poetics. And while Lowell's trope of "personal vibrance," and Warren's "envisionments" both point to a metaphysical approach to the poetic process, Lowell's angle of vision is more existential, narrow, even solipsistic—its vision centered more on the idea of validating selfhood—that the artist's existence becomes his art, and visa-versa. "He is born in it, and hardly exists without it" (Alverez 43).

Warren's focus, on the other hand, while not universal, does leave open the possibility of finding truths that might be applied to the wider scope of human experiences outside of self. As he says of *Audubon*: "The poem is about man and his fate—all along, Audubon resisted his fate and thought it was evil—a man is supposed to support his family, and so forth. But now he accepts his fate. Late in his life he said, 'I dream of nothing but birds.' Audubon was the greatest slayer of birds that ever lived: he destroyed beauty in order to create beauty and whet his understanding. Love is knowledge. And then in the end the poem is about Audubon and me" (Heirs et al. 244). While Warren sees the poem as a link between himself and others (Audubon *and* me), in Lowell's work, the sense of shared experience is always tempered with his anxiety about his otherness: "I'm afraid / to touch the crisp hair on your head—/ Monster loved for what you are, / till time, that buries us, lay bare" (Lowell, *Collected Poems* 395).

The reason for this difference largely comes down to theological temperament. Warren, who calls himself a nonreligious man, nevertheless pays religious reverence to poetry's redemptive power, and uses it as a means to discover man's relation not only to himself, but also to nature and to what he calls the "immanence of meaning in things." As he tells Peter Stitt in a 1977 interview:

> I am a creature of this world, but I am also a yearner, I suppose. I would call this temperament rather than theology—I haven't got any gospel. That is, I feel an immanence of meaning in things, but I have no meaning to put there that is interesting or beautiful. I think I put it as close as I could in a poem called "Masts at Dawn"—"We must try / To love so well the world that we may believe, in the end, in God." I am a man of temperament in the modern world who hasn't got

any religion. Dante almost got me at one stage, but then I suddenly realized, "My God, Dante's a good Protestant—he was! Where have I gone?" My poems reverse the whole thing, you see: I would rather start with the world. (Hiers et al. 243)

Warren is not anti-religious. As he told Thomas Conelly in 1984, "I have the deepest awareness of [religion's] importance" (382). But because he'd "rather start with the world," he is a "yearner" whose work embodies, he says in the same interview, a "quest for religion." And as a man in and of the world, he sees in poetry, and in the process of poetic creation, a force that can help humanity to reconcile the complexities of history and experience. Consequently, he argues at the close of his essay on *The Ancient Mariner*: "If poetry does anything for us, it reconciles, by its symbolical reading of experience (for by its very nature it is in itself a myth of the unity of being), the self-divisive internecine malices which arise at the superficial level on which we conduct most of our living" (*Essays* 398).

Despite his assertion that he doesn't have "any gospel," Warren's renunciation falters under the weight of his faith in the original sin of the divided self. For Warren, these "internecine malices" are the direct result of man's search for self-identity, which is complicated by the ambiguity of meaning that arises from man's divided nature—"men's heroism and depravity, in nature's beauty and horror" (Strandberg 191). Consequently, man's struggle to find meaning in such a world forces him into a dilemma in which he lives, unhappily, under the "terrible necessity of judgment" (Warren "Why Do We Read Fiction?" 84). In order to escape this dilemma, man must accept his complicity in the human condition.

According to Warren's essay, "Knowledge and the Image of Man," this acceptance of complicity can be brought about through a *vision* or *experience* of interrelationships" that he calls "the osmosis of being," which can produce a merger of "the ugly with the beautiful, the slayer with the slain," evoking "such a sublimation that the world which once provoked . . . fear and disgust may now be totally loved." Man is "in the world with continual and intimate interpenetration, an inevitable osmosis of being, which in the end does not deny, but affirms, his identity" (182). And since poetry, or envisionments brought about by the "poetic condition," is the vehicle through which one can bring meaning to experience, redemption is possible ("for we are all one flesh"), but not easy (Warren *Collected Poems* 240).

In a poem called "To a Little Girl, One Year Old, in a Ruined Fortress" (a series he dedicated to his daughter on the occasion of their first trip to Italy when she was a year old), Warren experiences just such a redemptive possibility. The five part poem opens with a section titled, "Sirocco," where the natural world and history collide in the "place of ruined stone" and "sea-reaches." Warren sets up the conflict in the poem by juxtaposing the frailty of man's "fastidious mathematic and skill" with the obliterating power of nature's "crag-cocked" sea cliff. Where stones had once lined the drawbridge, they "now languished / long in the moat, under garbage" while at the moat's brink "rosemary with blue, thistle / with gold bloom, nod."

The opposing dialectics of man/nature, decay/permanence, beauty/ugliness strain against the limits of meaning for the narrator, whose "heart aches" as he contemplates the sound of his child's innocent laughter in the midst of this "geometry of military rigor" that survives in "its own / ruined world." The weight of his dilemma is further complicated by the contrast between the "black-browed" and "anguished" man who once lived in the castle, "[f]or whom nothing prospered, though he loved God," and the blessed child whose head shines in Christ-like radiance, as the "sun regilds [her] gilt hair" in a golden halo. sun-gilded head. (*Collected Poems*103)

Then, in Section II, titled "Gulls Cry," Warren begins to sense a flicker of meaning while sitting with a group of villagers outside in the heat of the sirocco, so oppressive that he does not "think that anything in the world will move," while "under blue shadow of mountain, over blue-braiding sea-shadow, / the gull hangs white," before passing "into the astonishing statement of sun." Among the villagers is the wife of a *gobbo* (humpback) who is also the mother of a "defective child," who now "squats in the dust." The mother "sits under vine leaves, she suffers, her eyes glare." And against this backdrop of ugliness and despair, the child's laughter once again interposes itself, which arouses in the narrator a glimmer of hope—a faint possibility of unity as the images begin to coalesce into an osmosis of being: "But at your laughter let the molecular dance of the stone-dark glimmer like joy / in the stone's dream, / And in that moment of possibility, let gobbo, gobbo's wife, and us, and all, take / hands and sing: redeem, redeem!" (103-04)

Although this moment of joy is tempered by the ambiguity of "the stone's dream," there is yet the possibility of redemption. In Section III, "The Child Next Door," the focus of the poem centers on the reconciliation of man and his depraved nature. The section opens with the narrator observing the defective child (who represents a kind of fallen man), and his twelve-year-old sister who is teaching him how to wave *ciao*. She sits "beautiful like a saint" with "the monster all day, with sure love, calm eyes." At first, he scoffs at her existential happiness: "Fool, doesn't she know that the process / Is not that joyous or simple, to bless, or unbless, / The malfeasance of nature or the filth of fate?" But in the next stanza, he realizes how brutally arrogant and solipsistic his judgment is. Unlike the narrator's innocent baby daughter, this child is at the age of knowing, and therefore her gesture is even more powerful than the Christ-like joy of the infant. And in a moment of envisionment, he understands what beauty and power her benediction has as a means of recognizing one's complicity in the human condition. "I trust our hope to prevail / That heart-joy in beauty be wisdom, before beauty fail / And be gathered like air in the ruck of the world's wind!"(104). His trust in the human capacity for love in the face of the world's indifference is bolstered as he moves into the next section.

Section IV, "The Flower" is a longer verse, pastoral in its evocation of nature and its beauties. The trimeter and tetrameter lines push the reader quickly through a descriptive series of various flora and fauna as the narrator and his wife hike with their daughter up a hill in search of "the spot and hour" where a "white flower" grows. The flower is a gift of nature given by the parents to the daughter in a "ritual" of which she "compels" the observance. But the day is late, and the "season has thinned out," and though it is a private ritual, the outside world is beginning to intrude as "the shout / Of a late bather reaches our ear." The late season has also brought a change in the weather and now the "wind / nags the shore to white" turning the flowers "by season and sea-salt brown." Nevertheless, they offer the best one, "ruined, but will have to do," to their daughter, and another, blue, for their "own delight" that they place in the daughter's "drowsy gold nod." And despite nature's fickle indifference to the child's desire for a "bloom worthily white," she is still happy. "And you sing as though human need / Were not for perfection." The narrator is so taken by his daughter's response that he blesses the child with an invocation:

Let all seasons pace their power,

> As this has paced to this hour.
> Let season and season devise
> Their possibilities.
> Let the future reassess
> All past joy, and past distress,
> Till we know Time's deep intent,
> And the last integument
> Of the past shall be rent
> To show how all things bent
> Their energies to that hour
> When you first demanded your flower.
>
> And in that image let
> Both past and future forget,
> In clasped communal ease,
> Their brute identities. (106)

The anxiety, heartache, and confusion the narrator experienced at the beginning of the poem are now all but gone. The merger of "the ugly with the beautiful" has evoked "such a sublimation that the world which once provoked fear and disgust may now be totally loved." And as he moves into the last section, "Colder Fire," with this new conviction ("our joys and convictions are sure"), he is able to trust the language of "spirit past logical reason"—the redemptive language of the heart. But it is a language, as he tells his daughter, that she must find in her own "heart of a colder fire":

> I cannot interpret for you this collocation
> Of memories. You will live your own life, and contrive
> The language of your own heart, but let that conversation,
> In the last analysis, be always of whatever truth you would live.
>
> For fire flames but in the heart of a colder fire.
> All voice is but echo caught from a soundless voice.
> Height is not deprivation of valley, nor defect of desire,
> But defines, for the fortunate, that joy in which all joys should rejoice. (108)

The "fire" of inspiration that opens the "peephole to the other world," the narrator reminds us, comes out of a moment of yearning—when knowledge is limited, ambiguous, and therefore incomplete. And it is these moments, when the paradoxical "echo caught from a soundless voice" (the voice of God, the "all voice" of man, nature and spirit), combines with a heart tempered in the "colder fire" of knowledge, that redemption is defined: "in that joy in which all joys should rejoice" (107-08). For Warren, this "yearning" for ultimate knowledge, or God, is the glory of the poetic process. It is enough.

Lowell, on the other hand, believes, like Ezra Pound, that a concept of God is somewhere in sight in all poetry. Moreover, in a stance that closely mirrors that of Emerson, he believes that the function of the poet, like that of the prophet, is to surprise, shock, cajole, and horrify his listeners into seeing the world and its history for what it is: a mechanistic inhumane wasteland dislocated from the paradise from which it originated—a land where, if not yet, then surely just around the corner, the Apocalypse awaits. As Richard Eberhart, Lowell's long-time friend and early mentor writes, Lowell "[e]arly had begun the wrestling with the soul…the harsh struggle with the inner spirit against the outer world, the confrontation of intolerable opposites, the unresolvable realization (resolvable only in art) which are the crude and terrific fires that leap almost to madness in the mind, dancing with vision of poetic reality, that reality luring all sacrifice, all devotion, and the only power worth having" (48).

Consequently, Lowell's poems, as Steven Axelrod points out, "are designed to refute time entirely. They deny the importance of human events except as part of a cosmic, ageless pattern. They deny that history has any existence as a nonrecurring, non-symbolic, non-teleological movement through time" (47). Like Warren, Lowell is searching in his work for a solution to the suffering in man that arises from a complex sense of connection to and disconnection from the past, and hence from the self. But unlike Warren's redemptive vision, the apocalyptic vision of the world in Lowell's early poetry (informed and enlarged by the theological influence of his conversion to Catholicism) bears witness to his belief that God, not man, is the measure of all things.

For Lowell, the work of the poet is not about revealing the possibility of redemption through a unity of man, nature, and god (Warren's "osmosis of being"), but about revealing how far man, in his depraved nature, has come from the god-centered state of paradise. Further, since man, in this post-lapsarian state, is incapable of bringing all of the disparate and conflicting realities of the world into unity (and therefore has no possibility of a return to the paradisiacal beginnings), the poet's job, like that of Elijah, is to use those revelatory moments of "personal vibrance" to bring to light the horror of humanity's degenerate and corrupt condition (both historical and current). In this way, the poet's words are both a warning, and a prophecy—that the only hope for redemption must come through a humble admission that man is ultimately a lost and bewildered soul, and that his only expectation of lasting peace must lie in the faith that God's total annihilation of the world will make room for a post-apocalyptic paradise of heaven.

Hence, all of Lowell's early work (especially through *Life Studies*) wrestles, in one way or another, with three related themes: history, current events, and God. But even in his later verse, such as *The Dolphin* [1973], which some consider his most hopeful volume, the apocalyptic strain is evident. His poem, "Fall Weekend at Millgate," is a series of ruminations (written in a loose sonnet form) about his stay at the famous historical house in Bearsted, Kent. Section 1 opens: "The day says nothing, and lacks for nothing . . . God" (*Collected Poems* 659). Where Warren's poem ends with the paradoxical "soundless voice," toward which he yearns and by which he finds resolution to his metaphysical dilemma of otherness, Lowell's sound of "nothing" represents the beginning of his conflict. In a God-centered world that "lacks for nothing," yet "says nothing," the brief moments of "vibrance" that may reveal some kind of meaning in life serve only to remind the narrator, like the Christian "pilgrim on the hard-edge Roman road," how impossibly distant that search for true knowledge is. Therefore, the day becomes an intoxicating but confusing series of events that take away from life as much as they give: the "moonshine trying to gold-cap my life, / asking fees from the things I lived and loved." The price for nature's promise of sainthood ("gold-cap"), is too high and too illusory (nothing more than the drunken visions "moonshine"), coming, as it does, at the cost of his life and loves.

Even the study of history, represented by the mansion filled with the monuments of a decadent past, cannot reveal answers the narrator seeks. Nor can the representative human "face" mirrored on "a mat of plateglass sapphire, / mirror scrolls and claspleaves," its "huge eyes and dawn-gaze . . . unruffled" and "unlearning." The portrait serves only to remind the narrator how "astigmatic" and "humanly low" man has become.

In section 2, the narrator again turns to nature's "soaking leaves, green yellow" that "hold like rubber" in the "inundating air" for some deeper disclosure of reality. But here again, there is no movement toward a deeper revelation of the universal (compare to Warren's "white gulls" that "at an eye-blink" pass the "astonishing statement of the sun"). Instead, the leaves hang in a kind of limbo, where "none tumble." The scene reinforces for the narrator only the inadequacy of nature to bring perfect meaning to life. Nevertheless, he has gained *some* knowledge, even if it is but the knowledge of what can't bring meaning. At least, through this logic of negation (of that which will not bring meaning) he has found a truth on which to stand; and he emphasizes the importance of this revelation in the strict formalism of the next line: "A weak eye sees a miracle of birth." It is a weakness, in this view, to see birth as a miracle, for it is only nature's infinite repetition of non-movement: "only good for repeating what it does well: / life emerges from wood and life from life." The depraved nature of man can only beget again and again the depraved nature of man.

In the final section, the narrator tries to pull together the threads of man's past and present history and its relation to nature in a final effort to glean a more meaningful understanding of his relation to God, and therefore his relation to self and others. But comparing his own present state as landlord "for the month" (660), to *Milgate's* past landlords, who kept the hall "standing for four centuries," the "good" alternating with "derelict," he sees only "poison," in the "Jacobean brick," of the past.

Moreover, it is the present state of nature's "midday heat," that draws the poison to the bricks and "wilderness to our doorstep." And it is at this midpoint, in the heat of the narrator's thoughts, in the struggle to untangle the diffuse strands of knowledge, that he experiences a revelatory moment of vibrance. For the warm day also brings out "wasps to share our luck" (echoes of "Upon a Wasp Chilled with Cold" by the New England Puritan Edward Taylor). And he understands that the only question worth "debating" is whether he should "stay and drown" in the temptations of the flesh, like the wasps, those "suckers for sweets," or "by losing legs and wings, take flight." And here, finally, is the apocalyptic choice: abandon all hope of an answer on earth or in heaven, for there is more to heaven and earth that can be known to the mind of man. All we can hope for, in the end are the tender mercies of an unknowable, unnamable God.

Notes

1. Lowell to his grandmother, Mary Devereux Winslow, dated Monday. The letter was probably written in late August 1940.
2. The showy giant writer referred to here is Thomas Wolfe.

Works Cited

Alverez, A. "A Talk with Robert Lowell." *Encounter* Feb. 1965: 39-43.
Axelrod, Steven Gould. *Robert Lowell: Life and Art*. Princeton: Princeton UP, 1978.
Blotner, Joseph. *Robert Penn Warren: A Biography*. New York: Random House, 1997.
Eberhart, Richartd. "Four Poets." *Sewanee Review* 55 (1947): 324-36.
Hamilton, Ian. *Robert Lowell: A Biography*. Boston: Faber & Faber, 1983.
Hiers, John T., Floyd C. Watkins, and Mary Louise Weeks, Eds. *Talking with Robert Penn Warren*. Athens: U of Georgia P, 1990.
Lowell, Robert. *Collected Poems*. Eds. Frank Bidart and David Gewanter. New York: Farrar, Straus, & Giroux, 2003.
Mariani, Paul. *Lost Puritan: A Life of Robert Lowell*. New York: Norton, 1994.
Seidel, Frank. "The Art of Poetry #3: Robert Lowell." *Paris Review* 25: 9, 1961): 1-41.
Strandberg, Victor. *The Poetic Vision of Robert Penn Warren*. Lexington: UP of Kentucky, 1977.
Warren, Robert Penn. *The Collected Poems of Robert Penn Warren*. Ed. John Burt. Baton Rouge: Louisiana State UP, 1998.
———. "Knowledge and the Image of Man." *Sewanee Review* 63 (Winter 1955): 182-92
———. *New and Selected Essays*. New York: Random House, 1989.
———. "Why Do We Read Fiction?" *Saturday Evening Post* October 20, 1962: 82-84.

Warren, Bellow, and the Changing Tides

by Joseph Scotchie

Robert Penn Warren and Saul Bellow became friends in the mid 1940s. Both were then teaching at the University of Minnesota's renowned Department of English. Warren had been at Minnesota for four years, a refugee from Louisiana State University, where, along with Cleanth Brooks, he had edited the *Southern Review*. Warren liked his old job and had hoped to put down roots in Baton Rouge. However, with the forced austerity of World War II, the LSU administration began to look for savings. As all students of Southern literature know, LSU decided to keep Mike the Tiger, the football squad's popular mascot rather than continue funding the highly acclaimed *Southern Review*. With six published books behind him, Warren, at Minnesota, was deep into a working draft of his signature novel, *All The King's Men*.

Saul Bellow, on the other hand, was a relative unknown. He had published only one novel, *Dangling Man*, plus a handful of short stories, several of them in the *Partisan Review*, thus fulfilling a youthful dream for the author from Chicago. Warren liked Bellow, and he took the younger novelist under his wing, at least as much as the iconoclastic Bellow would permit. Warren read the typescript of Bellow's second novel, *The Victim* and predicted good things for it. Meanwhile, *All The King's Men* was published to great commercial and critical success. With the royalties from that novel, Warren was able to purchase a new automobile. He once let Bellow take it for a drive. Bellow, a city boy through and through, promptly wrecked the car on one of those drives, earning him a stern lecture from his generous friend.

Warren stayed at Minnesota until 1949. He then joined Cleanth Brooks at Yale University, the institution that would become Warren's professional home for the rest of his career. Bellow also left Minnesota that same year. He followed a more nomadic existence, teaching at, among other places, Bard College, Princeton University, and the University of Puerto Rico, before finally settling down at the University of Chicago's Committee for Social Thought.

Throughout the decades, the two remained friends. Bellow did not reach Warren's fame until the 1964 publication of *Herzog*. And so, the friendship, in its early years, remained one of Warren as the literary elder boosting the younger Bellow's career. Warren gave an especially generous review to Bellow's 1953 breakthrough novel, *The Adventures of Augie March*. Writing in the *New Republic*, Warren praised *Augie* as a "rich, various, fascinating and important book," declaring "any discussion of fiction in America in our time will have to take account of it" ("Man with No Commitments" 22).

Warren and Bellow corresponded for a good four decades. Bellow reserved much of his praise of Warren's work to private letters. In 1969, for instance, a typically beleaguered Bellow claimed that he had been reading Warren's poetry "with the greatest satisfaction," adding, "I say this as a man of disturbed mind, very hard to calm. There are few texts nowadays that can do it." In the late 1940s, Bellow sought out Warren as a reference for a Guggenheim grant that the novelist coveted. In 1950, Bellow further wondered if Warren could find work for him at the New School of Social Research in New York City.

On a personal level, Bellow was not above pouring out deep emotions to Warren. In a 1959 letter, one delivered from Poland, Bellow complains, "[The] gods refuse to grant me a peaceful life." Bellow was in the midst of a divorce from his second wife, Sondra. He hoped that Warren and he would soon "have the talk we never had." Here, Bellow may be referring to Warren's own earlier martial problems with his first wife, Cinina. Bellow's last known letter to Warren, written in the winter of 1983, is full of warmth and affection, one grand old man of American letters writing to another. Bellow congratulates Warren on becoming a grandfather for the first time. He also notes that his summer home in Vermont is near completion. "No small part of the happiness" in having the house is the fact that Bellow would be fairly close to Warren's residence in rural Connecticut. From now on, visits would be more frequent (Warren Papers).

The Warren-Bellow friendship was one free of competition or jealousy. Bellow enjoyed the connection to an established American author, while Warren took pleasure in seeing the upward trajectory of Bellow's career. The friendship was also one of two men identified with two significant strains of Twentieth Century American literature. Warren was a major force in the Southern Renaissance of the 1920s and '30s, while such Bellow novels as *The Adventures of Augie March* and *Seize The Day* helped to make Jewish-American themes and literature accessible to the wider public. As Thomas Fleming has observed:

> Southern fiction has so dominated the United States in this century that some people have said there are only two kinds of American writers, Southerners and Jews. This is an exaggeration, but just barely, and despite the…differences that separate Southerners and Jews, the success of both groups depends on their atavisms: loyalty to kinfolk, preservation of tradition, and suspicion of aliens. (15)

In addition, Warren and Bellow had the luck to come of age in pre-television America. Both men were avid readers from the start. Both read the classics, Warren cutting his teeth on Shakespeare, Marlowe, Pope, Dickens, Thackeray, Sherwood Anderson and especially, Milton's *Lycidas*. Bellow read Shakespeare, but also Chicago's own Theodore Dreiser, and the modern European masters: Balzac, Flaubert, Joyce, Dostoyevsky, Tolstoy, and Proust. Both were able to memorize long passages of their favorite works; Bellow with lines from Shakespeare and entire poems of Percy Shelley and John Keats, while Warren became legendary for his ability to recite T.S. Eliot's "The Wasteland" and Coleridge's "The Rime of the Ancient Mariner" to packed classrooms of amazed undergraduates.

As importantly, both found like-minded literary soul mates early on. Picked on by local bullies in his schoolboy days for his high marks, Warren found solace at Vanderbilt University. He matriculated there at the same time the Fugitive poetry movement was in full swing. Quickly becoming friends with Allen Tate, Donald Davidson, and John Crowe Ransom, Warren began contributing poetry to that group's flagship publication, *The Fugitive*. Decades later, Warren fondly remembered the "priceless education" he received while exchanging poems and ideas with Ransom and Davidson. Warren was welcomed into the Fugitive fraternity, and after publishing his thick 1929 biography of John Brown, he contributed "The Briar Patch" to *I'll Take My Stand*, the agrarian manifesto that assured lasting literary fame for the Nashville writers.

Bellow, for his part, enjoyed the company of fellow bibliophiles in his West Side Chicago neighborhood. "In Chicago…we dreamed of the literary life—we were mad for it," he recalled in a 1975 interview with *Newsweek*. Bellow and his friends met at Chicago's Humboldt Park on Friday evenings to discuss favorite authors and such topics as politics and religion. Still, Chicago, despite being home to such luminaries as Theodore Dreiser, Carl Sandburg, and Edgar Lee Masters, was not where Bellow and his closest literary friend, Isaac Rosenfeld, would seek their fame. Rather, New York City, home to both Greenwich Village and the *Partisan Review,* was the eventual destination. Bellow became a favorite of the *PR* crowd and was touted for future greatness by the prominent critic, Lionel Trilling. Eventually, however, Bellow tired of the literary pretensions that marked the Manhattan cultural scene, preferring life in Chicago, "that somber city," one that remained happily out-of-touch with East Coast trends and fashions. (Clemons and Kroll 33).

From our vantage point, where literature hardly matters in what passes for American culture, it is easy to look back on the heyday in which Warren and Bellow worked as a Golden Age, a Lost Eden even. In the 1950s, giants from the modernist era, especially Ernest Hemingway, T. S. Eliot, William Faulkner, and Robert Frost, had become international celebrities, receiving the same public adulation later reserved for rock stars. The public was at least aware of serious literature. For the post-war generation, the great American novel was still a prize to be won. Poetry, too, loomed large. As late as 1950, all the big name Manhattan publishers had poetry volumes on their "B" lists. Furthermore, with Europe and Asia still reeling from World War II, the American economy utterly dominated the world scene.

A large middle class was being born. Americans now had much disposable income to spend on books, even those of the highbrow variety. Cities and towns were populated by small bookstores, not impersonal jumbo-sized chain stores, where a book can be easily lost. Most importantly, certain mass media types knew what serious writers were up to. This had been true for some time. In 1939, for example, *Time* magazine reviewed *Pale Horse, Pale Rider*, a sequence of three novellas by Katherine Anne Porter, who then resided in Baton Rouge and was regularly published in the *Southern Review*. *Time* used the occasion to hail the "literary colony of Baton Rouge" and its growing contributions to American letters. Authors, such as Eudora Welty, who made their debuts in such small circulation quarterlies, often were published by the larger firms; in time, they would receive exposure in the mass media. Such a connection is vital to the survival of literature itself (Cutrer 102-03).

And so it went. By the 1950s, both Warren and Bellow had demonstratively "made it" in the highly competitive world of American letters: success meaning best sellers, profiles in mass circulation magazines and newspapers, awards, grants, prizes, and tenure at major universities. As the author of bestselling novels and co-editor of an important textbook, *Understanding Poetry*, and as a leading Southern liberal of his day, Warren was one of the select writers of that era—among them, Tate and Trilling and Delmore Schwartz—who revolved in the circles of those prestigious quarterlies—the *Sewanee Review* (unofficial home of the Southern Renaissance), the *Kenyon Review*, the *Hudson Review*, and the *Partisan Review* (which served the same purpose as the *Sewanee Review* for New York intellectuals). In addition, Bellow, with each new novel, was championed as a successor to

Hemingway and Faulkner.

Then came the 1960s. Perhaps the 1950s proved too normal for the fractured Western mind. Either way, the liberal optimism of the early 1960s gave way to mid-60s disillusionment and finally, to out-and-out chaos and disorder. Those certain restraints that keep civilization above ice were shattered. In a 1970 essay, the sociologist Robert Nisbet waxed gloomily. "[It] would be difficult to find a single decade in the history of Western culture when so much barbarism—so much calculated onslaught against culture and convention in any form, and so much sheer degradation of both culture and the individual—passed into print, into music, into art and onto the American stage as the decade of the Nineteen Sixties," he observed in a symposium on that tumultuous era published in *Encounter* magazine(11).

In 1968, Bellow had his own encounter with the new dispensation, a moment he would later dramatize in his 1970 novel, *Mr. Sammler's Planet*. Riding high on the fame earned by *Herzog*, Bellow was giving a talk titled "What Are Writers Doing In The Universities?" at San Francisco State University, itself a hotbed of student activism. The question-and-answer period turned ugly. A creative writing instructor, obviously no fan of Bellow's, got into an angry exchange with the novelist, accusing him of trying to make the university both "a haven from the vulgarities of the contemporary world" and "a genteel old maid's school." A non-plused Bellow refused to rise to the bait, and so the instructor used a string of obscenities to denounce the novelist. Bellow found few allies on the San Francisco State faculty. Some thought his talk was unduly provocative. Others claimed he had been cold and discourteous to his undergraduate questioners. At least he didn't use profane language (Atlas *Bellow* 374-77).

For Warren, inklings that things were going wrong came in the early 1970s. In 1973, he along with Cleanth Brooks and R. W. B. Lewis, published a magisterial textbook, *American Literature: The Makers and The Making*. Writing at the peak of his critical powers, Warren contributed sterling essays on such classics as *Adventures of Huckleberry Finn*, *The Red Badge of Courage*, *Winesburg, Ohio*, *The Great Gatsby*, and *A Farewell to Arms*. After its publication, Warren felt satisfied, declaring that he had come to a better appreciation of his "fatherland" and its literary achievements. By then, however, the New Criticism that Warren and Brooks had early popularized was itself under attack. Consequently, *American Literature* went through only one printing, never approaching the success that *Understanding Poetry* had enjoyed (Blotner 387-98, 412).

Also, by the 1970s, the faculty at Yale was undergoing some changes. The presence of William Wimsatt, along with Warren and Brooks, had long given the New Critics a beachhead at Yale. At the same time, deconstructionists such as Paul de Man had also made their way to New Haven. A new generation now filled the faculty offices. A 1971 *New York Times Magazine* profile celebrated, often tongue-in-cheek, two big best sellers recently published by Yale professors: Charles Reich's counter-culture favorite, *The Greening of America* and Erich Segal's tear jerker, *Love Story*. Warren, to be sure, was still a respected and admired member of the Yale faculty. But many in the new crowd also considered him "something of an anachronism," even a reactionary (Meehan).

A 1970 meeting, at which Warren invited Bellow to speak to a select group of Yale English majors was noted more for its indifference than confrontation. In her profile of Bellow for *Life* magazine, Jane Howard recorded the bland proceedings:

There he [Bellow] sat, captive, donnishly tweeded, physically slight and boyish despite his white hair and 54 years. And there they sat, longhaired, languid, and oddly unresponsive....To [a student] who sought Bellow's opinion of campus revolutionaries, he said, "The trouble with the destroyers is that they're just as phony as what they've come to destroy. Maybe civilization *is* dying, but it still exists, and meanwhile we have our choice: we can either rain more blows on it, or try to redeem it." Silence. His audience seemed unmoved by Bellow's implied attacks on the fashionable tenets that Black—and Youth and Social Consciousness and Relevance and Where It's At and Spontaneity—is necessarily Beautiful. "Well," he said, "I see I've reduced you all to silence." More silence. "Well," he said, "it's late and I have an early train to catch." It wasn't late at all; it was only 9 o'clock, but the group dispersed. "Ah well," said Bellow as he shrugged on his imposing sheepskin-lined coat, "they and I don't talk the same language." (Howard 58)

Warren held similar sentiments. By 1973, he was ready to retire. Warren wanted freedom from his academic duties. He also was tired of the intellectual climate at his longtime employer. Looking at an early 1970s Yale curriculum guide, Warren remarked to a friend: "One seminar...apparently consisted only on reading contemporary pornography. I suspect it was the first time in history kids got course credit for reading dirty books." His final class contained some drama. Meeting his seminar of 10 students, Warren went around the room, asking each student to recite a poem, any poem. If not, could they at least relate the plot of a short story? Both queries were also met with total silence. With that, Warren walked out of a Yale classroom for the last time. (Blotner 411).

Never the retiring type, Warren remained as prolific as ever. He devoted most of his efforts to poetry, his first literary love. But he also found time for one last novel, *A Place to Come To*; the 1974 Jefferson Lecture, published as *Democracy and Poetry*; and two memoirs, *Portrait of A Father* and *Jefferson Davis Gets His Citizenship Back*. The latter book was inspired by a 1979 weeklong celebration in Guthrie, Kentucky, Warren's hometown and also the site of an impressive monument to Davis himself. The U.S. Congress had recently restored American citizenship to the only president of the Confederacy (an honor that Warren correctly noted would have been rejected by Davis). This book represented a circle of sorts. Warren, as noted, began his career with a critical biography of John Brown, the murderous abolitionist.

By the time of the Civil War centennial in the early 1960s, Warren published *The Legacy of the Civil War*. That volume chastised both the South for holding onto "the Great Alibi" and the North for touting its "Treasury of Virtue." Warren also acknowledged how the tragic grandeur of that age, along with the old America's sense of community, still fascinated citizens of a more mobile nation. Finally, as the 1980s dawned, Warren celebrated the old-fashioned virtues—compassion, honor, and courage—that Jefferson Davis exemplified. In general, Warren now cast a colder eye on American notions of progress. According to Joseph Blotner, Warren, during the 1980s, became more critical of the New Deal, believing it had caused a "weakening" of the American spirit. Warren enjoyed good-natured bantering with his second wife, the award-winning novelist Eleanor Clark. Political arguments often ended with Clark scolding her husband, "you old Agrarian!" and with Warren returning the slight, labeling his spouse as "you old Trotskyite!" (Blotner ix).

When a second wave of left wing radicalism hit American culture in the late 1980s, Warren was active, but elderly. Bellow, now into his seventies, was still teaching. In the early 1990s, he finally gave up on Chicago, moving with his young wife to a position at Boston University. His cultural criticism remained as pointed as ever. In the 1960s, he had no use for the New Left assault on the academy. Likewise, he was a critic of multiculturalism, the great left wing cause of the 1980s and beyond. "Who is the Tolstoy of the Zulus? The Proust of the Papuans? I'd be glad to read them," Bellow joked in response to a question from James Atlas, who was doing a profile on Allan Bloom, Bellow's colleague at the University of Chicago and recent author of the runaway best seller, *The Closing of the American Mind*. Bellow's remarks were published in parenthesis; they were hardly central to the article. But in making them, he had mimicked the Left's latest fixation (Atlas, "Grumpy Guru" 31).

And so, the Nobel laureate found himself under attack from the usual suspects. Even Alfred Kazin, a one-time friend and admirer, declared that his "heart sank with each fresh report of Bellow's contempt for the lower orders." Several years later, Bellow explained the remark in a *New York Times* op-ed piece. He recalled reading, in his undergraduate days, a novel, "Chaka," by Thomas Mofolo, itself a tragic tale about a massacre of Zulu tribesmen by a deranged tribal chief. Zulu fiction did exist. Still, Bellow gave no endorsement to multiculturalism. In the old Chicago, Bellow related, people were allowed "a kind of openness" when confronting the realities of a multiethnic society. However, in an age of rage and guilt, all that was over. "We can't open our mouths without being denounced as racists, misogynists, supremacists, imperialists, or fascists," the novelist protested. ("Zulus and Pampuans").

Bellow was just as critical of political correctness, the other reigning ideology of our time. The electoral victories by Ronald Reagan in the 1980s had no effect on the state of American culture. Liberals still dominated the publishing and entertainment industries, not to mention all aspects of American education. The Reaganites did not, as pledged, abolish the Department of Education. Still, liberals felt threatened over the rise of conservative thought and ideas in the body politic. For instance, by the late 1980s, a plurality of Americans identified themselves as conservative. Consequently, liberals used their power bases to lay down the law, namely through the phenomenon of "political correctness," which basically declared any criticism of liberal orthodoxy to be beyond the pale of acceptable discourse. Not surprisingly, Bellow would have none of it. He was alarmed by the implications of p.c. It represented, he told a reporter, "a serious threat to political health, because where there is free speech without any debate what you have is a corruption of free speech, which very quickly becomes demagoguery. It's a bad moment in the history of the country" (Atlas, *Bellow* 575).

Neither Warren nor Bellow was a campaigning conservative. While skeptical over the New Deal, Warren, as far as I know, did not hold similar sentiments concerning the liberalism of the 1950s and '60s. Into the 1990s, Bellow still referred to himself as "some sort of liberal," while also attacking modern liberalism as a form of "mindless medallion-wearing and placard-bearing." In the 1980s, Bellow briefly was a member of the Committee for the Free World, a leading neoconservative organization. He soon quit, tiring of that committee's own cultural criticism and the belief held by Joseph Epstein that American novelists had no great subjects to write about (Atlas, *Bellow* 513-14).

If not conservative in politics, both men were traditionalists in literature. How could they not be? Both came of age when the classics were mandatory reading on college campuses. At the Vanderbilt of Warren's youth, prospective students had to translate a page of Latin before being admitted to that institution. Meanwhile, Bellow enjoyed recalling the Chicago public schools of his own adolescence, where students were required to read poetry by Robert Frost. As writers, both were moralists whose creative efforts struggled with those grand dramas where a man's soul was at stake. As literary traditionalists at a time of anti-Western ideology, both Warren and Bellow have been targeted for neglect and derision. Much humility is in order. Warren and Bellow are writers from an exciting and creative time in American literature. In the future, both should be taught and read, providing that the Western tradition somehow survives in these United States.

Works Cited

Atlas, James. *Bellow: A Life*. New York: Random House, 2000.
——. "Chicago's Grumpy Guru." *New York Times Magazine*, Jan. 3, 1988, pp 13-15, 25, 31.
Bellow, Saul. Letters to Robert Penn Warren in Robert Penn Warren Papers, Beinecke Rare Book and Manuscript Library, Yale University.
——. "Zulus and Pampuans." *New York Times*, March 10, 1994, p. A25.
Blotner, Joseph. *Robert Penn Warren: A Biography*. New York: Random House, 1997.
Clemons, Walter and Jack Kroll. "America's Master Novelist." *Newsweek*, Sept. 1, 1975, pp. 32-34, 39-40.
Cutrer, Thomas. *Parnasus on the Mississippi: The Southern Review and the Baton Rouge Literary Community, 1935-1942*. Baton Rouge: Louisiana State UP, 1985.
Fleming, Thomas. "Southern Men, American Persons." *Chronicles: A Magazine of American Culture*, May 1994: 15-17.
Howard, Jane. "Mr. Bellow Considers His Planet." *Life*, April 3, 1970, pp. 57-58.
Meehan, Thomas. "The Yale Faculty Makes the Scene." *New York Times Magazine*, Feb. 7, 1971, pp. 12-13, 48-52.
Nisbet, Robert. "The Nemesis of Authority." *Encounter* 39 (August 1972): 11, 16-17, 19-20.
Warren, Robert Penn. "The Man with No Commitments." *New Republic*, November 2, 1953, pp. 22-23.

"A Friendship That Has Meant So Much":
Robert Penn Warren and Ralph W. Ellison[1]

by Steven D. Ealy

Ralph Ellison was in residence at the American Academy in Rome as a fellow from 1955 to 1957. Robert Penn Warren was also at the Academy between May 1956 and early 1957. The two men and their wives apparently hit it off immediately, and this family friendship remained active until the end of Warren's life. Writing to Nathan Scott in 1989, Ellison noted that "it was in Rome that we really became friends. For it was there that [Warren] became the companion with whom I enjoyed an extended period of discussing literature, writing, history, politics—you name it—exploring the city, exchanging folk tales, joking, lying, eating and drinking" (Ellison Papers).

During late 1956 Ellison and Eugene Walter, editor of the *Paris Review*, conducted one of the most searching interviews that Warren ever gave. The interview took place in Ellison's apartment at the American Academy and was subsequently published in the *Paris Review*. Among the important topics covered are the question of race, the "combat" involved in writing, and Warren's resistance to reducing the complexity of experience to "correct" or "accepted" interpretations or answers.

Ellison characterized Warren's writings on race as an "exciting spiral." (Watkins et al. 32) He wondered if the movement from "The Briar Patch," Warren's contribution to the Southern Agrarian manifesto *I'll Take My Stand* in 1930, to *Brother to Dragons* (1953) and *Segregation* (1956) represented stages in Warren's "combat with the past." Warren took this question as an opportunity to speak directly to the issue of race, but also to make a more general comment on his whole approach to writing. "The Briar Patch," Warren recounted, was written in Oxford while he was a Rhodes Scholar, and reflected the then dominant constitutional position of "separate but equal" that had been articulated by the Supreme Court. Warren claimed that he had not reread the essay in the three decades since he had sent it from Oxford to Donald Davidson for inclusion in the agrarian collection, and admitted to "some sense of evasion" in writing it.

At the same time Warren was writing "The Briar Patch" he was also working on "Prime Leaf," a novella commissioned by the editors of *American Caravan*. "If you are seriously trying to write fiction, you can't allow yourself as much evasion as in trying to write essays," Warren told his interviewers (Watkins et al. 33). That is another way of saying that fiction is, at bottom, more concerned with truth than is nonfiction. Truth is deeper than factual accuracy, and deals with the motives of human action—what Warren in this interview calls the "moral shock" of human existence. In writing his novels he was looking for a "dramatic rub" deeper than that found in social realism. Warren maintained that one writes fiction "from the inside, not the outside—the inside of yourself—you have to find what's there—you can't predict it" (35). Warren held that the stories he told chose him, rather than he choosing them. Writing, for Warren, was a process of discovery. Warren told Ellison and Walter, "When you start any book, you don't know what, ultimately, your issues are. You try to write to find them" (28).

As to whether his writing on race reflected a combat with the past, Warren allowed, "As for combat, I guess the real combat is always with yourself. Southerner or anybody else" (34). This combat with one's self is two-fold, as Warren makes clear elsewhere. First, it is a struggle for truth. As Warren writes in his analysis of Joseph Conrad's *Nostromo*, the philosophical novelist "is willing to go naked into the pit, again and again, to make the same old struggle for his truth" (*New and Selected Essays* 160). Second, however, the combat with one's self actually involves the creation of the self—the choices that one makes as a writer not only reflect but also shape who he is as a person.

From the time of "The Briar Patch" (1930) to the 1950s the social and moral landscape had changed. In Warren's view, Southern loyalty and piety—which he recognized as real, or legitimate, values—came into tension with both the Southern religion and moral sense—also legitimate values. It was the "moral shock" caused by such a deep conflict of values—and the growing civil rights movement reflected such a shock—that generated "vital imagination" (Watkins et al. 30).

At a number of points in this interview Warren took aim at "right thinkers" who believe that they have the final answer on each and every question. Warren thought that he had been inoculated against "one-answer systems" by his encounter with Henry Thomas Buckle's *History of Civilization in England* as a teenager. To Warren's young mind, Buckle provided a simple answer to explain everything. He recounts, "History is all explained by geography. I read Buckle, and then I could explain everything. It gave me quite a hold over the other kids, they hadn't read Buckle. Buckle was my Marx" (26). Somewhere between his youth and his adult years, however, Warren "lost the notion that there was ever going to be just one key" to explain the universe (27).

Warren's opposition to single-cause explanations can be seen in his discussion of literary criticism. He began by arguing against the view that literary criticism and literary creativity were *necessarily* in opposition, although he recognized that in some individuals for some reason the critical faculty might kill the creative impulse. But, Warren argued, "criticism is a perfectly natural human activity, and somehow the dullest, most technical criticism may be associated with full creativity" (30). Any criticism that provides a deeper insight into the work of art is good—whether it be "how to" criticism, Marxian or Freudian analysis, or historical and social commentary. Warren then concludes his discussion with a caution: "there is no *one, single, correct* kind of criticism—no *complete* criticism. You only have different kinds of perspectives, giving, when successful, different kinds of insights." These different approaches to criticism, Warren adds, may vary in importance during different historical periods.

Warren's opposition to single-answer systems is reminiscent of Ellison's critique of the liberal or "sociological" understanding of the experience of American Blacks. Ellison stated his position succinctly in "The World and the Jug," a response to the critic Irving Howe. Howe had praised Richard Wright as the model for Black writers and criticized James Baldwin and Ellison for not following Wright's example. Ellison did not deny that Wright's approach to the oppression that Blacks experienced in their lives, the "protest novel," was one possible reaction to those circumstances. He did, however, maintain strongly that protest was not the only legitimate response. Other responses might include singing the blues, writing a symphony, or looking deeper into the inner conflict and humanity even of those responsible for the oppression (*Collected Essays* 164, 176).

One did not have to understand oneself as beaten or victimized. In referring specifically to Wright, Ellison puts his objection to Howe (and perhaps in part to Wright also) in these terms: the social conditions and pressures that Wright experienced allowed him to grow into a person who could imagine Bigger Thomas (protagonist of *Native Son*) and write his story, but he developed Bigger Thomas as a character in such a way Bigger himself could never have the imagination or creativity of Richard Wright. That is, Ellison implies, Wright's life to some extent belies Wright's art, because his life shows the human possibility in a way that the protagonists in his writing do not manifest. The example of Wright's life allows for richer possibility than does his fiction (162, 167).

Nine years after Ellison interviewed Warren for the *Paris Review* Warren interviewed Ellison for *Who Speaks for the Negro?* Warren's reflections on Ellison, including excerpts from his two interviews of Ellison, constitutes the concluding section of a chapter entitled "Leadership from the Periphery." Among the others discussed in this chapter are Judge William Hastie, novelist James Baldwin, columnist Carl Rowan, and Dr. Kenneth Clark. All of these men, in Warren's view, had not only successfully competed with whites in the larger world, but had also confronted "the painful consequences of success," (*Who Speaks for the Negro?* 269).

Ellison's response to a question about the split of the Negro psyche asserted by W. E. B. Du Bois was to suggest that the issue was more complicated than Du Bois thought. Ellison's concern was not with whether he would accept or reject American values, for it was inevitable that he would be influenced by these values, because "they're coming at me through the newspapers, through the books, through the products I buy, through all the various media—through the language." Rather, for Ellison the problem was to put himself "into a position where [he could] have the maximum influence upon those values" (*Who Speaks for the Negro?* 327). Additionally, Ellison wanted to see the ideas embedded in the Declaration of Independence "made manifest." Thus he was committed to an affirmation, rather than rejection, of certain fundamental American values.

Ellison's emphasis in his discussion of the Black experience in America focuses on questions of "culture, social experience, and political circumstance," rather than blood. He rejected the view of Negro life, articulated both by Black leaders and whites, that characterized it primarily as deprivation, suffering, and alienation. He feared that this view might become "an excuse and a blinder," and lead young Blacks to reject their individual talents "in favor of reducing [themselves] to a generalized definition of alienation and agony." Should this occur, the individual himself would bring about "what the entire history of repression and brutalization has failed to do: the individual reduces himself to a cipher" (*Who Speaks for the Negro?* 328-29). This suggests a peculiar difficulty that might be called "self-stereotyping," which should be understood in connection with the general problem of stereotyping.

Warren noted a change in Ellison's perspective over time. In the late 1940s Ellison argued that the Black experience was characterized by self-hatred and a search for identity, but his later view was that Blacks could fully achieve their individuality even under repressive conditions. This later view is articulated in Ellison's review of *Blues People*, a study of black music by Le Roi Jones.

"A slave," writes Le Roi Jones, "cannot be a man." But what, might one ask, of those moments when he feels his metabolism aroused by the rising of the sap in the spring? What of his identity among other slaves? With his wife? And isn't it closer to the truth that far from considering themselves only in terms of that abstraction, "a slave," the enslaved really thought of themselves as *men* who had been unjustly enslaved? (*Collected Essays* 284)

The problem of stereotyping begins with a generalization, and then proceeds to fitting the individual into a "type" rather than treating him as a person. It is this phenomenon that makes the "invisible man" invisible—he is not seen as an individual but as a case or as a unit to be used, and as a type or case the person disappears. This is the dynamic at play throughout Ellison's novel, *Invisible Man*, in which the protagonist is not seen as an individuated person by those he encounters, neither by the white elite who watch him in the battle royal, nor Dr. Bledsoe, President of the College, nor Mr. Norton the college trustee whose "fate" he was, nor the Brotherhood leadership (*Invisible Man* 42, 427). The exception to this unwillingness to see him as a person in his own right is Mary, who urges him to live in her house until he recovers from the wounds he received in the explosion of the paint factory. One of the reasons that the Brotherhood insists that he leave Mary's house is that his identity must be erased, for individual identity is seen as a threat by the Brotherhood.

"Invisibility" is one of the experiences that brought Ellison and Warren together as friends—they both experienced being seen as representative of a caste, which of course means that they both experienced being not seen, or being invisible. Ellison tells Warren that he "very often found people who think that they know me as an individual reveal that they have no sense of the experience behind me, the extent of it and the complexity of it. What they have instead is good will and a passion for abstraction" (*Who Speaks for the Negro?* 336). Warren's response to Ellison's comment reflects a similar sensibility. "I encounter the same thing, I suppose, in a way. I've been congratulated by well-meaning friends who say, 'It's so nice to [meet] a reconstructed Southerner.' I don't feel reconstructed, you see. And I don't feel liberal. I feel logical, and I resent the word—I resent the word *reconstructed*" (337).

The Southern Historical Association's annual meeting in November, 1968, held in New Orleans, featured a panel organized by C. Vann Woodward of Yale University on "The Uses of History in Fiction." The panelists, in addition to Woodward as moderator, were William Styron, who had recently published *The Confessions of Nat Turner*, Ralph Ellison, and Robert Penn Warren. In his opening remarks for this roundtable discussion, Warren attempted to distinguish history from fiction, first by dismissing what might be assumed to distinguish the two: relation to time and relation to imagination. First, Warren argued, both history and fiction are written "in the past tense." In order to write fiction, even science fiction set far in the future, "you get yourself to a point beyond the story that you are telling." (Graham and Singh144) Second, both fiction and history are imagined. But there is a difference in the quality of imagination and the knowledge it gives to the historian and to the novelist. The crux of the matter appears to be the difference between external and internal knowledge. "Historians are concerned with the truth *about*, with knowledge *about*, the fiction writer with the knowledge *of*" (143; italics in original).

In his prepared remarks, Ellison argued that the origins of American historiography were found in the same attitudes that led to the development of tall tales, and maintained that "historians are responsible liars" (146). While both American fiction and history share the same foundation, they part company fairly quickly, because the historian is "dedicated to chronology" in a way that the novelist is not. For the novelist, according to Ellison, time is an enemy, because he seeks "to manipulate or even to destroy" chronology (147). The novelist's manipulation, both of time and of reality, is designed to uncover 'those abiding human predicaments which are ageless and timeless." Ellison concluded that if one wants to know something of interpersonal racial relations in the South, one is better off turning to Faulkner than to historians, including Negro historians. For Ellison a key difference between American history and American literature is that history avoids tragedy and literature concerns itself with tragedy.

The third member of this panel, William Styron, was at the time embroiled in a controversy over *The Confessions of Nat Turner*. This novel, based on an historical slave rebellion in Virginia, had generated tremendous anger among some members of the black community. Among the allegations directed at Styron was the charge that he falsified the historical record (for example, his Nat Turner was not married, and yet the historical figure had been), and Ellison's comments about the relationship between fiction and history need to be understood as his caution to avoid such confrontations, which (in his mind) work only to the disadvantage of the novelist. Thus the foundation for Ellison's warning directed to Styron was to highlight the trap of being stuck with a historical record that one couldn't manipulate: "the moment you put any known figures into the book, then somebody is going to say, 'But he didn't have that mole on that side of his face; it was on *that* side'" (Graham and Singh 159). The "autonomy of fiction" (158) that Ellison desires to protect requires that the novelist keep his distance from history, for "facts are a tyranny for the novelist" (159).

Both Ellison and Warren rejected Styron's cavalier attitude toward historical facts as essentially unimportant for the artist. Styron had used Georg Lukacs's *The Historical Novel* to argue "that facts *per se* are preposterous. They are like the fuzz that collects in the top of dirty closets. They don't really mean anything." Ellison's response was, "They *mean* something. That's why you're in trouble." Warren's response to Styron is a more ambiguous, "I wouldn't go that far" (159).

Warren's view was perhaps somewhere between those of Styron and Ellison. He had previously explained his understanding of the relationship between literature and history in the introduction to *Brother to Dragons*, where he maintained that poetry "is more than fantasy" and famously argued, "if poetry is the little myth we make, history is the big myth we live, and in our living constantly remake" (xii).

For Ellison written history is related to social action in the same way that myth is related to ritual. "History is sacred, you see, and no matter how false to actual events it might be." (Graham and Singh 148) For this reason Ellison warns novelists to steer clear of history, for involvement with history can only deflect the novelist from his real concerns. While implicitly criticizing Styron, he explicitly praises Warren for having the good sense not to make *All the King's Men* a historical novel—"Thanks to Warren's art we may now view that man [referring to the historical Huey Long] through the heightened sense of the past which both history and literature grant to all who are truly involved with the mystery of human existence" (149).

I

Echoes of Ellison's massive and masterful *Invisible Man* can be found in a number of Warren's works, and echoes of Warren can be found in Ellison. James Grimshaw, for example, notes that Warren's *Wilderness* contains allusions to *Invisible Man* (Grimshaw 77). One of the reasons for these resonances are that concerns with the nature of history and the place of the individual in history provide the subtext for the fiction of both writers.

Jack Burden concludes his reminiscence which is *All the King's Men* with the memorable reflection that he is preparing to leave his childhood house "and go into the convulsion of the world, out of history into history and the awful responsibility of Time" (438). This whole novel can be seen as Burden's effort to reach the point of understanding the nature of human responsibility and the individual's place in the drama of human history. Jack's story as he himself relates it is one of avoiding knowledge on both of these fronts. Jack makes use of various gimmicks as he avoids the terror of personal responsibility, at times by assigning responsibility to mechanistic historical forces ("the Great Twitch") and at others by convincing himself that he is merely an agent of someone greater than himself ("the Boss") and therefore is not acting. He finally comes to understand the individual responsibility for one's actions by reflecting on his dead friends Willie Stark and Adam Stanton. "He had seen his two friends…live and die. Each had killed the other. Each had been the doom of the other…. But at the same time Jack Burden came to see that his friends had been doomed, he saw that though doomed they had nothing to do with any doom under the godhead of the Great Twitch. They were doomed, but they lived in the agony of will" (436). As another character in the novel tells Jack, "History is blind, but man is not."

Jack's growth in understanding is symbolized by the status of his doctoral dissertation. Early in the novel's chronology Jack had been unable to complete his dissertation on Cass Mastern. Although he knew the facts of Mastern's life, he couldn't understand the truth of that life, especially Mastern's decision to carry the burden for his actions in his future conduct. By the end of the novel, however, Jack is able to begin to tell the tale of Cass Mastern.

During the course of the novel, Jack also learns that he is not an isolated and atomistic being, free to do whatever he wants, but that his story is part of a greater story, begun before his time and continuing on after him. As he tells Anne Stanton near the end of the novel, "if you could not accept the past and its burden there was no future, for without one there cannot be the other, and how if you could accept the past you might hope for the future, for only out of the past can you make the future" (435). Accepting the burden of the past is perhaps the most difficult option that one can take in dealing with the past, for the easy options are either the total embracing of one's past—the moonlight and magnolia version of the Old South, for example—or the total rejection of that history—the stance of the New South that sees no value or virtue in understanding the old ways. Accepting the burden of the past places a tremendous burden on the actor, for he must sort through the good and the bad before deciding what to accept and what to reject. Further, accepting the burden of the past forces one to realize that there are skeletons in the family closet that most prefer to ignore. Moreover, every family closet has its share of skeletons.

This struggle with the past also characterizes the narrator of *Invisible Man*. Throughout the novel he wrestles with his grandfather's deathbed description of himself as a traitor and a spy and with his grandfather's final advice: "Agree 'em to death and destruction" (574-75). This advice, given to the narrator's father along with the admonition to "Learn it to the younguns" (16), has truly become a burden for the narrator, for throughout the novel he seeks to understand the meaning and the significance of this oracle statement. This understanding takes on both a personal and a political dimension in the mind of the narrator.

On the first level, he tries to understand how his mild-mannered grandfather could think of himself as a traitor and a spy. On the political level, he struggles with the meaning and implications of the command to "agree 'em to death." Should one "affirm the principle on which the country was built and not the men" or should one "take responsibility for all of it, for the men as well as the principle, because we were the heirs who must use the principle because no other fitted our needs?" (574).

One character in *Invisible Man* provides a distorted echo of Jack Burden's claim that he is going to step "out of history into history." Tod Clifton first enters *Invisible Man* as a leading figure on the Brotherhood's Harlem committee, serving as director of youth activities. The narrator, just appointed to be the Brotherhood's spokesman in Harlem, initially sees Clifton as a potential rival, but they work well together planning a series of rallies against tenant evictions. Together they confront Ras the Exhorter, a black nationalist who opposes cooperation between the races. In the aftermath of their initial confrontation with Ras, Clifton says, "I suppose sometimes a man has to plunge outside history." Ras had tried to recruit Clifton to his cause, and Clifton explains that by "plunging outside history" he means turning his back on forces that might cause him to "go nuts" (377). The possibility of Clifton "going nuts" is reinforced later when the narrator is told that Clifton was quick with his fists and that he "goes wild when he gits mad" (396).

The narrator is transferred from Harlem by the Brotherhood, and in his absence Tod Clifton has disappeared, leaving his assignment incomplete. The narrator is instructed to return to Harlem, where he happens upon Tod Clifton selling "Sambo, the dancing doll" on a street corner. In revulsion, he spits on one of the dolls and thus becomes an inadvertent part of Clifton's impromptu minstrel show. Clifton quickly moves to avoid being arrested by a policeman, for he is vending his dolls without a license. The narrator is so disheartened by his discovery of Clifton in these circumstances that he cannot confront Clifton. He interprets this obscene venture as Clifton's effort to "fall outside of history," but also believes that Clifton's personal decision is a threat to the Brotherhood. At this point the narrator still thinks the Brotherhood is essential—"only in the Brotherhood could we make ourselves known, could we avoid being empty Sambo dolls" (434).

Soon he again spots Tod Clifton, this time being shoved down the street by a police officer. He watches Clifton turn on the officer after being pushed, punch the officer to the ground, and sees the officer shoot and kill Clifton (436-38). He cannot understand Clifton's actions or motives—why would he "deliberately plunge out of history"? Why would he go off on his own and "leave the only organization offering him a chance to 'define' himself"? (438).

The narrator's reflections on Clifton's death lead him to begin to question or rethink the view of history articulated by the Brotherhood: "What if Brother Jack were wrong? What if history was a gambler, instead of a force in a laboratory experiment…? What if history was not a reasonable citizen, but a madman full of paranoid guile…?" (441). He organizes a funeral service for Tod Clifton, and although it is well attended, he thinks the

Brotherhood would not approve because in his oration he does not emphasize the political (or historical) dimension of Clifton's deadly encounter with the police. He is right about the Brotherhood's reactions to the funeral, but for the wrong reasons. Clifton is seen by the Brotherhood as a racist traitor undeserving of a hero's funeral, and the Brotherhood has changed its program for Harlem.

John Burt draws a provocative parallel between *All the King's Men* and *Invisible Man*. "Jack's commitment to Willie is like the Invisible Man's commitment to the Brotherhood: we cannot doubt that either springs from political motives that the novelist finds to be as credible at the end of the novel as he did at the beginning. At the same time, the political institutions that are supposed to represent those values keep falsifying them" (335-36). While it is true that both Willie Stark and the Brotherhood "falsify" the values they represent, the claim that both retain credibility is problematic.

Consider that within the context of the two novels Willie Stark shows a self-critical consciousness that allows him to see that he himself has subverted the values he holds, and to engage in self-corrective action. The Brotherhood shows no such self-reflective dimension that might allow for robust learning and modification of behavior. What is true of both Jack Burden and the narrator of *Invisible Man* by the conclusion of their respective novels is that each is ready to act, and each is ready to write. One major difference between the two novels is that race serves as a minor backdrop for Jack Burden and is a major concern for Ellison's narrator.

Tod Clifton serves as a model that Warren adapts in his later novel, *Flood*. Although the question of race in America is not the primary focus of *Flood*, published in the mid-1960s, it provides one of the most extended treatments of race found in Warren's fiction. Here I focus only on one minor character, Mortimer Sparlin, because of the ways he mirrors Tod Clifton. Sparlin, like Clifton, is shown stereotyping the black experience. Like Clifton, Sparlin proves to be handy with his fists. Unlike Tod Clifton, however, Mortimer Sparlin dons his stereotype—literally and figuratively—as a way to disguise his essence, and is able to discard his costume as he prepares to enter a new stage of his life. Tod Clifton appears to embrace his "dancing Sambo" as a way to plunge out of history while Mortimer Sparlin uses his disguise as a way to step into history—and perhaps to change it—even if in a small way.

Sparlin, an honor graduate in romance languages from the University of Chicago, had come south to study the French writers Corneille and Racine at Fisk University in Nashville before taking up a graduate fellowship at the University of Rome. He enters the novel, however, not as an honors student in romance languages but as "Jingle Bells," the attendant who pumps gas at The Seven Dwarfs Motel. He wears a costume out of a fairy tale—a jerkin with bells and tights with a red right leg and a yellow left leg—and affects a Stepin Fetchit manner as he performs his tasks under a billboard advertising the hotel. The billboard features "the bloated, minstrel-show-white lips of a benignly grinning black face," which advertises breakfast served in the individual cottages and concludes with "Yassuh, Boss!" (*Flood* 4-5). Thus Mortimer Sparlin is, at first glance at least, a live model of Tod Clifton's "dancing Sambo" doll.

Sparlin has come South for two reasons: to study with a distinguished professor at Fisk whose work had interested him and "because he wanted to know what it felt like to be a Negro in the South" (366). My presumption is that he took the attendant's job at the Seven Dwarfs Motel—forty-five minutes away from Fisk University on his Lambretta motor scooter—to provide a laboratory where he could gather data related to his second concern. His interaction with the novel's protagonist, Brad Tolliver, suggests that Sparlin is willing to play his assumed role only so far. At the opening of the novel Tolliver pulls into the Seven Dwarfs Motel to gas up, and Sparlin remains in character for the most part. When Tolliver drives off after giving Sparlin a tip, "Jingle Bells" breaks character by saying, "Thanks, Mac" out of the corner of his mouth and giving Tolliver a large, non-servile smile. This is especially jarring to Tolliver, who had anticipated stereotypical behavior from a stereotypical character (9-10).

Near the end of the novel Tolliver takes Leontine Purtle, blind daughter of the sheriff, to the Seven Dwarfs Motel for an afternoon sexual dalliance. As he is settling Leontine back into his car after their romp in the motel room, Tolliver is approached by "Jingle Bells," who asks, "How do you like blind tail?" Before Tolliver can call him a "black bastard," Sparlin hits him with a right jab and knocks him to the ground. He advises Tolliver not to fight back because he was ranked in Gold Gloves. When Tolliver heads to the office, Sparlin tells him that he can't be fired because this is his last day of work, and that if he calls the Sheriff he will subpoena "the blind tart" to testify. Tolliver climbs into his Jaguar and calms the bewildered Leontine Purtle: "It was nothing much. Just an argument about change. And…they were right." As he drove away, "he repeated the word *change*, and began to laugh. As he laughed he felt like both the laugher and the laughed-at" (365).

After his tiff with Tolliver Mortimer Sparlin thinks he has the answer to the question of what it felt like to be a Negro in the South. "It felt like being himself" (366). He reflected on his future at the University of Rome, where he had imagined that everything would be different, and realized that he himself would not be different, but would remain the same self he was. For Mortimer Sparlin, as for the other characters in Warren's fiction, the creation of the self is primarily an internal rather than an external phenomenon.

II

In a letter to Ralph and Fanny Ellison dated December 2, 1985, Robert Penn Warren recounted the highlights of their relationship, beginning with the publication party for *Invisible Man* and concluding with a recent dinner together at the home of Albert Erskine, who was editor for both Warren and Ellison at Random House. "In between there fell, of course, that wonderful time when we were in Rome together." Warren concluded this brief communication by noting that his wife, Eleanor Clark, joined him "in gratitude for a friendship that has meant so much" (Ellison Papers).

The draft of a letter to Warren that Ellison never sent describes the shocked reaction of a young black reporter to seeing a photograph of Warren on a shelf along with portraits of other writers and composers. He promises to explain the nature of friendship the next time something similar occurs (Ellison Papers). In a letter to Nathan Scott, Ellison explains the importance of their time together in Rome as the foundation for their friendship.

> A vigorous man, he damn near walked my legs off as we covered miles of what
> for him were familiar historical sites, restaurants, and bars. And it was through

such pleasurable roaming that any bars to our friendship that might have been imposed by Southern manners and history went down the drain and left the well-known Fugitive poet and the fledgling writer and grandson of Freedmen marvelously free to enjoy themselves as human beings. (Ellison Papers)

According to Ellison's account to Scott, one thing that the two men did not discuss when they got together was their work in progress, although they did share their writings immediately upon publication. Perhaps a key to their friendship was the fact that both men had experienced what it meant to be taken for granted—to be invisible—because of external characteristics. While at the American Academy in Rome, Ellison wrote to his friend Albert Murray: "Warren is a man who's lived and thought his way free of a lot of irrational illusions and you'd like him." He also told Murray, "it took Rome to let us discover one another—which might be the most important thing to happen during these two years" (Murray and Callahan 158).

Warren promoted Ellison both privately and publicly. In 1963, Warren nominated him for membership in the prestigious but secretive Century Club of New York. The next year he helped Ellison secure a grant from the Rockefeller Foundation—one that allowed him to write with no teaching responsibilities. In 1965 Warren reviewed Ellison's collection of essays, *Shadow and Act*, for *Commentary*. Under the title "The Unity of Experience" (for the source of the title, see Ellison's *Collected Essays* 170), Warren wrote, "Ellison is... more concerned with the way a man confronts his individual doom than with the derivation of that doom; not pathos, but power, in its deepest inner sense, is what concerns him. He is willing, pridefully, to head into responsibility" ("Unity" 92).

It also must be noted that the origin of their friendship was as much social as it was intellectual. While in Rome the two families, not just the writers, grew close together, and this closeness remained after the year in Rome ended, and extended to Warren's children, who were always asked after in the Ellisons' letters—some written by Ralph and some by his wife Fanny. The Ellisons became regular invitees to the annual holiday bash thrown by the Warrens, and if they missed a year there was much consternation on both sides. Ellison described these gatherings to Nathan Scott: "We were introduced to an array of people—writers, artists, curators, publishers, academics—whom otherwise we might not have encountered.... I suspect that a few who took part were bewildered by the easy Americaness of the mixture, their talk of equality notwithstanding. For as far as we were aware no other writers gave parties that encompassed such a diversity of backgrounds and talent" (Ellison Papers).

Robert Penn Warren died on September 15, 1989. Along with Cleanth Brooks, C. Vann Woodward, Albert Erskine, and Saul Bellow, Ralph Ellison was invited to deliver a brief reminiscence at the memorial service held at Stratton Church. Ellison also was at the memorial service held at Yale University. After the Yale service, Ellison told Brooks that he had dreamed of Warren the night before. In the dream, Red was swimming out to sea. As he got closer to an island barely visible from shore, he turned around, waved to Ralph, and disappeared (Winchell 454).

Note

1. The author would like to thank John Burt, literary executor for the estate of Robert Penn Warren, and John F. Callahan, literary executor for the estate of Ralph Ellison, for permission to quote from unpublished correspondence. John F. Callahan also kindly granted the author access to restricted files containing the Ellison-Warren correspondence in the Ralph Ellison Papers housed in the Manuscripts Division of the Library of Congress.

Works Cited

Burt, John. "After the Southern Renascence." In *The Cambridge History of American Literature, Volume 7: Prose Writing 1940-1990*. Edited by Sacvan Bercovitch. Cambridge: Cambridge UP, 1999. 313-424.
Ellison, Ralph. *The Collected Essays of Ralph Ellison*. Edited by John Callahan. New York: Modern Library, 1995.
———. *Invisible Man*. 1952. Reprint New York: Vintage International Paperback. 1995.
Ralph Ellison Papers. Manuscript Division, Library of Congress.
Graham, Maryemma and Amrijit Singh, Eds. *Conversations with Ralph Ellison*. Jackson: UP of Mississippi, 1995.
Grimshaw, James A., Jr. *Understanding Robert Penn Warren*. Columbia: U of South Carolina P, 2001.
Murray, Albert, and John F. Callahan, Eds. *Trading Twelves: The Selected Letters of Ralph Ellison and Albert Murray*. New York: Modern Library, 2000.
Warren, Robert Penn. *All the King's Men*. 1946. Reprint New York: Harcourt, 1982.
———. *Brother to Dragons: A Tale in Verse and Voices*. New York: Random House, 1953.
———. *Flood*. New York: Random House, 1964.
———. *New and Selected Essays*, New York: Random House, 1989.
———. "The Unity of Experience." Review of *Shadow and Act*, by Ralph Ellison. *Commentary* May 1964, 91-96.
———. *Who Speaks for the Negro?* New York: Random House, 1965.
Watkins, Floyd C., John T, Hiers, and Mary Louise Weaks., Eds. *Talking with Robert Penn Warren*. Athens: U of Georgia P, 1990.
Winchell, Mark Royden. *Cleanth Brooks and the Rise of Modern Criticism*. Charlottesville: UP of Virginia, 1996.

A Pair of Moles:
Robert Penn Warren and William Styron

by Robert Cheeks

"We are a pair of moles burrowing away in the same direction."
—Ivan Turgenev to Gustave Flaubert,
May 26, 1868

Robert Penn Warren and William Styron were friends for at least twenty and perhaps as many as thirty years. They celebrated this shared comity at every opportunity with good food, a postprandial libation (or two), and the intellectual introspection that is expected of the literati. They wove their friendship around and through their families, binding them together in a cheerful camaraderie whose joyful memories linger to this day. Beyond the fact that these men exhibited a decided literary genius, the single most important element of their friendship was, as Styron said, "a commonality of interest in the sense that we were both from south of the Mason-Dixon line" (Allen). Theirs was a mutual understanding that even though a generation separated them, they shared a unique Southern historical and cultural heritage that resisted the assault of modernity. This heritage defined a "way of thinking," a unique conservatism, that lay firmly rooted in feudalism, the code of chivalry, the ideal of the gentleman, and a particular religiousness that, according to Richard Weaver, "stands close to the historic religiousness of humanity. It is briefly, a sense of the inscrutable, which leaves one convinced of the existence of supernatural intelligence and power, and leads him to the acceptance of life as a mystery" (*Southern Tradition* 31-32).

Beyond this friendship, which enjoyed its share of tumult, Warren and Styron stayed true to their art. As Cleanth Brooks said in his book, *The Hidden God*, "The genuine artist presumably undertakes to set forth some vision of life—some imaginative apprehension of it which he hopes will engage our imagination. He gives us his own intuition—his own insight into the human situation" (2). For Warren and Styron, both of whom were "genuine artists," each with his distinctive style and force, the human condition represented not only disorder and anarchy, brought about by the exigencies of modernity, but also a search, sometimes sentimental, sometimes grotesque, for the restoration of the imagination.

While neither man claimed to be Christian, each may have been, as Flannery O'Connor once famously wrote, "Christ-haunted." That is, being raised in the South, they were environmentally imbued with the Christian tradition and, at the least, found certain aspects of the sundry doctrines propitious. It is, I think, instructive that both men were raised in Presbyterian households although neither family was particularly "churchy," as Warren once commented. Presbyterianism, at least its liberal version, had commenced the journey from ecclesial concerns to a more secular and intellectual worldview that reached its denouement with a successful effort to propel America into war with Germany in 1917 (See Gamble).

In the intellectual milieu in which they lived, Warren and Styron were constantly subjected to the ideologies and philosophies of their day: Marxism, liberalism, pragmatism, determinism, rationalism, and relativism. Considering these perfervid and alluring influences, it is quite remarkable that both men succeeded to the extent they did in recognizing and denouncing the deadening effects of modernity, the ultimate achievement of which was to establish a sterile, atheistic, humanism, to purge the world of the core doctrines of Western civilization, and to recast the individual as a rational automaton—a being devoid of soul and moral imagination.

Warren and Styron, through their literary art, were among the vanguard of American intellectuals who examined the stultifying effects of an inflexible secular orthodoxy that required the "displacement of God" in man's order of things and His replacement with the New Man. As Nietzsche illustrated, the "death of God" was required in order to bring forth the new man and free him from the bondage of two thousand years of Western culture, philosophy, and ethics. Man would thus be reduced to the nothingness of being, an entity defined by a materialistic and bourgeois society powered by the machine, technology, and technique (Tonsor 204-05). According to Cleanth Brooks, Warren "subjects the claims of twentieth-century man to the sternest testing and he is suspicious of the doctrine of progress and of the blandishments of utopianism" (99). For Styron, who was profoundly influenced by both William Faulkner and Warren, the problem was to develop his own style while retaining certain broad affinities with the men he admired. But his initial challenge with his first book, *Lie Down in Darkness*, was to examine the effects of modernity on the family. "I would also be able to anatomize bourgeois family life," Styron wrote, "of the kind I knew so well, the WASP world of the modern urban South" ("Recollections").

Although one is tempted to proclaim a Christian core at the center of their intellectual efforts, that is going a bit too far. Flannery O'Connor reminds us of the possibilities, the what-might-have-beens, when she writes that, "the chief difference between the novelist who is an orthodox Christian and the novelist who is merely a naturalist is that the Christian novelist lives in a larger universe. He believes that the natural world contains the supernatural" (146). For Red Warren and Bill Styron this would not do; they were far too pragmatic and rational. Still, the reader can find traces, perhaps a yearning, for that "older religiousness" that clung to them like a shadow on a summer's day.

I

Two events proved particularly providential in Red Warren's life. The first occurred when his ten-year-old brother, Tom, quite innocently, pitched a chunk of coal high over a nearby hedge. It happened to hit Red, who was lying on the grass on the other side, severely damaging his left eye (years later the eye had to be surgically removed). Because of the injury he would have to give up his recent appointment to the United States Naval Academy and accept his second choice, Vanderbilt (Blotner 30).

During his freshman year (1921), the sixteen-year-old prodigy found Vanderbilt to his liking. One of his professors was the former Rhodes scholar John Crowe Ransom, and one of his earliest friends was Andrew Lytle. As the school year advanced, he lost the nickname "Rob" and gained the sobriquet, "Red." His sophomore year he studied literature under Donald Davidson, who loaned Red and some of his other students a copy of a magazine that contained T. S. Eliot's newly published poem, *The Waste Land*. Incredibly, Red memorized the entire poem and considered it a "watershed" of his literary life. Red Warren was profoundly influenced by the most scintillating and abstract criticism of modernity ever written (Blotner 31-35).

Eliot wrote *The Waste Land* in the ideogrammic method, that is he juxtaposed historic events and personal memories without providing any discernible rhyme or reason. As Daniel Taylor observes: "[T]he reader is invited not to receive a predigested message but to participate in the creation of meaning" (42). Eliot's poem is a critique of modernity's decadence, its spiritual ennui, and cultural emptiness accomplished by mining historical consciousness and refusing to pander to the "scientific worldview." Cleanth Brooks thought that the poem was a "unified whole," in which various historic recollections provided a solid construction and an understanding of the poet's intention. Given Eliot's conversion to Christianity, five years after the poem was published, his Tory affiliations, Monarchist inclinations, and prose writings that stoutly defended not only the Christian faith but Western culture as well, it is obvious that Eliot rejected modernity's dehumanizing and deleterious effects on mankind (Williamson 214-15).

As a rational, pragmatic intellectual, Warren believed that the quest for truth was predicated on the need not only to understand the past, but to accept it as well. This "historical consciousness" was tied directly to his Southern origins, where men are raised on stories and anecdotes about their ancestors and neighbors, about their county, village, and state. The stories were a source of enjoyment for him. Growing up in a border state (Kentucky), he took a certain pride in knowing that his kith and kin were a hard-boned, straight-backed, and fiercely independent people. Red's grandfathers, Gabriel Penn and William Henry Harrison Warren, Jr., both served under the illustrious Bedford Nathan Forrest during the War Between the States.

Back at Vanderbilt for his junior year, Red was now fully involved with the Fugitives, a group of poetry aficionados that was initially composed of what Donald Davidson called "Southernized Jews and art-minded Gentiles." Red's education at Vanderbilt was a very good one; his education with the Fugitives was sublime. Soon they published a magazine, *The Fugitive*, and with Red as one of the sixteen editors. He was eighteen years old (Blotner 140-45). In 1930, after matriculating at Oxford for his B.Litt. degree, Warren received an invitation from his mentor, John Crowe Ransom, to write an essay on "ruralism as the salvation of the Negro." Ransom and Davidson were putting together a group of twelve essays in a book to be titled *I'll Take My Stand*. Fugitives wrote four of the essays, with the balance written by Southern intellectuals who had witnessed the adverse impact of industrialism and modernity on culture and hoped to spark a return to agrarianism in the South. However, their primary concern was that "industrialism" would be wedded to a virulent and pernicious statism that would together implement "the same economic system as that imposed by violence upon Russia in 1917." Davidson wanted Warren to write "an essay on the Negro," to "prove that Negroes are country folks—'bawn and bred in the briar-patch.'" He accepted (Blotner 105 and Winchell 285).

Warren's thesis, in his essay "The Briar Patch," was quite simple and mirrored the position of the vast majority of white America, circa 1930—that negroes should, indeed must, have the same opportunity for "equality" as whites, that they were "different but equal." He agreed with Booker T. Washington when Washington said, "that any man, regardless of color, will be recognized and rewarded just in proportion as he learns to do something well—learns to do it better than some one else—however humble that thing may be" (See Warren "Briar Patch" 250).

Admitting a lack of "justice" in the South, Warren writes: "It will be a happy day for the South when no court discriminates in its dealings between the negro and the white man"(252).

He explains why "industrialization" was taking place in the South, "The factory may have come to be near its requisite raw materials, but it has also come to profit from the cheap labor, black and white, which is to be had there." He goes on to argue that the negro's "mere presence is a tacit threat against the demands which white labor may later make of the factory owner" (256). Many Southerners must have seen Warren as radical in calling for negroes to be admitted to labor unions rather than serving as perpetual scabs during strikes. For Warren, however, there was only one way out of the racial calamity besetting the South (not to mention the North), and that was for the "white workman ... [to] learn, and his education may be as long and laborious as the negro's, ... that he may respect himself as a white man, but, if he fails to concede the negro equal protection, he does not properly respect himself as a man" (260).

Warren saw a possible solution to the racial dilemma not in the "industrialization" of the negro but in his finding a place in the small town and rural environment where, with the "poor white man," his hope for inclusion and equality might come to fruition. In the end Warren makes a prescient statement: "If the Southern white man feels that the agrarian life has a certain irreplaceable value in his society, and if he hopes to maintain its integrity in the face of industrialism or its dignity in the face of agricultural depression, he must find a place for the negro in his scheme." He concludes with the pithy metaphor, "Let the negro sit beneath his own vine and fig tree. The relation of the two [races] will not immediately escape friction and difference, but there is no reason to despair of their fate" (264).

Perhaps Warren's most significant achievement in "The Briar Patch" was his recognition of one of the most important causes for prejudice in the South—Reconstruction. Following the War Between the States, Reconstruction brought forth a federal army of occupation and a train of scalawags and carpetbaggers; the newly freed slave was their pawn, and they played him mercilessly. Blacks benefited from newly acquired voting rights, while the Confederate veteran found himself disenfranchised. Blacks were voted in and the white man took his place at the back of the line. The white Southerner would not forget. The negro "sadly mortgaged his best immediate capital," Warren wrote; ". . . that capital was the confidence of the Southern white man with whom he had to live. . . . Reconstruction badly impaired the white man's respect and gratitude. The rehabilitation of the white man's confidence for the negro is part of the Southern white man's story since 1880" (248). In the end, "The Briar Patch" became something of a millstone around Warren's neck. He abandoned his segregationist views, embraced integration, and proclaimed rather loudly his affection for and agreement with the Civil Rights Movement in general and Martin Luther King in particular. As Red's daughter, Rosanna observed, Robert Penn Warren "grew" (telephone interview).

II

Like all good writers, William Styron was an omnivorous reader, a habit that was encouraged when he enrolled in English 103, taught by Professor William Blackburn, late of the faculty of Duke University. Blackburn and Styron shared similar personality traits. They were "reserved and distant," and yet, through the talent displayed by the student and the teacher's ability to recognize and draw out that talent, the two assumed the role of mentor and pupil. Professor Blackburn's great gift to his fledgling freshman writer was the admonition that if he wanted to write, he must first read. Styron, to his credit, did just that, filling his mind with the classics: Thomas Mann, Marcel Proust, the Russians,

Conrad, Shakespeare, and the Elizabethans. Styron's success is rooted in the wisdom of this gentle Duke University professor (See West 93-109).

William Styron was as good a non-fiction writer as he was a novelist and storyteller. His essay on William Faulkner's funeral is written with a decided panache, conjuring a magic and mystery that draws the reader not only into Faulkner's private chambers but also into his family and life. Styron's moving and eloquent description of the great writer's funeral cortege, where white and negro "stand watching the procession in the blazing heat, in rows and groups and clusters, on all sides of the courthouse and along the sidewalks in front of Grundy's Café and Earl Fudge's Grocery and the Rebel Food Center," is given a decidedly Southern twist that Faulkner himself would have enjoyed, when Styron adds the aside of a native commentator: "But funerals are a big thing around here. Let the Baptist deacon die and you'll *really* get a turnout" (*Quiet Dust* 261-62).

Styron's essay on the death of his friend and fellow novelist, James Jones, a Midwesterner, sounds an elegiacal lament that discloses the writer's overwhelming grief; his loss becomes the reader's loss. "You were the most *American* writer of your generation," Styron wrote in tribute and in love (*Quiet Dust* 269). He recalled that they shared the great question, "What does it all mean?" both in ribald humor and in the earnest, nearly monish quest, for a solution to a mystery already revealed. Styron's grief upon visiting his friend at the hour of his death is simple, facile, and profound: "So, Jim, you found me out weeping for you in Mrs. Charlotte Ford Forstmann's elevator (*Quiet Dust* 268).

In late December of 1947, with the snow pounding against the basement windows of his Lexington Avenue apartment in New York and the ice covering street and stoop, William Styron, a "penniless" would-be writer, sat down to read Robert Penn Warren's *All the King's Men;* it was Styron's epiphany. "The book itself," he wrote, "was a revelation and gave me a shock to brain and spine like a freshet of icy water. I had of course read many novels before, including many of the greatest, but this powerful and complex story embedded in prose of such fire and masterful imagery—this, I thought with growing wonder, this was what a novel was all about, this was *it,* the bright book of life, what writing was supposed to be" (*Quiet Dust* 247). Warren's book propelled Styron to the typewriter to begin his career, "I began my first novel before that snow had melted; it is a book called *Lie Down in Darkness,* and in tone and style, as any fool can see, it is profoundly indebted to the work which so ravished my heart and mind during that long snowfall" (*Quiet Dust* 247-48).

III

William Styron and Robert Penn Warren met at the house of Van Wyck Brooks in Bridgewater, Connecticut, either in 1958 or 1959. There, friendship was "immediate" and pleasing. "He was everything I expected him to be," Styron said. "He was friendly, and outgoing and responsive and generous" (Allen). The friendship blossomed, and often when one or the other was enjoying a European vacation they exchanged letters. At the end of July, 1962, Styron sent Warren, who was vacationing with his family at Saint-Jean-de-Luz in the south of France, his account of William Faulkner's death. The essay had been commissioned by *Life* and had appeared in the July 20 issue. It was titled "As He Lay Dead, a Bitter Grief." "Thanks for the letter and article," Warren wrote in reply, "Your piece on Faulkner was extremely effective. A difficult thing, very well done. It has been circulated a little by hand here, and well received" (Duke, Sept. 1, 1962).¹

Warren was home by the first of the new year, and on January 21, 1963, he wrote Styron that if he "had no objections," he would propose him for membership in the Institute of Arts and Letters. Apparently, this was an effort on Warren's part to boost the literary prestige of his friend. However, something went amiss, and there seems to have been some hesitancy on the part of the Institute concerning Styron's proposed membership. "I honestly don't think the 'rejection' is 'embarrassing,'" Warren wrote to Styron on February 12, 1965, "though it made me God-damned sore. . . . I'm going to insist—or someone else will, whether you know it or not—on going ahead. Then you can do what Sinclair Lewis did, decline. Also, its [the institute] not entirely filled with shit-heels, broke-down book-reviewers, puff-artists, and hatchet-men" (Duke, Feb. 12, 1965).

In August of 1966, this time vacationing in France on the isle of Port Cros and in the company of novelist Shirley Hazzard and her husband, Francis Steegmuller, Warren sent Styron a chatty letter and a new poem, "Internal Injuries." The poem, realistic and powerful, tells the story of an elderly black woman struck down by a car. In a postscript Warren says, "I am sticking in a poem done this spring and summer, in the hope that you find it interesting. I am not setting up as the bard of the CR (Civil Rights) movement. This poem isn't even about that" (Duke, August 13, 1966).

A few months later, after he'd moved the family to Magagnosc, Warren penned a particularly moving letter to Styron and his wife: "You two—Bill and Rose—have made me very happy—not for the first time, I may say, and not only in the way I am about to describe—by being so kind about my poems, you, Bill about "Internal Injuries" and you, Rose about the book. There's nobody I'd rather have such kind words from, and I keep telling myself that you are both monuments of integrity and would make Cordelia sound like a flatterer. But I know, in my heart of hearts you are kind, too." He continues, switching to a favorite subject:

> It is great news, Bill, that Nat [Styron's Pulitzer Prize winning novel *The Confessions of Nat Turner*] is turning into the home stretch. Everything is right for this book, chiefly you, but it is the right moment historically, the right moment in your career, and the right literary context, by which I mean that nothing remotely like it, in material or method, is around, it will seem fresh, not a bit like *Naked Lunch*, or *The Group*, or *American Dream* or—to refer to the work of a real writer for a change—*Herzog*. Get it done. For one thing, I want to read it. (Duke, Nov. 28, 1966)

On February 16, 1967, Warren wrote to Styron that he'd just returned from giving a lecture at the University of Freiburg (Germany) and told him of meeting "an American named Rattner" who was writing a book about him and was holding up publication until *The Confessions of Nat Turner* was published. "Half the people I met at Freiburg asked about your work and you, student and profs," Red wrote, "There's a big back log of expectation for you and Nat" (Feb. 16, 1967). Late in March the two families rendezvoused in Cairo where the required lectures and readings were given at the American University. Then, with their obligations met, they journeyed on a wonderful trip up the Nile. "Fighting fleas and gnats and drinking literally tank cars full of Evian water," Bill Styron said. "And plus a little whiskey on the side" (Blotner 371, Allen).

Upon his return home, Styron sent Warren a copy of his *Confessions of Nat Turner* as soon as it became available. On June 8, while continuing at Magagnosc, Warren wrote his personal review for the author:

> Last night I finished Nat. It is terrific! I lay awake in the night thinking about it—a great experience. The book has the real paradoxical qualities of tragedy in it—that mixture of simplicity and innocence on one hand and depth of subtle implication on the other. And the narrative drive is irresistible—simple thrust of action with the delicate pauses, shifts, delays, and moments of inwardness. It is remarkable how you make the inwardness of Nat become, in itself, a matter of suspense, an integral part of the action and the thrust. There are dozens of great moments. The new sense of Travis that Nat has at the moment he sees the face for the first time—the moment before the murder. The death of the girl is so bold and moving and simple—a stroke of genius. (You'll catch a little hell from some quarters about the girl motif—but shit on 'em.) The final effect, the very end of the book couldn't be better. Everything pays off. That last bit about Mark—a fine stroke, it opens the book to a new feeling outside of Nat's involutions.

Warren was not only delighted with the book but with the author as well: "Bill, I'm so proud of you, and no crap. You have done it. Anybody who starts talking about the death of the novel now is going to be out on a limb. One more thing, this book has a certain scale and dimension of human feeling, a sense of the significance of experience as something different from scab-scratching—it's a new kind of novel, for our period, I mean" (Duke, June 8, 1967).

The Confessions of Nat Turner was not met with universal approbation. The most serious attack was launched in a book titled *William Styron's Nat Turner: Ten Black Writers Respond* published in August, 1968. "To anyone educated to observe basic standards of logic and decorum," Styron's biographer, James West III wrote, "*Ten Black Writers* is an appallingly poor performance. Many of the essays are based on shaky scholarship, and most are flawed by emotionalism, some of it theatrical" (386). "Theatrical" or not, *Ten Black Writers* produced enough heat to get certain tentative, one might say intimidated, critics to retract their positive reviews of Styron's *Nat Turner*. However, Red Warren was not on the sidelines. "Thanks for the mare's nest of a book by the Black Power people on Nat," he wrote on August 20. "It is a mare's nest. Of illogic, anguish, and God knows what else" (Duke, August 20, 1968).

The literary and sociological war over Nat Turner reached its denouement on November 6, 1968, when Styron appeared on a panel at the Southern Historical Association meeting held in New Orleans. Alongside him were his friends, Red Warren, and the famous black writer, Ralph Ellison. C. Van Woodward acted as moderator. Each gave a talk about the relationship of history and literature and then "offered further comments, most of them centering on *The Confessions of Nat Turner*." During the question and answer period a Black activist who'd questioned him during a similar gathering in Massachusetts the past summer confronted Styron. The confrontation was heated and insulting and in the end Styron said, "We're at an impasse, my friend." Following the Southern Historical Association meeting Styron withdrew, for a time, from the public square (West 393-95).

During the 1960s the Styrons often traveled to Warren's home in West Wardsboro, Vermont. There they would visit for a weekend and, on some occasions, a week. Neither man skied, so they traveled by snowshoe and spent hours by the fire (Warren took a certain pleasure in "getting in the wood" at his Vermont home) talking and imbibing. Styron has admitted abusing the hair-of-the-dog but declared he was no alcoholic. Warren drank as well, but the novelist Shirley Hazzard said that in all the years she knew him she never saw him drunk: "He never, never was out of control in any way" (Hazzard).

IV

The Warren / Styron friendship, and particularly the friendship between the families, suffered a severe setback some time in the late 1970s. The Warrens gave annual parties, usually a couple of weeks before Christmas. These were black tie affairs, and Warren reveled in the wine, music, and good company. One such occasion included a wide range of friends from academia and the literary world—notable writers, poets, editors, and publishers. Bill Styron happened to be at one end of the dinner table among a group of guests, including Harold Bloom. Bloom "was telling everyone within hearing that Warren should quit writing novels and stick to poetry. The novels were not very good and the poetry was good." Styron considered Bloom to be "terribly rude to say such things at the host's dinner table" and he rose to Warren's defense, "just as loud and direct as [Bloom] had been" (Hackney).

Apparently, some time after this clash, Styron was conversing with Albert Erskine's wife, Marisa. They were talking about his latest novel, soon to be published, *Sophie's Choice*. During the conversation Bloom walked over to Styron to engage him in conversation, but Styron refused to be interrupted and continued to talk with Mrs. Erskine. After a few moments, Bloom left the table and "went upstairs." Mrs. Erskine, who must not have heard the earlier confrontation said: "I don't think anyone at the table even noticed" (Erskine). The only mention of this fracture in Blotner's biography of Warren reads: "But after a time, to Styron's great sadness, the two couples no longer saw each other. Bill thought [that Red's wife] Eleanor had been offended somehow and that they had been walled out" (410).

The incident may reveal Bloom's affection and admiration for Warren. Perhaps he made his comments in the hope of persuading Warren to pursue what he considered a more advantageous course at this stage of his career. While we may question his method, speaking at the dinner table before a group of guests rather than privately with Warren, there is no question of Bloom's fondness for Warren. Likewise, Styron's defense of his old friend mirrors a distinctly Southern cultural trait, the ideal of the "gentleman," and reveals a close and enduring friendship that had a profound effect upon the lives and the art of both men.

Friends and family members have said that the two men continued their friendship, but Warren's letters sent to Styron located in the Duke University Rare Book, Manuscript, and Special Library stop after a letter dated, May 27, 1979. The letter itself may reveal the year of the contretemps:

> I am delighted to see the start that your book [*Sophie's Choice*] is getting, and I know that this is only the beginning. I am, God knows, not surprised, for long back I became convinced that you belong in only one place—the top bracket of the American writers of our time. But enough of that. You know what I think, anyway. But "of our time" may turn out to be only a minimum.... But the fact that we can't come to your party of celebration arises from something else. I seem

to have a slight infection of the bladder (as I had once years ago), and that means no alcohol and early to bed for a month or so.

V

For the "real" Southerner, at least that Southerner of an aesthetic, historical, or literary bent, there are two underlying themes related to the nature of man. Richard Weaver brilliantly illustrated these themes in his seminal study, *The Southern Tradition at Bay*. The first is the idea of self-denial, gleaned from a remembered history that included the sacrifice and suffering of total war and the obliteration of the Southern homeland. It must be remembered that the Southern people struggled through a prolonged period of self-restoration that required a sacrifice and a self-denial that carried with it the marks of redemption. The second is tragedy, that fundamental component that links intellect to spirit, providing an opportunity truly to accept nature and live in the mystery of God.

William Styron was a humanist, absorbed in his own time and place, which was not meant to detract from his literary art or his mastery of language. Styron's concern was with social justice, arising from his Southern roots, its associated racial guilt, and his appreciation for the Greek concept of tragedy—all themes that mirror the "unsentimental sentiments" of Southern culture. He was present during the faux-revolution of the New Left celebrated on the streets of Chicago during the 1968 Democratic National Convention, visited the Soviet Union in 1968, and served as a witness for Abbie Hoffman during the trial for the Chicago 7 (West 389-91, 395).

Eschewing Christianity, Styron's intellectual roots can be traced to the skepticism of certain Southern aristocrats following the French Revolution. Jefferson with his Deism and rationalism is the best example but this skepticism also flourished among a small coterie of the wealthy and educated until 1830 (See Weaver 91-92). Avoiding Faulkner's recognition of the South's "older religiousness," Styron, then, was condemned to follow the well-worn path of his Northern, nihilistic, literary contemporaries in a poignant and relentless search for "the meaning of man." It is a search that has produced a plethora of literary characters, victims of a bourgeois, technological society that has cast God aside and conjured a convoluted order that "transcends a providentially ordered history" (Tonsor 204).

Red Warren too, shared in the great metaphysical quest. At the age of seventy-five Red was "willing to tackle some of the eternal questions," and provide some insight into his thoughts, "'I think a man just dies,' he says, "No heaven, No hell…I'm a naturalist. I don't believe in God. But I want to find meaning in life" (Blotner 450). Red's daughter, Rosanna, relates a heartfelt observation she made as a young adult: "I was so aware of these great dark spaces that Pa had inside him, his melancholia." She recalls her father's denunciation of Emerson ("that optimism that he thought cut against reality") and his ambivalence toward "'that very old God,' an Old Testament God he hates but respects" (Blotner 373). And she remembers one of her father's favorite phrases, "Original Sin." It was a term she heard over and over again, "That was pounded into my ears. He was constantly joking about it, but it meant he believed in it."

Warren's genius is his acceptance of "Original Sin." How else can man begin to define himself, to know the essential nature of his own being? Cleanth Brooks said, "Dedication to his art . . . would not necessarily bring the artist to Christianity. It would be foolish to claim *that*. But dedication to his art may well protect the artist from some of the deceptions endemic to our time" (99). Warren, then, knew and wrote of modernity's decline. He weighed his time and found it wanting. He was born and raised in an era when the "Christian component" played a very real part in the drama of mankind; he experienced, first hand, the sentiments of the South. As he went through his life, that component began to unravel—the transcendentals were mocked, belittled, and extirpated. Man was left to rationalize and reorder the modern world, to "desacralize time" which resulted in an endless and purposeless cycle, the "abomination of desolation."

Both Warren and Styron are the products of what Weaver called "the last non-materialist civilization of the Western World," the American South. Their literature—their art—describe the decline of society, an annihilation of culture. It also projects a knowledge of the eternal struggle, forever bound by memory and the inherent yearning for a civilization that "is the refuge of sentiments and values, of spiritual congeniality, of belief in the word, of reverence for symbolism, whose existence haunts the nation" (*Southern Tradition* 275).

Note

1. From a collection of twenty-seven letters and poems sent by Robert Penn Warren to William Styron, which are housed at the Duke University Rare Book, Manuscript, and Special Collections Library. These will be cited parenthetically in the text by date.

Works Cited

Allen, Susan. Interview with William Styron. May 5, 1980.
Blotner, Joseph. *Robert Penn Warren: A Biography*. New York: Random House, 1997.
Brooks, Cleanth. *The Hidden God: Studies in Hemingway, Faulkner, Yeats, Eliot, and Warren*. New Haven: Yale UP, 1963.
Erskine, Marisa. Personal interview. Sept. 12, 2005.
Gamble, Richard. *The War for Righteousness*. Wilmington Delaware: Intercollegiate Studies Institute, 2003.
Hackney, Sheldon. Personal interview, Sept. 25, 2005.
Hazzard, Shirley. Telephone interview with the Author. August 16, 2005.
O'Connor, Flannery. *Mystery and Manners*. Eds. Sally and Robert Fitzgerald. New York: Farrar, Straus, & Giroux, 1974.
Styron, William. "Recollections of a Once Timid Novelist." *Hartford Courant*. Jan. 3, 1992.
———. *This Quiet Dust*. New York: Random House, 1982.
Taylor, Daniel. "Living with the Big Poem." *Books and Culture: A Christian Review*. September 2005: 42-43.
Tonsor, Stephen. *Equality, Decadence, and Modernity*. Wilmington, Delaware: Intercollegiate Studies Institute, 2005.
Warren, Rosanna. Telephone Interview with the Author. August 17, 2005.
Warren, Robert Penn. "The Briar Patch." In Twelve Southerners. *I'll Take My Stand: The South and the Agrarian Tradition*. New York: Harper & Brothers, 1930. 246-64.
West, James L. III. *William Styron: A Life*. New York: Random House, 1998.
Weaver, Richard M. *The Southern Tradition at Bay: A History of Postbellum Thought*. Chicago: Regnery Gateway, 1989.
Williamson, Chilton, Jr. *The Conservative Bookshelf*. New York: Citadel, 2004.
Winchell, Mark Royden. *Where No Flag Flies: Donald Davidson and the Southern Resistance*. Columbia: U of Missouri P, 2000.

Modern Primitives: Mergings in the Poetry of Robert Penn Warren and James Dickey

by Daniel Cross Turner

Nature is but an image or imitation of wisdom, the last thing of the soul; nature being a thing which doth only do, but not know.
                                                    Plotinus (205?-270?)

The biographical and aesthetic intersections between Robert Penn Warren and James Dickey are many and deep. Both held degrees from Vanderbilt University, with Warren earning his Bachelor of Arts in 1925 and Dickey completing a Bachelor as well as a Master of Arts at the Nashville institution in 1949 and 1950, respectively. On a broader scale, both the Kentucky-born Warren and the Georgia-reared Dickey were sons of the South, growing up in view of the general Southern history of racial segregation, socioeconomic deprivation, and cultural "backwardness." Both were novelists of note, with Warren's *All the King's Men* (1946) winning the Pulitzer Prize and Dickey's *Deliverance* (1970) becoming a national best-seller, and both novels being converted into successful film versions. They were also of course two of the best known and most prolific poets in America during their lifetimes. Among myriad other honors, Warren earned two Pulitzers for his later poetry and was named the first poet laureate of the United States in 1985. Despite a decade-long hiatus from writing poetry in the 1940s and early 1950s, Warren distinguished himself as one of the most productive and wide-ranging poets of the twentieth century.

For his part, Dickey earned a National Book Award for *Buckdancer's Choice* in 1966 and was appointed poetry consultant at the Library of Congress from 1966-68. Although his collecting of poetry prizes dropped off after these notable early honors, this was perhaps largely the result, as critic Ernest Suarez has argued, of Dickey's conservative political stances. Warren and Dickey were impressed with one another's work, and each one's poetry bears the mark of the other. Each poet dedicated at least one work to his counterpart: Dickey honored Warren with "Under Buzzards" (1968)—writing his fellow craftsman that he felt "some root-deep kind of affinity with [Warren's] poetic effort" (Bruccoli 281)—and Warren returned the favor with "Rattlesnake Country" (1973) and *Chief Joseph of the Nez Perce* (1982). Dickey read the sweeping final section of *Audubon: A Vision* (1969) as the eulogy at the funeral of his first wife Maxine, explaining this choice in a 1980 letter to Warren: "I could think of nothing of my own so fitting, or so likely to last, or to hang longer in the bearded oaks of Waccamaw Cemetery, at Litchfield, where we were all together" (Bruccoli 389). Warren and Dickey shared a long personal friendship and were even filmed together in Connecticut and South Carolina as the subjects of a CBS documentary titled *Two Poets, Two Friends* in 1982.

Deborah Dickey, James Dickey's widow, was generous enough to share with me some stories about her husband's friendship with Warren. In particular, she recalled that Warren was the first great writer she had met (besides of course her husband) when Dickey introduced her during a visit to Washington, D.C., soon after they were married in December 1976. At only twenty-four years old, she was self-conscious about meeting a man admired greatly by her husband. She remembered Warren as "very sweet, very kind—a wonderful old Southern gentleman," who took pains to make her feel at ease. At a later encounter at the American Academy of Poets, she informed Warren that she and James had quit drinking nine months before. In his thoroughly gracious manner, Warren replied in his rich Kentucky drawl that, as he had gotten older, he had noticed that after his evening cocktail "a terrible torpor" often came over him. Warren also sent along a memorable note to the Dickeys upon the birth of their daughter Bronwen, telling them that he was sure that they were "still examining the new creature, finger by finger." Her last memories of her husband and Warren together were when they were at the Dickeys' house on Pawley's Island, South Carolina, during the filming of *Two Poets, Two Friends*. She regrets that she was not able to take better care of them then, since they were both beginning to show their age.

As modern primitivist poets, Warren and Dickey were interested in forging an original relation of the self to the underlying rhythms of the natural world. Although the terms used here invoke the language of Emerson's famous search for an "original relation" of self to universe in *Nature* (1836), primitive metaphysics diverge significantly from Emerson's ideas in at least two respects: (a) although modern primitivist poets focus on renewal through the individual's fuller integration into the workings of the natural realm—even at times extending to the level of mystical transcendence—they also emphasize the necessary role of the violence inherent in nature to the process of human as well as natural regeneration, and (b) the primitivist definition of the human relation to the universe is original not so much in the sense that it originates with the individual's imaginative consciousness, as for Emerson, but in the sense that immersion of the self into the natural world enables reconnection to a collective human past, to a kind of instinctual memory that reunites the modern individual with his primitive origins.

This impulse is what Casey Clabough has aptly described in *Elements: The Novels of James Dickey* (2002) as the phenomenon of "merging": the assumption of the individual into the essence of nature, producing a kind of energized fugue state when unconsciousness takes over. Although both Warren and Dickey were deeply involved with modern primitivist thought, Dickey's work typically exploits such primal returns as an escape from the social realm, whereas Warren is more often concerned with the political dimensions of primitivism. Dickey views the primitive as a denial of history; Warren uses it as a means for historical confrontation.[1]

In his earlier poems, Dickey manipulates incantatory rhythms and ritualistic repetitions in order to articulate a willful denial of the ultimate contingency of human existence. These techniques underlie his attempt to counter the loss of stable definitions of individual and collective identity in the postwar era by espousing primitive transcendence in his verse. Though fully aware of the existential predicament—a concept given not merely philosophical but personal significance through his experience as a bombardier in World War II[2]—he attempts to lend some kind of temporary permanence to existence by merging with primal nature.

Perhaps the quintessential manifestation of Dickey's poetic primitivism is "The Heaven of Animals" (1962), a poem that delivers on its titular promise by offering a primal vision of a starkly animalistic heaven. This bestial Eden reflects a level of undivided consciousness where the Adamic power to name holds no sway. In *The Immense Journey* (1957), Loren Eiseley offers a literal-minded interpretation of the mythic fall in the Garden. The fall of man was the fall into consciousness, into imagination, into the capacity to dream other realities beyond the present: "The Eden of the eternal present that the animal world had known for ages was shattered at last. Through the human mind, time and darkness, good and evil, would enter and possess the world" (120). Eiseley provides a description of the evolutionary shift in human biology (the enlargement of the brain) that created the mythic fall away from instinctual reliance on the rhythms of nature and into a fully conscious state—a fall away from a preconscious integration with the things of the world into the symbolic use of language:

> [Man] was becoming something the world had never seen before—a dream animal—living at least partially within a secret universe of his own creation and sharing that secret universe in his head with other, similar heads. Symbolic communication had begun. Man had escaped out of the eternal present of the animal world into a knowledge of past and future. The unseen gods, the powers behind the world of phenomenal appearance, began to stalk through his dreams. (120)

In "The Heaven of Animals," Dickey attempts through adept manipulation of symbolic language to return us to a time before symbols, before the rise of consciousness when, like animals, humans were motivated wholly by instinct. The poet's implicit faith in the power of imagination is ironic since it is the imagination itself that condemns man to awareness of time and death, of possibilities other than present actualities. The conscious ability to imagine a better condition—and ultimately a life without death—is exercised by the poet in this instance to create an ideal set of conditions, not for humans, but for animals. Paradoxically, Dickey creates a heaven that is marked by its earthiness:

> Here they are. The soft eyes open.
> If they have lived in a wood
> It is a wood.
> If they have lived on plains
> It is grass rolling
> Under their feet forever. (78-79)

This heaven is not a blanched-out abstraction, replete with disembodied souls plucking out celestial harmonies on golden harp-strings, but a place where the preconscious instincts of animals can "wholly bloom" (79). That the full realization of these instinctual drives involves violence and death is an inevitability, for "It could not be the place / It is, without blood" (79). Even those animals marked forevermore as prey acquiesce in full compliance with the natural order, "Fulfilling themselves without pain / At the cycle's center" (79). The poem's rhythmic repetitions underscore these verbal reiterations, imbuing the poem with a sense of heavy-handed fixity, and the decided stresses evoke an almost shamanistic cadence. Dave Smith notes that Dickey's early style reflects "the slow and steady development of the dense, drummingly cadenced poem that was intensely personal and privately imagistic in statemental lines alternately composed of kinetic verbals and mystic assertions with the present tense" (171).

Robert Kirschten further describes Dickey's "preference for marchlike anapests—hypnotic, compulsive, primitive" (37) and suggests that his "rhythmic music conveys the persistent power of his principles by constituting a recurrent ground rhythm that itself seems magically independent of the speaker" (37). In "The Heaven of Animals," sound and sense, like the paradisal predators and prey, seem bound together in unalterable blood marriage. The initial statement of the poem, "Here they are," announces the fixity of the cycle of violence and renewal, as it forcefully declares the whereabouts of all the animals, leaving no place for the reader to imagine them elsewhere; we, like the animals, seem to be stuck in the eternal present. There is no space for imagination, a human liability. Here, without question, whatever is is right. This sense of permanence is seen again in the repetition of particular words or phrases (e.g., "The soft eyes open," "Outdoing," "It is") and in the repetition of like rhythms throughout the poem.

The centrality of the phenomenon of savage violence and renewal to Dickey's sense of primitive essentialism is evident in the permanence of the natural order fulfilled by the animals and in the inescapability of each animal's instinctual role. As Thom Gunn notes in his review of *Drowning with Others*, the poem expresses "an almost feudal vision of order: The hunted are as satisfied with their place in creation as the hunters; they are part of 'the cycle'" (14). The final stanza merges form to content, as the rhythmic repetition shadows the fixed repetition of the primitive cycle of predators and prey:

> At the cycle's center
> They tremble, they walk
> Under the tree,
> They fall, they are torn,
> They rise, they walk again. (79)[3]

That all of the animals, predators as well as their victims, fully embrace this pattern is emphasized by the repetition of active verbs in the final stanza. Even though it describes the victimage of the hunted animals, it contains only one passive verb ("they are torn"); the predominance of active verbs suggests that completing their instinctual role as victims is not a mark of their sheer passivity, but is the active fulfillment of the primary and pre-ordained reason for their existence.

Although these animals have no souls and have come here "beyond their knowing," they are later described as existing "in full knowledge" of their condition. This apparent contradiction alludes to the implications of the Eden myth and signals the divide between human experience and that of preconscious animals. The animals designated as prey are rewarded by walking "Under such trees in full knowledge / Of what is in glory above them" (79). According to the myth of Eden, full knowledge of good and evil led to human awareness of guilt and regret. By contrast, the only kind of "knowledge" the animals experience is purely instinctual. As a result, they are able to kill without remorse and to die without regret, each in its ordered place. If this arrangement is translated into the human realm, it starts to resemble—chillingly—the politics of social Darwinism. Kept safely out in the primitive netherworld, however, the poem represents a fantasy of returning to a preconscious state of being, of reconnecting to the primal reservoir of our collective origin, of remembering our instincts. Yet the poem itself cannot effect such a return; it can only approximate this experience, and the reconstruction will always be tainted by the intrusion of the rational, conscious mind. That is, there are both conscious and unconscious elements at work in Dickey's poetic description of the heaven of animals, which is the product of the poet's highly conscious arrangement of materials drawn from the realm of the unconscious, such as the ostensibly "primal" rhythms and the recurrence of archetypal images.

Although a number of Warren's poems would fit neatly alongside "The Heaven of Animals" as depictions of escapes into a primitive otherworld ("Rattlesnake Country," "Red-Tail Hawk and Pyre of Youth," "Heart of Autumn," and arguably even *Audubon: A Vision* would meet this description[4]), much of Warren's poetry is intensely interested in the friction between primal nature and cultural nurture. Nowhere is this friction more apparent—or more shockingly imparted—than in *Brother to Dragons* (1953; 1979).[5] To invoke Warren's description of the emergence of fascism, this volume-length narrative poem reveals the unmasking of a blank oblivion of power. In *Brother to Dragons*, modern primitivism takes the historical turn, posing the question: if the primal impulse is an implacable part of the modern unconscious, personal and collective, then how do we confront the social and political problem of primitivism?

The volume recounts the story of two of Thomas Jefferson's nephews, Lilburne and Isham Lewis, who had removed themselves from Virginia to establish a plantation on the western Kentucky frontier. After their mother, Jefferson's sister Lucy, passed away and was buried in Kentucky, their father Charles returned to Virginia and left the plantation for Lilburne to manage. Falling into alcoholism and marital troubles with his second wife, named Letitia, Lilburne became increasingly harsh in his treatment of his slaves. One young slave named George (renamed "John" in the 1979 version) seemed particularly to draw Lilburne's ire. On the night of December 15, 1811, while a series of severe earthquakes shook the territory, even causing the Mississippi River to flow backward momentarily, Lilburne and Isham had the slave tied to a table in the meat-house and hacked him to death with an axe, casting his mutilated body parts into a roaring fire before the eyes of the other slaves. The supposed reason for this brutality was that the slave had broken a favorite pitcher of Lilburne and Isham's dead mother. Eventually news spread about the murder (a fire-blackened bone was discovered, having been sniffed out and gnawed by a curious hound), and the brothers were arrested and indicted. After they were released on bail, Lilburne convinced his younger brother to engage in a suicide pact, according to which each brother would fire a fatal shot simultaneously into the other. Things did not go according to plan, with Lilburne being killed, while his brother survived unscathed. Isham was taken into custody again but escaped and fled before being brought to trial. There were reports that he was killed while serving under Andrew Jackson at the Battle of New Orleans. As Warren himself noted in a 1953 letter explaining the genesis of his poem, "the story is a shocker" (Robert Penn Warren Papers).

According to Warren's version of this real-life horror story, Lilburne plays the part of the primitive monster revealed. Isham is the incompetent, but doggedly loyal younger brother who is pliable to Lilburne's direction. John is given only a few lines; he is less a character in his own right than a vehicle for demonstrating the stark irrationality of the slaveholding mentality. Even in light of his famous statement about the poetic quality of historical representation in the foreword, Warren takes considerable poetic license in adding and inventing characters, most notably the figure of Jefferson and an ironic stand-in for the poet himself, aptly named R.P.W, who serves as a kind of meta-narrator for the poem, Warren's fictive doppelgänger. Jefferson is depicted as naive and is made complicit in his nephews' murder of the slave for believing too much his own Enlightenment principles, which, by poem's end, have been reduced to nothing more than the rotting corpse of a long-buried ideology. The other additions of note are Aunt Cat, Lilburne's former wet-nurse and a stereotypical "Black mammy" figure, and Meriwether Lewis, of Lewis and Clark fame and another of Jefferson's kin. The figure of Meriwether Lewis brings to light the issue of manifest destiny in the territorialization of the American frontier, and his suicide provides another graphic spectacle that returns to haunt Jefferson. All the characters are long dead, gathered together again in a psychically tortuous afterlife.

Although the poem is set in "no place" and at "any time," there is continuous tension between the "eternal" time of instinctual memory and the historically bound brutalities we are made to witness. Warren's brand of historicized primitivism is announced early as one of the poem's major themes, as he positions his depictions of unleashed primal savagery squarely in the realm of American and Southern history. In one of their initial conversations, R.P.W. interrupts Jefferson to give his description of the fall of the literal house of Lewis, a landscape replete with the remains of an undying familial and regional past:

> R.P.W.: Yes, I have seen it. Or saw,
> Rather, all that remained when time and fire
> Had long since done their kindness, and the crime
> Could nestle, smug and snug, in any
> Comfortable conscience, such as mine—or the next man's—
> And over the black stones the rain
> Has fallen, falls, with the benign indifferency
> Of the historical imagination, while grass,
> In idiot innocence, has fingered all to peace.
> Anyway, I saw the house— (9)

As it turns out, the "historical imagination" is not so benign, nor indifferent. Nature may forget, but human memory is not yet done with this place. The historical primitive is reiterated through the figure of the black snake that haunts the ruins of the Lewis estate. This primal, yet historical serpent is encountered by R.P.W. and his father as they make a field trip to view the remains of the former plantation's bloodstained past:

> Well, standing there, I'd felt, I guess, the first
> Faint tremor of that natural chill, but then,
> In some deep aperture among the stones,
> I saw the eyes, their glitter in that dark,
> And suddenly the head thrust forth, and the fat, black
> Body, molten, out-flowed as though those stones
> Bled forth earth's inner darkness to the day—
> As though the bung had broke on that intolerable inwardness. (24)

Though the snake is literally nothing more than "just a snake, / Black Snake, Black Pilot Snake, the Mountain Blacksnake, / Hog-snout or Chicken Snake" (25), it irrepressibly takes on symbolic meaning as a figure combining the primitive ("the black lust all men fear and long for") with the political ("spirit of the nigger boy named John, / Whose anguish spangled midnight once like stars") (25). Thus, the serpent's primal form, "the ictus of horror," converts R.P.W.'s "natural tremor of fatigue" into "the metaphysical chill, and [his] soul / Sat in [his] hand and could not move" (24). It is perhaps wishful thinking on R.P.W.'s part that the snake offers a kind of *quid pro quo* absolution to its human intruders, past and present, "As though it understood our human limitation, / And forgave all, and asked forgiveness, too" (25), apologizing for the shared darkness of the reptile brain. However, as communicative, self-conscious "dream animals," humans, though equally marked by primal impulses, must accept the existential limitations of judgment and responsibility; as the subsequent narrative of Lilburne's murder of John makes clear, human action carries with it social liability. The serpent does not exist wholly in a primitive netherworld, but is set in a recognized time and place and is therefore historically bound to the ruins of Southern history, physically embodied in the plantation's ruins. Its black skin metonymically plays on the recurrent figures of blackness throughout the volume, as moral blackness becomes intertwined inextricably with violently enforced racial divisions, the blackness of the human heart with that of human skin.

This connection is made clear in Warren's depiction of Lilburne, which shows that his primitive will to power is expressed within the historical context of chattel slavery, for his primal urges are fired and channeled through his own abject fears of contamination by contact with his slaves. In the wake of his mother's death, he begins to consider the servants as an intolerable threat to her good memory and responds by overmastering his slaves beyond the bounds of "rational" (i.e., socially sanctioned) master-slave relations. This leads to a vehement form of primal regression on Lilburne's part that culminates in the brutal spectacle of John's death. In his notes for the poem, Warren describes Lilburne's failed attempt to reject his "dark self":

> If Lilburn killed George [John] because he saw in the Negro the "black parody" ...& the dark "self" to be expurgated—(ie a purified & therefore an "ideal" act perverted)—then Jefferson's repudiation of Lilburn is a parallel crime—that is, an attempt to purify "the self" by exclusion, suppression, not by "love," ie absorption— "Evil" the "food of good"—eat it assimilate it, love it (Robert Penn Warren Papers)

The image of darkness doubles as a sign of Lilburne's repressed primal nature, his attraction to antisocial sexuality and violence, as well as his attempted rejection of his connection with his Black slaves. Indeed, after he hears of the death of his mother, he tells Aunt Cat that he would spit out her breast milk in order to spit back out "all her niggerness" (98). He thus performs "the old charade where man dreams man can put down / The objectified bad and then feel good" (21). This charade is the "sadistic farce whereby the world is cleansed," though all the while "in the deep / Hovel of the heart the Thing lies / That will never unkennel himself to the contemptible steel" (30).

According to Warren, primal savagery is inextricable from the work of the historical imagination: the Thing may "never unkennel himself to the contemptible steel," but its darkness must be acknowledged through historical reflection. In the concluding section of *Brother to Dragons*, R.P.W. returns in wintertime to the plantation house ruins, remembering the figure of the serpent among the ruins, this time marking its absence as "winter makes things small, all things draw in" (129) and noting the inaccuracies of his earlier view of the place:

> I had plain misremembered,
> Or dreamed a world appropriate for the tale.
> One thing, however, true: old *obsoleta*
> Had reared that day, and swayed against the sun.
> But not today. He's keeping home this weather,
> Down in the rocks, I reckon, looped and snug
> And dark as dark: in dark the white belly glows,
> And deep behind the hog-snout, in that blunt head,
> The ganglia glow with what cold dream is congenial
> To fat old *obsoleta*, winterlong. (129)

The fact that the snake is in hibernation suggests something for hope at poem's end. Although the "cold dream" of primitivism may be "congenial" to the human condition, this image of a "looped and snug" serpent buried deep beneath the rocks implies the possibility of temporarily containing our collective impulse towards unleashing the primal drive to power, "dark as dark."

The final passages of *Brother to Dragons* reveal some hope of living with the confirmation of our darker drives, of sublimating these at least partially into the social and legal restraints of liability, as R.P.W. crosses the evening barnlot, opens the sagging gate, and prepares himself "To go into the world of action and liability" (132). It is no accident that Warren invokes the legal term "liability" in these final lines, since here and elsewhere in the volume he suggests that our effort to draw in the primitive rests in the strength of collective responsibility and the bonds of law, which have at least the potential to construct and enforce "a world / Sweeter than hope in that confirmation of late light" (132). Although no ledger "in the great bookkeeping / Of History" (127) has balanced yet, there is still the human duty to keep strict account of "the dark audit of blood" (127).[6] The law may well be a means of performing the old charade of objectifying good and bad, yet this social act of rationalizing human conscience into codes of action and liability is the only way to contain for the time being the violence of our instinctual nature and therefore to purge our history momentarily of blood.

Warren and Dickey, two poets and two friends, shared a sustained interest in the philosophical argument of modern primitivism. While both accepted the primal underpinnings of human nature, Dickey offers instinctual memory as an escape from the pressures of modernity, while Warren exploits images of the primitive as a means of engaging himself with the recurrent savagery of our historical conditions. Even if modern primitivist poetry could enable us to enter fully into a preconscious state and erase the divide between instinctual experience and the conscious rearrangement of poetic form, it could offer us only temporary reprieve. In the concluding pages of *James Dickey and the Politics of Canon*, Ernest Suarez wonders whether Dickey had not been disappointed that in all his years he had not experienced "revelation, some kind of Old Testament vision, that he expected his poetry or his life to yield, and that would allow him to deliver the 'immortal message to mankind' he spoke of in *Sorties*" (157). He poses the question to Dickey, then in his late sixties, by invoking the final lines of "Circuit" from *The Eagle's Mile* (1990) and asking why the poem ends not with a confirmation of "meaning, consequence, [and] a positive assessment of the savage ideal" (158), but with an "expression of desire" (158), the hope, left unanswered, for revelation and transcendence. Dickey responds with a sincere acknowledgment of the limits of his modern primitivist art: "Because those things can't happen" (158).

Ultimately, Dickey confesses that primitive transcendence is one of those things that can't happen, but the magnitude of the creative force with which this lie is told contains its value. By contrast, much of Warren's work suggests that primitivism presents a means not of escaping, but of confronting the historical cycle of violence. For Warren, instinctual memory is not an avenue for mystical transcendence; rather, he is more blunt than Dickey in his assessment that primitivism is a symptom of, not a cure for our historical condition. To turn the phrase of Plotinus that serves as epigraph for this article, Warren contends that human nature must be a thing which doth do *and* know. History is blind, but man is not.

Notes

1. Dickey himself noted Warren's penchant for history in a 1954 letter to Andrew Lytle. Dickey suggests parallels between the historical concerns evident in both Lytle's and Warren's work:
   "Do you like [Warren's] work? I very much do. "History is blind, but man is not," Warren writes in *All the King's Men*. Critics have not said much about this side of Warren, but it seems to me to be the central preoccupation of all his work to define and evaluate the past. That is, can we see in certain happenings behind us, on which we have a kind of perspective, symbolic patterns? If so, what are their value to us? How can this be assimilated to our lives?" (Bruccoli 63).

2. Dickey was a radar specialist during World War II, not a pilot, as he sometimes claimed. In fact, he washed out of flight training. Like Faulkner, Dickey was prone to exaggerate his military achievements, among other things, consciously exploring the creative possibilities of the lie. This is the overriding thesis of Henry Hart's recent biography of Dickey, which is appropriately titled, *James Dickey: The World as Lie* (2000).

3. The rhythmic repetition of the final two lines is reminiscent of the rhythm of the opening stanza of Emerson's "Brahma" (1856):
   If the red slayer think he slays,
   Or if the slain think he is slain,
   They know not well the subtle ways
   I keep, and pass, and turn again
   Whereas Emerson's vision of an essential order in the universe is explicitly theological, supporting itself under the framework of the Hindu belief system, Dickey's creation of a heaven for animals can be read on one level as an implicit parody of religious belief (certainly of traditional Christian belief), pointing out the flimsy and unimaginative nature of conventional Christian representations of the afterlife in contrast to his own creative, though equally far-fetched, vision of an animal afterworld.

4. For primitivist readings of *Audubon: A Vision*, see Robert S. Koppelman's *Robert Penn Warren's Modernist Spirituality* (1995) and Keen Butterworth's "Projections and Reflections in *Audubon: A Vision*" (2003). Koppelman posits that "immersion into primary nature is central" in the poem (149), while Butterworth examines the presence of Jungian archetypes in *Audubon*, arguing that the poem explores the primal territory of "the powerful reservoir of patterns or archetypes which inform our understanding of life that is otherwise nothing more than unrelated events.... Here psychology is elevated to the realm of metaphysics

and theology" (90).

5. All quotations are from the 1979 version of *Brother to Dragons*, which Dickey praised above and beyond the original poem in a 1980 letter to Warren:
   Later, when I have more time to dig into comparisons, I will write you at length about the new version of *Brother to Dragons*. I haven't had time to do the poem justice under the present circumstances, but do know that though I believed the original version to be a classic, I now think that you have made of it a super-classic, and I plan to tell you in detail later on why I think so. (Bruccoli 389)

6. In *Robert Penn Warren and American Idealism* (1988), John Burt contends that the closing lines of *Brother to Dragons* reassert some hope in the human, but only after wisely noting that it is precisely this kind of humanist philosophy that has been battered throughout the poem.

Works Cited

Bruccoli, Matthew J., and Judith S. Baughman, eds. *Crux: The Letters of James Dickey*. New York: Knopf, 1999.
Burt, John. *Robert Penn Warren and American Idealism*. New Haven: Yale UP, 1988.
Butterworth, Keen. "Projections and Reflections in *Audubon: A Vision*." *Southern Literary Journal* 36 (2003): 90-103.
Clabough, Casey Howard. *Elements: The Novels of James Dickey*. Macon, Georgia: Mercer UP, 2002.
Dickey, James. "The Heaven of Animals." *The Whole Motion: Collected Poems, 1945-1992*. Middletown, Connecticut: Wesleyan UP, 1992. 78-79.
Dickey, Deborah. Phone interview with the author. November 6, 2005.
Eiseley, Loren. *The Immense Journey*. New York: Vintage Books, 1957.
Gunn, Thom. "Things, Voices, Minds." In *"Struggling for Wings": The Art of James Dickey*. Edited by Robert Kirschten. Columbia: U of South Carolina P, 1997. 13-15.
Hart, Henry. *James Dickey: The World as a Lie*. New York: Picador, 2000.
Kirschten, Robert. *James Dickey and the Gentle Ecstasy of Earth*. Baton Rouge: Louisiana State UP, 1988.
Koppelman, Robert S. *Robert Penn Warren's Modernist Spirituality*. Columbia: U of Missouri P, 1995.
Smith, Dave. "The Strength of James Dickey." In *Local Assays: On Contemporary American Poetry*. Urbana: U of Illinois P, 1985.
Suarez, Ernest. *James Dickey and the Politics of Canon: Assessing the Savage Ideal*. Columbia: U of Missouri P, 1993.
Warren, Robert Penn. *Brother to Dragons: A New Version*, 1979. Reprint. Baton Rouge: Louisiana State UP, 1996.
———. Papers. Yale Collection of American Literature. Beinecke Rare Book and Manuscript Library, Yale University.

Robert Penn Warren, David Milch, and the Literary Contexts of *Deadwood*

by Joseph Millichap

Although the enduring significance of Robert Penn Warren, Renaissance man of modern American letters, in our popular culture was revealed by the second movie adaptation of *All the King's Men* in 2006, more than a century after his birth and six decades after the novel's first publication, the pervasive influence of his creative example also is demonstrated by the award-winning productions of David Milch, maverick genius of contemporary television. The second season of his popular and provocative HBO series *Deadwood* in 2005 occasioned a *New Yorker* profile by Mark Singer in which Milch revealed his profound respect for Warren both as writer and as man. From 1965 to his death in 1989, Warren successively acted as Milch's teacher, mentor, and colleague, and the profile also reveals that the senior figure still serves as a role model for the younger in terms of his life as well as his work. Warren's creative canon demonstrates a number of influences on and intertextualities with Milch's diverse productions, providing insight into the literary contexts that make *Deadwood* high quality television.

At first glance, critical comparison of the Hollywood eccentric with the Yale conservative, of the self-proclaimed addictive Milch with the austere Warren, may seem something of a stretch, but their parallels prove too numerous to ignore. In addition to Milch's revealing commentary on Warren, the two writers also share many subjects, modes, and styles—albeit in differing genres. The film adaptations of *All the King's Men* in 1949 and 2006 provide a link here, however, especially when we recall that Warren wrote his own theatrical versions of his novel and assisted director Robert Rossen with its first movie production. In *Deadwood*, Milch presents a dramatized and filmed serial novel in one-hour installments, while drawing on literary sources ranging from Shakespeare to Dickens to the classic movie Western, a genre Milch attributes to Jewish studio moguls (Havrilesky). While Warren is more concerned with popular culture than his academic critics will acknowledge, Milch is more involved in a high culture critique of the American experience than his reviewers have recognized.

Robert Penn Warren was born in 1905, the first child of Robert Franklin Warren and Anna Ruth Penn Warren, devoted and ambitious parents who had recently settled in Guthrie, Kentucky. Warren's hometown was the thriving agricultural and railroad center of the Black Patch, the dark-fired tobacco country in western Kentucky and Tennessee. Both Warren's parents were descended from established agrarian families, and, coincidentally, both of their fathers had served as captains in Nathan Bedford Forrest's Confederate cavalry corps. Warren grew up only a generation after the Civil War, and as a boy he lived through one of its many aftershocks in the bitter Tobacco Wars of his region during the early twentieth century. Wherever he would live and whatever he would write, Robert Penn Warren would remain a Southern writer at heart, if not always in mind.

Warren's literary genealogy was a great deal less provincial, however. Both sides of his family were educated and well read; his mother was a schoolteacher before and after her marriage, while his father had studied the classics and published verse as a young man. Encouraged by his parents and teachers, Warren excelled at local schools, and in 1921 he enrolled at Vanderbilt University in nearby Nashville. In some respects the university was still a Methodist backwater, but no place could have proved better suited for the development of a young Southern writer. Although the burgeoning Southern Renaissance had its other outposts, the Nashville Fugitives were already in residence when Warren arrived there. No other venue would prove as amenable to the shock of modernity, as the younger Fugitives often considered Southern subject matters in terms of modernist forms. In particular, the most significant inheritance for Warren was T. S. Eliot's *The Waste Land*, as evidenced by his not only reading but memorizing this modernist masterpiece on its publication in 1922.

Perhaps the pure bravado of young Warren's appreciation of Eliot reveals the intellectual intensity and the artistic ambition that would drive the public aspects of his career. Warren remains the only person to have won Pulitzer prizes for both fiction and poetry, the former in 1947 for *All the King's Men* (1946) and the latter in 1958 for *Promises* (1957) and again in 1979 for *Now and Then* (1978). The Warren canon includes nine other novels, a volume of short fiction, a score of poetry collections, a verse drama, several plays and screenplays, as well as significant cultural criticism, such as *The Legacy of the Civil War* (1961). In a series of influential texts written with Cleanth Brooks, Warren also helped found the New Criticism that dominated American letters for a generation. So Warren would have remained a formidable figure on the literary scene of mid-twentieth century America even if he had published nothing after reaching the customary retirement age of sixty-five in 1970. The writer he was at that point is the one created by the traditional criticism—the Renaissance man of American letters. Recently, readers have recognized that Warren's collections published between 1970 and 1985 reveal a different writer, a major twentieth century poet; his later poetry is less derivative from the early modernists and therefore more open in form, more evocative in tone, and more personal in subject matter.

On the centennial of his birth, it becomes more clear that Warren's *alterswerk,* his "age work," to translate literally that useful critical term, forms only one part of his life-long project of bridging the gulf between high and popular culture in America. This effort began as early as the 1930s when the economic and social dislocations of the Depression decade transformed the Fugitives, essentially an aesthetic gathering focused by the traditions of high culture, to the Agrarians, a broader intellectual grouping aware of popular culture as well. Warren's contribution to the Agrarian anthology *I'll Take My Stand* in 1931 was a conflicted essay on race in the South; written from the perspective of his Rhodes scholarship at Oxford and entitled "The Briar Patch" after a Brer Rabbit tale, the piece recognized racial injustice in the region but offered only the impractical solution of agrarianism in an industrial age. Almost immediately, Warren published his first fiction, the long story "Prime Leaf" (1931), that clearly dramatizes the persistent failures of the Southern tradition in the depredations of night riders during the earlier Tobacco Wars in the Black Patch.

In the 1930s and into the 1940s, Warren's impulses toward high culture were confined for the most part to his poetry and literary analysis, while his fiction and cultural commentary were involved to a greater extent with popular culture. Exceptions exist, of course, as with his long narrative poem, "The Ballad of Billy Potts" (1944), which was based on a Kentucky folk tale and popular history. His first published novel, *Night Rider*

(1939), extends the compass of the earlier story "Prime Leaf," while *At Heaven's Gate* (1943), his second novel, dramatizes the turbulence of Tennessee politics in the two preceding decades. With his third and best known novel, *All the King's Men* in 1946, Warren truly entered the realms of popular culture. Loosely centered on the historical figure of the colorful Louisiana politician Huey Long, Warren's narrative skillfully weaves the popular story of his political persona with that of a faintly autobiographical narrator who allows the incorporation of high culture perspectives on Southern history. The novel was chosen a Book-of-the Month Club selection, then earned the Pulitzer Prize for Fiction; a movie adaptation of *All the King's Men* appeared in 1949, and it in turn won the Academy Award for Best Picture.

Born in 1945, just before Warren achieved popular success, David Milch grew up in suburban Buffalo, New York, where his father was a prominent surgeon and his mother a member of the school board. As Milch told Warren's biographer Joseph Blotner in a 1988 interview, he became "a Jewish country day school boy" (3). At Yale, Milch's major advisor in English was R. W. B. Lewis, an eminent scholar of American literature, and his teachers included Cleanth Brooks, theorist of the New Criticism, as well as Robert Penn Warren. Milch went on to earn an MFA at Iowa, later teaching there and at Yale while publishing poetry and fiction. During the early 1970s he assisted his three distinguished professors with the editing of their anthology, *American Literature: The Makers and the Making* (1973). About this experience Milch says: "I never really got an education until I began to do that work for them" (Blotner 1). Careful considerations of his television productions, especially *Deadwood*, reveal not only how much Milch learned from his mentors by way of their own creative and critical legacies, but how much he was influenced by the great traditions of American literature he discovered through them. "Warren spread out all the literary artifacts of American culture for me to study, as part of my working for him on that history of American literature" (Singer 205).

In 1982, a former Yale classmate recommended Milch as a writer for the breakthrough television series *Hill Street Blues*; his initial script, "Trial By Fury," dramatized the murder of a nun and earned him both an Emmy and the Humanitas Award. With this initial success, Milch left academe for full-time work on the series as a writer, an editor, and finally a producer. After *Hill Street Blues* concluded in 1987, Milch produced the unsuccessful spin-off *Beverly Hills Buntz* and the short-lived press drama *Capital News* (1989). In 1992 he once again teamed with *Hill Street Blues* producer Stephen Bochco to create the highly praised and recently concluded series *NYPD Blue*. Milch came to control these productions to the point that he became their *auteur* in filmic terms, complicating the collective methodology of a television ensemble and eventuating in his separation from *NYPD Blue* in 1997. Since then he has been involved with a number of critically acclaimed projects, most notably *Big Apple* (2001), an hour-length drama series set in the New York City FBI office. Admitting that he struggled with personal demons, including the abuse of multiple substances as well as compulsive gambling even while at Yale, Milch confesses that these problems were exacerbated by the entertainment world. His personal life did take a more positive turn after marriage to documentary producer Rita Stern and the births of their three children in the 1980s, though only health problems in the late 1990s scared him into sobriety. He still bets, though, often on his own horses.

Like the best of Warren's works, Milch's finest creations, especially *Deadwood*, employ a distinctive, diverse, and mannered style to delineate a harshly naturalistic vision of the dark and divided depths within the American national character, an identity simultaneously and paradoxically both innocent and corrupted. In an introduction to a selection of Herman Melville's Civil War poems for an American literature anthology, Warren characterized the nineteenth century master's style as "metaphysical" in both poetry and prose. Warren recognized that, like the English poets of the seventeenth century, Melville fused physical with psychological imagery. In describing and analyzing Melville's poetry, Warren really describes his own work as well: "[Melville] was aiming at a style rich and yet shot through with realism and prosaism, sometimes casual and open and sometimes dense and intellectually weighted, fluid and various because following the contours of the subject, or rather the contours of his own complex feelings about the subject" (*Melville* 12). Thus, Warren's formulations here might be applied to Milch's methods in *Deadwood* as well; the style Warren inherited from Melville he left in turn as his literary legacy for Milch.

The most notorious aspect of *Deadwood* has become its dialogue, a striking conflation of flowery rhetoric, often verging on Shakespearean verse or Victorian prose, with rough slang and crude profanity. *Deadwood's* negative critics have reacted to this torrent of vulgarity even more vehemently than to its callous depiction of sex and violence. One commentator counted the "f-word" used some 870 times in the 12 episodes of *Deadwood's* first season (more than once a minute), and this profusion is nearly matched by the plethora of other even more startling expletives. Both poles of his characters' speech have been challenged in terms of historical realism, but Milch resolutely defends his practice in recent interviews. While he probably is enjoying his freedom from the network censors who constantly snipped at *Hill Street Blues* and *NYPD Blue*, Milch also may be insuring the attention of cable viewers already inured to shock from earlier HBO series such as *The Sopranos, Six Feet Under,* and *Carnivale*.

Milch also is following Warren's lead in both fiction and poetry. For example, *All the King's Men* is narrated by Jack Burden, a failed scholar become cynical political operative, who combines philosophical terminology with tough-guy slang to tell the story of Governor Willie Stark. Warren also extended this practice into his poetry. Notable examples include "The Ballad of Billy Potts" (1944) and *Audubon* (1969), both narrative poems set on a Kentucky frontier of the early nineteenth century not so much different from frontier South Dakota in the later half of that century. The narrator of *Chief Joseph of the Nez Perce* (1983), a Western epic poem set like *Deadwood* in the years of gold fever and Indian hysteria following the first strikes in the Black Hills and the Battle of the Little Big Horn, complains of how the frontier power brokers "slick-fucked a land" (*Collected Poetry*, hereafter *CP*, 520). Even in the more personal revelatory lyrics of his later career, Warren balances capitalized abstractions such as "Time" and "Truth" against vulgarities similar to those heard so often on the streets or in the saloons of Milch's fictionalized Deadwood.

Other than the characters' language, Western buffs have found little to complain about in *Deadwood's* recreation of the frontier West; indeed, several critics have proclaimed it the most realistic example of the genre ever made. Milch prides himself on the historical accuracy of his production, personally overseeing even the smallest details of sets and costumes. The total effect of this surface realism mirrors a deeper, more naturalistic vision of the human experience as seen on the frontier between wilderness and civilization. All aspects of the life process are presented in a somber naturalistic vision: birth and death, youth and age, sex and violence, illness and decay, even nutrition and elimination.

Perhaps the most repulsive instance is the constant disposal of murdered corpses as fodder for the pigs of Deadwood's Chinatown. Again, all of these elements mirror Warren's own naturalism; even the flesh-eating swine are found in "Go It Granny—Go It Hog," part of the deceptively titled collection *Promises*. *All the King's Men* is filled with other Darwinian examples, intertextual with the Realists and Naturalists Warren admired, from Stephen Crane and Theodore Dreiser to Ernest Hemingway and William Faulkner.

In *The Mind of the South* (1940), W. J. Cash speculates that Southern history was different from that of other American regions because it evolved through the frontier mode not just once, but twice—in the ante-bellum and post-bellum eras. Warren writes consistently about both Southern frontiers—other examples not mentioned above include *World Enough and Time* (1949), *Brother to Dragons* (1953), and *Band of Angels* (1955). Writing in the 1960s, no less a critic than Leslie Fiedler considered these narratives the heart of Warren's achievement: "Warren...has attempted the risky game of presenting to our largest audience the anti-Western in the guise of the Western, the anti-historical romance in the guise of that form itself" (392). Warren's works also consider the Western frontier directly—from the Willie Proudfit plot strand of the early *Night Rider* to the lyrics focused by the Western landscape which predominate in Warren's last poetry collection, *Altitudes and Extensions* (1985).

Warren's later lyric poetry, so much admired by its contemporary readers such as David Milch, likewise presents many examples of Western landscapes and Naturalistic visions. Warren's "Going West" (1981) provides a paradigmatic example, with its startling central image of a pheasant smashed against the windshield of a car speeding across the Great Plains, so that poet and reader can see the shining mountains only through a sudden curtain of blood.

> I have seen blood explode, blotting out the sun, blotting
> Out land, white ribbon of road, the imagined
> Vision of snowcaps. (*CP* 455)

As the poem's persona sums the experience up, "This is one way to write the history of America" (*CP* 455). In his 1974 Jefferson Humanities Lecture "Democracy and Poetry," Warren characterizes the "corrosive" vision of America's history found in our art: "and man, moving ever westward, was redeemed from the past, was washed in the blood of a new kind of lamb" (8). "Going West" also anticipates the manner in which David Milch would rewrite the accepted history of his America in *Deadwood*, moving from the decaying cities of the East to the final frontier of the great West, like Warren in this poem, but discovering the same patterns of human violence that deny the American Dream. Significantly, the opening episode of *Deadwood's* second season is titled "A Lie Agreed Upon"—Napoleon Bonaparte's skeptical yet fitting definition of history.

A powerful pattern of imagery in *Deadwood* presenting this reading of American history is the exploitation and betrayal of youthful innocence. Because few children were found in a mining camp such as Deadwood, they become natural points of narrative focus. In fact, two episodes are organized around this theme, as their titles indicate: the eighth of Season 1, "Suffer the Little Children," and the eighth of Season 2, "Childish Things." The most significant children are the orphaned Sophia Metz, discovered after her family's massacre in the first season, and the fatherless William Bullock, adopted in the second season by his uncle Seth who dutifully weds his brother's widow in an act of patriarchal piety. Both of these pre-pubescent children seem to represent the innocent hopes forfeited by almost all the adults in Deadwood, and in so doing they become bright little pawns in their elders' shady relations. Although Sophia's life seems constantly in danger from villainous Al Swearengen through the first season, it is William who is killed in the second season, seemingly by chance, though some suspect foul play. William's funeral provides a thematic focus for Season 2, somewhat the same way as Wild Bill's last rites served for Season 1.

Another young pair just the other side of puberty from William and Sophia are the putatively innocent Miles and Flora Anderson, who arrive in Deadwood searching for their "lost" father—significantly from Buffalo—in Episode 8 of Season 1, "Suffer the Little Children." Although their Victorian names are realistic enough for the time period, readers of American literature will recognize that they are recycled from those of the lost children in Henry James's chilling story of psychological horror, *The Turn of the Screw* (1898). Interestingly, James's biographers reveal that the author set *The Turn of the Screw* in the English country house he had just purchased because he was working through his own unhappy youth in several fictions at that moment. In Milch's intertextual retelling, the young pair, ostensibly brother and sister like James's earlier children, arrive already corrupted and attempt to seduce and swindle several of the adult denizens of Deadwood by playing on their childhood disappointments. When suspected and then detected by Machiavellian and murderous Cy Tolliver, Miles and Flora of Buffalo are savagely beaten, brutally slaughtered, and callously tossed to Mr. Wu's pigs as their episode ends.

Deadwood also develops this theme of innocence betrayed in many autobiographical revelations by adult characters, both female and male, of the youthful experiences that shaped their present lives. Almost all of these Deadwood residents capable of any self-awareness and self-expression have such moments. The major female figures—ranging from the barely reputable Alma Garret and Calamity Jane, to the completely disreputable Joanie Stubbs and Trixie the Whore—all imply duplicity and perhaps physical and/or sexual abuse by literal fathers or other patriarchal figures. Interestingly enough, many of these revelations between and among the women of Deadwood come as they flock together, reputable and disreputable, in protection of the orphaned Sophia Metz, as if to prevent their past fates from befalling her in the future.

The male characters prove more reticent, though their betrayed naïveté becomes apparent in their relations to these same women: Seth Bullock to Alma, Al Swearengen to Trixie, Cy Tolliver to Joanie, and Charlie Utter to Calamity Jane. The most significant of these confessions come in Al's drunken dialogues while being pleasured by Dolly, a barely post-pubescent substitute for Trixie, who can only grunt her response to his tortured monologue. In the first of these, at the close of the Season 1, Al says that he too is an orphan, abandoned by his prostitute mother at a Dickensian workhouse in Chicago run by "Mrs. Fat Ass…Anderson." After little William's funeral near the end of Season 2, Al reveals that the family who purchased him from Mrs. Anderson beat him mercilessly after the death of their natural son from "falling sickness." Swearengen also calls the orphanage overseer a "pimp," probably because she sold him not just Dolly but all his whores whenever he passes through Chicago to revenge himself on his own past (Havrilesky). Perhaps because he was sexually abused himself, Al's uncharacteristically benevolent attitudes toward both young Sophia and William might be explained by the trauma of his own life journey at the same ages as these youngest inhabitants of Deadwood.

This thematic pattern may prove most important, however, in unraveling Al Swearengen's complex relations with Seth Bullock, the central conflict of character driving *Deadwood* as a series. Despite the fact that both men can be merciless killers if their circumstances demand it, both are strangely distanced from their base behaviors. Seth, in particular, often seems a naïf pulled between principle and pragmatism, though Al also is sometimes unaware of his motivations, especially his better ones as with Sophia and William or with the grotesques Jewell and the Reverend Smith. Milch has compared the complex characterization of Al Swearengen to the heroic if flawed Detective Andy Sipowicz of *NYPD Blue*—a drunk, a racist, as well as a character "very much like my dad, who was complicated and driven" (Havrilesky). Elmer Milch was not only a respected surgeon but a compulsive gambler, who early on involved young David with the manic part of his personality and through it with the seamier side of Buffalo. As Milch put it in the *New Yorker* profile: "I was the surrogate demon who was to act and sort of expurgate the demonic in my dad" (Singer 200). Milch also implies to his interviewer that he was sexually abused by a counselor when he was packed off to camp so that his parents could enjoy the racing season at Saratoga; as Singer sums it all up: "What Milch has made of such fraught relationships, betrayals, and traumas is, in essence, his life's work as a writer" (197). So, if Al Swearengen proves another imperfect father figure, Seth Bullock then becomes something of another betrayed surrogate son seeking out his place after the death of his own adopted boy, young William.

Such themes of disillusioned innocence can be found throughout Warren's voluminous canon, but particularly in his early short fiction and his late lyric poetry, as these both explore memories of his own childhood. Perhaps the finest example in fiction is his best known and most often anthologized story, "Blackberry Winter" (1946). While many of the later poems Warren once called his "shadowy autobiography" (*CP* 441) might serve us just as well, a fine instance is the one most often quoted by Milch in interviews, "I Am Dreaming of a White Christmas: The Natural History of a Vision" (1973). The logic of this tripartite lyric involves the subconscious psychology of dreams, and its settings triangulate a dreary December in western Kentucky during the 1910s of the poet's youth, a smoggy summer in the New York City of his 1970s present, and his timeless future as implied by the first snow of the season falling on the Nez Perce Pass between Idaho and Montana, named to honor Chief Joseph's gallant flight dramatized in Warren's later epic poem, a symbolic locus not that far from Deadwood in the real or the imagined geography of the West.

The poem then evolves into a naturalistic "vision" through the process of finding consequential continuities among past, present, and future. In this grim, fairy-tale world, three small chairs are placed for the three Warren children, and under the desiccated cedar Christmas tree wait "three packages. / Identical in size and shape" (*CP* 278). Unable to open his present, the persona is fearful of its implication that his parents' primal legacy is only their mortality. (In this regard, it seems interesting to wonder why Swearengen maintains a running dialogue with a parcel wrapped in brown paper, one that ostensibly contains the severed head of a Native American killed for the bounty Al offered in the initial episode.) Then the "brown-lacquered" scene of the Kentucky past and the hazy skies, "yellow as acid," of New York City's present are altered to the West's universal whiteness (*CP* 276, 279). Although he will never know the exact nature of his childhood gift, Warren realizes the true nature of his birthright from his parents,

> This
> Is the process whereby pain of the past in its pastness
> May be converted into the future tense
>
> Of Joy. (*CP* 281)

In his profile in the *New Yorker*, David Milch told Mark Singer that he embraced "this as a creative manifesto" (199); in fact, Milch entitles one of the chapters in his course on screenwriting "Future Tense Of Joy." Summing up his influence on him, Milch has said "Mr. Warren maintained certain disciplines that were the best lessons he gave me. As a model he was crucially important" (Singer 127).

Thus, the most significant connections between David Milch and Robert Penn Warren are more deeply personal than simply professional. As Milch puts it, Warren taught him how to be a human being by giving himself up completely to his art. He told Joseph Blotner in the 1988 interview, "You had the sense in his presence of what it took, of just how whole-souled the commitment was…and that it was a way to stand in the world" (2). Milch, like most of Warren's more recent critics, values his mentor's poems more than his fictions, and, though he left poetry early on in his own writing career, the television *auteur* frequently rereads Warren's poetic works. Milch then emulates Warren's creative methods by preparing himself to be found by his muse, an aesthetic version of the religious spirit. So Friedrich Kekule's remark, after his discovery of the Benzene ring in a dream, that "Visions come to prepared spirits," made its way as a salient example from Warren's creative writing seminars at Yale to Milch's screenwriting classes in Hollywood (Blotner 5, Singer 195). After watching Milch's scripting sessions for *Deadwood*, Singer judges them "equal parts master class and séance—the comparison that strikes me as most apt is channeling" (195). Warren taught Milch that even careful research and preparation must inevitably give way to a psychological, moral, and artistic commitment that cannot be compromised by any consideration aside from the personal vision of the artist.

Moral commitment may seem a strange formulation to use in regard to *Deadwood*, yet Milch insists that despite its vulgarity and violence all his work, including *Hill Street Blues* and *NYPD Blue*, is "profoundly moral," judgments born out by his several Humanitas awards for his writing on these earlier shows (Nyhuis). His next project, *Big Apple* in 2001, was so named he says "not for New York City, but for the fruit from the Tree of the Knowledge of Good and Evil" (Boles). Likewise, in his own historical notes for the *Deadwood* website, Milch characterizes the thematic premise of the show as "a kind of original sin—the appropriation of what belonged to one people by another people." Similar themes are found throughout Warren's canon in works of fiction, poetry, and cultural criticism as seen above—and in "Original Sin: A Short Story" (1942), *The Circus in the Attic* (1947), or *Segregation: The Inner Conflict in the South* (1956).

In *Deadwood*, one stylistic counterpoint to the characters' incessant profanity is found in the poetic diction of the King James Bible. To underline these contrasts, a preacher arrives in Deadwood for each season. In the first, the Reverend H. W. Smith, a demented Civil war chaplain, preaches Wild Bill's funeral, reading from St. Paul's epistles comparing the community of the church to the human body: "And whether one member suffer all the members suffer with it." Later, Smith is doomed by a brain tumor and mercifully suffocated by Al Swearengen, who secretly shares his suffering. In Season Two, Andy Cramed, a cardsharp abandoned by Cy Tolliver to die with plague, returns born again as a self-ordained preacher who conducts young William's funeral, reading extensively from the Psalms. It is as if through his art Milch is exploring the possibilities of both individual and collective redemption in nineteenth century Deadwood, the very place where it would seem least likely, as well as in contemporary America, where it often seems, if anything, even less so.

As Milch says of Warren in this regard, "his poetry is an expression of a unified state of being and really is…[a]s close to an exalted state as one who hasn't God can get" (Blotner 5). Thus Warren became not just a mentor for Milch, or even an "avatar" to use Mark Singer's formulation in the *New Yorker* profile (194), but a humane, artistic father figure who empowered his devoted surrogate son to find his own selfhood and to create in *Hill Street Blues, NYPD Blue,* and *Deadwood* some of the most real, complex, and memorable characters ever to grace American television. Milch's expanding canon continues to demonstrate a number of important influences from and intertextualities with Warren's diverse works, providing insight into the literary contexts of *Deadwood*. The carefully cross-cut conclusions of the second season—with its intricate weave of the wedding celebration in the muddle of Main Street, the territorial treaty signing in the depths of Al's Gem Saloon, and the sacrificial slaughter in the shadows of Chinese Alley—only promise more of the same for Season 3 of David Milch's *Deadwood,* as it pursues its course as Robert Penn Warren's literary legacy.

Works Cited

Blotner, Joseph. "Telephone Interview With David Milch" (Sept. 2, 1988). Unpublished typescript in Robert Penn Warren Collection, Western Kentucky University Library.
Boles, David. "David Milch's Active Imagination." *Go Inside*. May 17, 2002. <http:// goinside.com/02/5/milch.html>.
Fiedler, Leslie. *Love and Death in the American Novel*. Cleveland, OH: World Publishing, 1962.
Havrilesky, Heather. "The Man Behind *Deadwood*." *Salon*. March 5, 2005. <http://www.salon.com/ent/feature/2005/03/05/milch/>.
Milch, David. "The Real Deadwood." *Deadwood*. 2005. <http://www.hbo.com/deadwood/behind/therealdeadwood.shtm>.
Nyhuis, Philip. "David Milch's Deadwood." *Buffalo Spree Magazine Online*. January 2, 2005. <http://www.buffalospree.com/archives/2005_0102/010205Milch.htm>.
Singer, Mark. "The Misfit." *The New Yorker*. Feb. 14, 2005, pp. 192-205.
Warren, Robert Penn. *The Collected Poems*. Ed. John Burt. Baton Rouge: Louisiana State UP, 1998.
———. "Democracy and Poetry." *Southern Review* NS 11 (Winter 1975). 1-28.
———. Ed. *Selected Poems of Herman Melville*. New York: Random House, 1970.

www.ingramcontent.com/pod-product-compliance
Lightning Source LLC
Chambersburg PA
CBHW021937160426
43195CB00011B/1126